Bringing Freud to America

Bringing Freud to America

*Publishers, Pirates
and the Popularization
of His Ideas*

MICHAEL EDMONDS

McFarland & Company, Inc., Publishers
Jefferson, North Carolina

ISBN (print) 978-1-4766-9223-4
ISBN (ebook) 978-1-4766-5007-4

LIBRARY OF CONGRESS AND BRITISH LIBRARY
CATALOGUING DATA ARE AVAILABLE

Library of Congress Control Number 2023026907

Front cover: Sigmund Freud (bottom left) and A.A. Brill at Clark University
in September 1909 (*American Magazine,* November 1, 1910)

Printed in the United States of America

McFarland & Company, Inc., Publishers
Box 611, Jefferson, North Carolina 28640
www.mcfarlandpub.com

For my daughter Julia,
who was there when it all started
at an antiquarian bookshop in Minneapolis

Contents

Introduction

"No ideas but in things"

In 1900, hardly anyone in America had heard of Sigmund Freud. By 1920, almost everyone had. How did that happen?

Ideas don't travel telepathically through the ether. They live in concrete objects. Freud's ideas had to be printed on paper before they could become conversations in living rooms, lectures from podiums, or broadcasts on radios. His theories were banged out on typewriter keys, cast into metal plates, smeared with black ink, pressed onto sheets, and bound into books that were gripped by millions of hands in homes, libraries, cafes, and classrooms. To stretch William Carlos Williams' famous maxim, there are "no ideas but in things."

This is not a book about Freud's theories and their acceptance or rejection. It's a book about books and the people who made them. It describes the scoundrels and scholars, prudes and libertines, reactionaries and radicals who turned Freud's ideas into physical objects that changed millions of American minds. How did the people who first promoted Freud's works in the U.S. acquire his texts and then translate, edit, manufacture, and sell them? What did they believe, desire, and value? What did they hope to achieve?

Freud's ideas spread so successfully that, to paraphrase a well-known economist, we're all Freudians now. Concepts he introduced or promoted are woven so tightly into our daily lives that like gravity or air we hardly notice them. We say our friend is in denial, or our neatnik roommate is anal, or our boss is neurotic. We know that if we swallow our anger at work, it bubbles up later at home. We admit that slips of the tongue expose hidden wishes or worries. We think sex is natural and talk about it openly. Advertisers play relentlessly on our unspoken fears and desires. We know that unconscious drives can turn even priests and Scout leaders into child molesters or help transform liberal democracies into racist dictatorships. Most current assumptions about society, human nature, childhood,

1

health, and happiness can be traced in large part back to Freud's revolutionary work at the end of the 19th century.

As a young doctor in the 1880s, he was puzzled by patients whose symptoms had no physical cause. When research convinced him that repressed impulses and buried memories were making patients sick, his medical colleagues scoffed. When he claimed that nearly all neurotic illnesses were due to "disturbances of the erotic sphere," they called him pornographic. When he declared that young children felt sexual urges toward their parents and that the failure to resolve them caused mental illness in adulthood, his character was attacked and his writings condemned. "I was completely isolated," he later wrote. "In Vienna I was shunned; abroad no notice was taken of me."[1]

Freud was pushing against boundaries that seem almost absurd today. "The world took anything even slightly approximating the truth as one of the rankest and most criminal offenses possible," recalled novelist Theodore Dreiser. "One dared not 'talk out loud,' one dared not report life as it was, as one lived it."[2] In 1900 editors couldn't print the words "orgasm" or "homosexual" for fear of offending readers. When in 1906 *Ladies Home Journal* ran articles about sexually transmitted diseases, 75,000 readers cancelled subscriptions and advertisers fled. A conspiracy of silence prevented any discussion of sex. One newlywed was shocked by her first orgasm: "No one had ever told me about this definite, so definite and surprising thing," she wrote, "and I had never read of it." Describing birth control in public was punishable by a $2,000 fine and a year in prison. When one doctor described the sexual origins of a patient's obsessions at a 1911 conference, the entire audience stood up and walked out. Plays, films, and books with sexual references were banned and their publishers were arrested, including four of Freud's.[3]

Leading the campaign for Freud in America was energetic Dr. Abraham Brill (1874–1948), his first English translator. "If psychoanalysis now plays a role in American intellectual life," Freud wrote in 1931, "or if it does so in the future, a large part of this result will have to be attributed to this and other activities of Dr. Brill's." After Brill died, a colleague recalled, "we almost can visualize him, machete in hand, fighting against ignorance and hypocrisy [with] the cheerful aggressiveness that was characteristic of him, always certain that he was right."[4] Though Brill did more than anyone else to establish psychoanalysis in America, he's all but forgotten today. Many eccentric characters populate the following pages, but few of them rival irrepressible Dr. Brill.

By 1920 America had fallen in love with Freud, but the feeling wasn't mutual. Freud was a dignified Viennese professor steeped in Old World culture who dressed, spoke, and behaved like a bourgeois conservative.

He was disgusted by America's aggressive commercialism. "America is a mistake," he told his British disciple Ernest Jones, "admittedly a gigantic mistake, but a mistake nevertheless." He deplored "the two big vices of America, the greed for money and the respect of public opinion." During his only visit here, in 1909, he found the pace exhausting, the food indigestible, and the public restrooms too far apart. Most American publishers were afraid to issue his books, while others printed and sold them without his permission. One of them had to be repeatedly threatened with lawsuits before paying royalties. "American publishers," he told translator Helen Downey, "are a dangerous breed." In his letters he called them rascals, liars, swindlers, pirates, and crooks.[5]

Sigmund Freud (front) and A.A. Brill at Clark University, September 1909 (*American Magazine*, November 1, 1910).

"Considering Freud's enormous influence," wrote historian Geoffrey Meynell 40 years ago, "remarkably little has been said of how his books and papers came to be made accessible to English-speaking readers."[6] That's still true. Thousands of books have been written about Freud's ideas but almost nothing about the tangible objects that carried them into people's hands. WorldCat lists more than 40,000 works under the subject heading "Freud," but almost none of that research examines how Freud's ideas moved through editorial offices, printshops, bookstores, and libraries into the minds of readers.

A cursory glance at this book's chapter notes will reveal my indebtedness to classic works by Nathan G. Hale, John Burnham, Peter Gay, and others. But in recent years, new editions of letters and documents by Freud and his allies have been published for the first time. Digitization of literally millions of pages from rare books, newspapers, magazines, and manuscripts has unearthed previously unknown sources and provided new analytical tools. Publishers' archives, private papers, contemporary news-papers and magazines, court records, government documents, memoirs, letters, and interviews have become accessible. I've used all these sources to investigate how Freud's ideas first reached American audiences.

The following pages describe the history of each of Freud's American books published between 1900 and 1924, from its translation and first publication until its inclusion in the *Standard Edition of the Complete Psychological Works of Sigmund Freud* between 1953 and 1967. Detailed explanations describe how each work was translated, edited, printed, and distributed, including print runs and sales figures when known; careful bibliographic descriptions of first American editions are given in the appendix. Later printings and editions, however, are summarized only briefly, and Freud's books published in the U.S. for the first time after 1924 are hardly mentioned since by then his reputation was well-established. Chapters 1, 4, and 6 don't focus on books at all but rather on how medical journals and popular magazines spread his ideas between 1882 and 1918. The final chapter describes the dissemination of his works in the U.S. through the 1960s.

Freud's bibliographic history is a microcosm of 20th-century American publishing. His writings were shared in scholarly journals, mass-market periodicals, little magazines, nationwide syndicates, and immigrant newspapers. His books were published by venerable family firms who'd flourished for a century and by pirates who vanished almost overnight. They appeared as scientific monographs, retail books, best-selling reprints, and polemical tracts. They were sold not just in bookstores but also in wire racks at drugstores, by direct mail, through subscriptions, and door-to-door. They were issued in deluxe hardcover bindings intended to grace library shelves for decades and as flimsy booklets meant to be thrown away after reading. His ideas were packaged in experimental shapes like 1920s paperbacks, pocket-sized books bound in imitation leather, 10-cent "Little Blue Books" the size of a credit card, and plastic-coated "Permabooks." They were admired, denounced, hyped, flaunted, concealed, censored, and celebrated. And they were bought. Between 1910 and 1960 Freud's books were printed over 100 times in more than 40 editions which sold more than a million copies.

In recent years Freud has fallen out of fashion. A generation of historians attacked him for conceptual, methodological, and character flaws. His therapeutic approach was replaced by medications that assume mental activity is nothing more than biochemistry. The most popular form of treatment today is cognitive behavioral therapy, which helps clients observe and interrupt negative thoughts. Freud would have said that it only treats symptoms and ignores the disease. Even among psychoanalysts, his classic books are viewed as little more than the foundation on which decades of innovation rest.[7]

Yet Freud refuses to go away. His ideas still permeate not just the discipline of psychology but also education, marketing, literature, cinema, parenting, medicine, law, politics, and religion. More than 100 books about him appeared in the year 2022 alone. As I write, the latest biography promises to reveal "a Freud beyond patriarchy, beyond colonialism, beyond heterosexuality and gender inequality, beyond privilege ... a Freud who is useful and relevant for making sense of the contemporary world."[8]

Because Freud's books were so popular, most library copies were read to tatters and then rebound or replaced. Contemporary copies in original condition are scarce. Archivists, librarians, and rare book dealers around the country have generously examined their copies for me, patiently answered my questions about trivial details of binding and pagination, and provided dozens of photographs enabling me to untangle Freud's publication history. I want to thank the following people for their help: Tara Craig, Columbia University; Jim Danky, University of Wisconsin; Cara Dellatte, New York Public Library; Eric Dillalogue, University of Pennsylvania; Jonathan Eaker, Library of Congress; Simon Elliott, UCLA; Mary Fiorenza, for helpful comments on an early draft of the book; Matthew Goetz, George Washington University, who conducted research for me at the National Archives and the Library of Congress; Beth Harper, University of Wisconsin; Tom Hayes, Case Western Reserve University, who sent more than 40 photos of first editions in original bindings; Katie Heiserman, New York University, who examined manuscript collections for me in several New York City repositories; Steffen Kowalsky, West Coast Rare Books, Westport, County Mayo, Ireland; John Leonard, Chicago Institute for Psychoanalysis; Matt Mason, Yale University; Katie Mullen, Library of Congress; Steven Novak, Columbia University's Irving Medical Center; Deanna Parsi, St. Paul's School, Concord, New Hampshire; Isabel Planton, Lilly Library, Indiana University; Cynthia Shenette, Clark University; Micaela Sullivan-Fowler, University of Wisconsin; Kerrie Cotten Williams, Library of Congress; the staff at Wonder Book in Frederick, Maryland, who far exceeded normal customer service to unearth a volume with S.E. Jelliffe's bookplate; J. Wyatt Books, Ottawa, Ontario; Lewis Wyman, Library of Congress; the staff of the New York Public Library's local history division; and the seemingly indefatigable interlibrary loan team at the Madison, Wisconsin, Public Library.

Despite all that assistance, this book undoubtedly contains its share of errors and omissions, which I'll be grateful to hear about through www.michael-edmonds.com. Detailed notes and raw data that couldn't fit between these covers will be posted there if readers' interest seems to warrant it.

Timeline

1883—Freud's first American publication appears in *The Medical News.*

1894—William James calls attention to Freud's methods in *The Psychological Review.*

1900—Freud's first separately issued American work, *What Are Dreams?*, is pirated by Benjamin Tucker.

1906—James J. Putnam reports on the first American application of Freud's techniques.

1907—The first popular article about Freud's research appears, in *Harper's Monthly.*

1908—A.A. Brill visits Freud in Vienna and is appointed his American translator and literary agent.

1909—Freud makes his only visit to America, to lecture at Clark University in September.

1909—*Selected Papers on Hysteria...* is published by Jelliffe and White at the end of September.

1910—The first *New York Times* article about Freud appears in May.

1910—Freud's Clark lectures are printed by the university in October.

1910—Articles about Freud's theories begin to appear in popular magazines.

1911—*Three Contributions to the Sexual Theory* is published by Jelliffe and White in January.

1913—*The Interpretation of Dreams* is published by Macmillan in March.

1914—*On Dreams* is published by the Rebman Company in July.

1914—*Psychopathology of Everyday Life* is published by Macmillan in August.

1914—Freud's ideas begin to captivate the Greenwich Village avant-garde.

1915—*Modern Sexual Morality and Modern Nervousness* is pirated by Dr. William Robinson in October.

1915—A dozen mass-market magazine articles about Freud reach more than three million readers.

1916—*Wit and Its Relation to the Unconscious* and *Leonardo da Vinci* are published by Moffat, Yard and Co. in September.

1917—*The History of the Psycho-analytic Movement* is published by Jelliffe and White in February.

1917—John Toohey's account of Freud in *Ladies Home Journal* reaches 1.6 million readers.

1917—*Delusion and Dream* is published by Moffat, Yard and Co. in September.

1917—Mabel Dodge's advice columns in Hearst newspapers reach three million people twice a week.

1918—*Reflections on War and Death* is published by Moffat, Yard and Co. in April.

1918—*Totem and Taboo* is published by Moffat, Yard and Co. in May.

1919—*Leonardo da Vinci* is brought to court by the New York Society for the Suppression of Vice.

1920—*A General Introduction to Psychoanalysis* is published by Boni and Liveright in June with the help of Freud's nephew, Edward Bernays.

1920—Freud's writings on dreams are pirated by André Tridon and James McCann in December.

1924—Freud's English-language rights are centralized in the Hogarth Press and the International Psycho-Analytic Institute in May.

1924—*Group Psychology and the Analysis of the Ego* and *Beyond the Pleasure Principle* are published by Boni and Liveright in September.

1924—Freud's five Clark lectures are published by the Modern Library in *An Outline of Psychoanalysis* in September.

1938—*The Basic Writings of Sigmund Freud* is published as a Modern Library Giant in May.

1939—Freud dies in London on September 23.

1942—Freud's works begin to appear as mass-market paperbacks. At least 89 paperback printings totaling more than a million copies are issued between 1946 and 1966.

1948—Abraham Brill dies in New York on March 2.

1952—*Major Works of Sigmund Freud* is issued as volume 54 of the Encyclopædia Britannica's *Great Books of the Western World*.

1953—*The Standard Edition of the Complete Psychological Works of Sigmund Freud* begins to appear. Its final volume of texts is published in 1967 and its index in 1974.

People

Appleton, Robert (1865–1945)
editor at Moffat, Yard & Co., 1916–1918.

Bernays, Edward (1891–1995)
Freud's nephew and U.S. representative, 1920–1921.

Brett, George P. (1858–1936)
president of Macmillan who published Freud's first two trade books in 1913 and 1914.

Brill, Abraham A. (1874–1948)
Freud's friend, translator, literary agent (1908–1919), and chief advocate in the U.S., 1908–1948.

Bruce, H. Addington (1874–1959)
journalist whose articles on psychoanalysis reached more than a million readers, 1910–1915.

Cerf, Bennett (1898–1971)
Modern Library publisher whose books by Freud reached hundreds of thousands of readers.

Coit, Joseph (1865–1930)
editor at Moffat, Yard and Co. 1908–1917 who acquired five of Freud's books.

Eder, M.D. (1865–1936)
British psychoanalyst and translator of Freud's *On Dreams*.

Goldman, Emma (1869–1940)
Greenwich Village anarchist and early supporter of Freud.

Hall, G. Stanley (1846–1924)
president of Clark University who brought Freud to America in 1909.

Jelliffe, Smith Ely (1866–1945)
co-editor and publisher of the *Journal of Nervous and Mental Disease* and its *Monograph Series*, 1900–1945.

Jones, Ernest (1879–1958)
Freud's most energetic proponent in Britain, 1912–1958; founder of the International Psycho-Analytical Press, 1921.

Jung, Carl (1875–1961)
Swiss psychologist, early mentor of Brill, who broke with Freud in 1912.

Kuttner, Alfred (1886–1942)
Brill's translation assistant and proponent of Freud in Greenwich Village.

Liveright, Horace (1884–1933)	New York publisher who issued four of Freud's books, 1920–1924.
Macfarlane, Peter (1871–1924)	journalist whose 1915 *Good Housekeeping* articles on Freud reached 350,000 readers.
McCann, James A. (1887–1952)	New York publisher who pirated Freud's writings on dreams in 1920.
Putnam, James J. (1846–1918)	Harvard psychologist and early supporter of Freud, 1906–1918.
Rank, Otto (1884–1939)	psychoanalyst and Freud's U.S. representative, 1921–1924.
Rebman, Frank (1852–1940)	medical publisher who issued Freud's *On Dreams* in 1914.
Robinson, William (1867–1936)	New York physician and editor who pirated Freud's work, 1915–1931.
Strachey, James (1887–1967)	British translator of Freud, 1922–1967, and general editor of the *Standard Edition*.
Sumner, John S. (1876–1971)	leader of the New York Society for the Prevention of Vice, 1915–1950.
Toohey, John (1879–1946)	journalist and publicist whose 1917 *Ladies Home Journal* article on Freud reached 1.5 million readers.
Tridon, André (1877–1922)	Greenwich Village popularizer of psychoanalysis, 1915–1922, who pirated Freud's writings on dreams in 1920.
Tucker, Benjamin (1854–1939)	anarchist who printed Freud's first separately issued American publication in 1900.
Unwin, Stanley (1884–1968)	British publisher of Freud's *Interpretation of Dreams* in 1913.
Unwin, T. Fisher (1848–1935)	British publisher of Freud's *Psychopathology of Everyday Life* in 1914.
Van Teslaar, James (1884–1926)	Boston psychoanalyst and editor of *An Outline of Psychoanalysis* in 1924.
Viereck, George (1884–1962)	German American editor, journalist, and translator who popularized Freud in the 1910s and 1920s.
White, William A. (1870–1937)	co-editor and publisher of the *Journal of Nervous and Mental Disease* and its *Monograph Series*, 1907–1937.
Woolf, Leonard (1880–1969)	British publisher who represented Freud after 1924 and issued the *Standard Edition* beginning in 1953.

Publishers

Publishers of First Editions, 1900–1924

Boni and Liveright (1917–1974). First published Freud's work in 1920. The company was known as Boni and Liveright 1917–1928, Horace Liveright 1928–1933, simply Liveright during 1933, and Liveright Publishing Corporation 1933–1974, when it was acquired by W.W. Norton. Its editions of Freud's *General Introduction to Psychoanalysis* sold more than 45,000 copies, not including reprints licensed to others. Its Modern Library imprint published his Clark lectures in 1924, the same year it published *Beyond the Pleasure Principle* and *Group Psychology and the Analysis of the Ego*. See Chapter 10.

Critic and Guide Publishing Co. (1909–1931). Founded in 1909 by Dr. William J. Robinson, who pirated Freud's essay "Modern Sexual Morality and Modern Nervousness" from 1915 to 1931. See Chapter 7.

Hogarth Press (1917–). Founded by Leonard and Virginia Woolf, it became Freud's official English-language publisher in 1924 in partnership with the International Psycho-Analytical Press. During the 1920s and 1930s Hogarth distributed Freud's books directly to U.S. customers and also licensed reprint rights to American publishers. Produced the *Standard Edition* in 24 volumes, 1953–1974. See Epilogue.

Macmillan Co. (1896–). Separated from its London parent in 1896, Macmillan grew into an American publishing empire that survived until the 1990s. First issued Freud's *Interpretation of Dreams* and *Psychopathology of Everyday Life* in 1913 and 1914 and kept them in print for decades. See Chapter 5.

James A. McCann Co. (1919–1924). Stole long extracts from two of Freud's books and sold them as the piracy *Dream Psychology* in 1920–1921. See Chapter 11.

Moffat, Yard and Co. (1905–1924). Founded as a general trade publisher, this firm became a leading publisher of "the new psychology" before and during World War I. They issued five of Freud's books between 1916 and 1918, including *Wit and Its Relation to the Unconscious* and *Totem and Taboo*. Bought by Dodd Mead in 1924. See Chapter 8.

Nervous & Mental Disease Publishing Co. (1907–1951). Founded in 1907 to publish medical works which U.S. trade publishers considered too controversial to print. Issued 68 titles in its *Monograph Series*, 1909–1945. Published Freud's first American book, *Selected Papers on Hysteria* (1909), and first editions of *Three Contributions to the Theory of Sex* (1911) and *History of the Psycho-analytic Movement* (1917). See Chapter 2.

Tucker Publishing Co. (1875–1915). Anarchist Benjamin Tucker published more than 80 books including a series of daily pamphlets in the spring of 1900 called "The Balzac Library." This included Freud's first separate publication in the U.S., a pamphlet consisting mainly of long excerpts from *The Interpretation of Dreams*, under the title *What Are Dreams?*. See Chapter 1.

The Most Important Publishers of Later Works and Reprints, 1924–1967

Avon (1941–). Independent paperback house that issued titles in initial print runs of 50,000 copies. Published at least seven printings of Freud's *Three Essays on Sexuality, Interpretation of Dreams, Studies on Hysteria*, and *Future of an Illusion* during the 1960s.

Basic Books (1945–1969). Founded in 1945 as a psychoanalytic book club, it began publishing books in 1950; acquired by Harper & Row in 1969. Published Freud's correspondence with Wilhelm Fliess in 1954, Ernest Jones's official three-volume biography 1954–1957, the first U.S. edition of Freud's *Collected Papers* in 1959, and six other Freud titles, including three more volumes of letters 1954–1964.

Encyclopædia Britannica (1952–). Published *Major Works of Sigmund Freud* as volume 54 in its *Great Books of the Western World* series, starting in 1952. The series sold 30,000–40,000 sets annually through the 1990s for a total of approximately 525,000 copies by 1967. Most were purchased as decorative status symbols and the historian of the *Great Books* argues that few were actually read. See Chapter 12.

Garden City Publishing Co. (1923–1959). Doubleday's reprint division that issued inexpensive hardcover books through the 1950s. Sold more than 160,000 copies of Freud's *General Introduction*, 1938–1949.

Haldeman-Julius Publishing Co. (1919–1964). Sold more than 300 million five- and 10-cent Little Blue Books through direct mail. LBB no. 203, containing Freud's essay "The Sexual Enlightenment of Children," may have sold as many as 500,000 copies between 1925 and the early 1940s. See Epilogue.

Modern Library (1917–). Created in 1917 by Albert Boni and Horace Liveright, sold to Bennet Cerf and Donald Klopfer in 1925, and still thriving today. In 1924 published Freud's five Clark lectures in *An Outline of Psychoanalysis* which may have sold approximately 100,000 copies over the next three decades. Also issued *Leonardo Da Vinci* and *Totem and Taboo* in its short-lived Modern Library Paperbacks series (1955 and 1960) and an abridged edition of *The Interpretation of Dreams* in 1950. Its 1938 anthology, *Basic Writings of Sigmund Freud,* sold more than 345,000 copies through 1967. See Chapter 12.

W.W. Norton (1924–). Founded in 1924 to publish books on psychology and science, it licensed Freud's later works from the Hogarth Press starting in 1933 and issued 20 texts from the *Standard Edition* as they became available in the 1950s and 1960s.

Permabooks (1948–1963). A division of Garden City Publishing Co., which was itself a subsidiary of Doubleday; sold to Pocket Books in 1954. Published inexpensive hardcover and paperback reprints of Freud's *General Introduction*, 1949–1958. See Chapter 10.

Pocket Books, Inc. (1939–). Paperback publisher aligned with Simon & Schuster. It quickly became the most successful paperback house in the U.S., with sales of 1.5 million copies in 1939. Issued paperback reprints of Freud's *General Introduction* between 1952 and 1963.

1

Anarchists and Alienists, 1882–1900

Historians thought for many years that Freud was unknown in the U.S. until he came to lecture at Clark University in September 1909. Clark president G. Stanley Hall (1846–1924) probably created this myth by claiming in his 1924 autobiography that "the influence of Freudian views in this country, where they had been little known before, from this date developed rapidly, so that in a sense this unique and significant culture movement owed most of its initial momentum in this country to this meeting." In the years that followed, Hall's explanation was widely repeated. For example, an early historian of psychoanalysis wrote in 1941 that "except for a handful of people Freud was unknown and without influence in American psychology until his addresses of 1909 had been published in the *American Journal of Psychology* the ensuing year." The prevailing narrative claimed that Freud's 1909 Clark lectures first alerted American doctors and scientists to his work, which was afterward promoted in medical journals, then picked up by the Greenwich Village avant-garde, who finally spread it to the general public.[1]

But in 1970 Detroit psychoanalyst and bibliographer Alexander Grinstein discovered articles by Freud published in the U.S. as early as 1883. Other investigators gradually found more evidence that challenged the myth of Freud bursting onto the American scene in 1909. Recent mass digitization of primary sources has now revealed more than 60 significant references to Freud's work published in American medical and scientific journals prior to his 1909 visit, beginning with an 1882 report on his research on the structure of nerve cells (listed in the "Publications by or about Freud Prior to His September 1909 American Visit" section of the Bibliography).[2]

Freud's first American publication appeared anonymously in Philadelphia in 1883, just two years after he earned his M.D. degree.[3] "The great news of the day," he excitedly wrote to his fiancée, "is that I was requested by Fleischl to look at my article in the Philadelphia Medical News at his place. It has appeared there without alteration with some printing errors, and it is printed so narrowly, that it takes up only 2 columns and will bring in only 10 florins…. It is our first connection with America." This and his other early publications were scientific notes on tuberculosis, syphilis, the anesthetic properties of cocaine, and the anatomy of nerve cells. They were very brief notices printed in the weekly *Medical News*, which had been started by Philadelphia scientist Isaac Lea in 1843 to "record discoveries as they are made and passing events as they occur." In 1883–1884 it printed three short notes under the headline "Vienna—From Our Special Correspondent" and a long book review by the 27-year-old Freud.[4]

During the 1880s Freud began to investigate the psychological causes of illness and over the next decade published papers that culminated in 1895 in his first book, *Studien über Hysterie* (*Studies on Hysteria*), co-authored with Josef Breuer. Although not published in English until 1909, its main points were reiterated in the American medical press at least 14 times before the new century dawned; the first article was an abstract by William James when its opening essay appeared in German in 1894.[5] Between 1882 and 1909, before any of his books were published in the U.S., Freud's research was referred to, abstracted, or published in American scientific journals dozens of times.

Another journal reporting on Freud's early work was the quarterly *Alienist and Neurologist* ("alienist" was a Victorian term for psychiatrist). Edited by Dr. Charles H. Hughes (1839–1916) in St. Louis, it described itself as a "journal of scientific, clinical and forensic psychiatry and neurology intended especially to subserve the wants of the General Practitioner of Medicine." Hughes ran an open forum for new ideas, sharing Freud's early psychoanalytic theories even though he personally found them "foolish," "wildly conjecturable" and indicative of the "absurd lengths to which medical men will go in their conclusions, either when seeking medical notoriety or when they take leave of their reason."[6]

Because Freud often sounds like one of our contemporaries, it's important to remember how different the U.S. was in 1900 from how it is today. In 1900 most Americans lived in small towns or on farms rather than in cities and suburbs. They never saw a car, truck, bus, or airplane. Bicycles, telephones, recorded music, and electric lights were cutting edge technology. Information existed only on paper or ephemerally in conversations. Streets were unpaved and regularly churned into mud by horses and wagons. Women struggled into corsets and men wore bowler hats. It was called the Gilded Age, but most people worked six 10-hour days each week or had at most a half-day off on Saturday. No Social Security, unemployment compensation, or Medicaid protected them from starvation and illness. One in five babies died before its first birthday. People suffering from anxiety or depression endured it untreated; there was no Xanax or Zoloft to be prescribed. The few psychotherapists available recommended rest cures and healthy diets. Patients with severe mental illnesses were sent to asylums that resembled medieval dungeons more than modern psychiatric hospitals.[7]

In 1895, Freud and Breuer claimed in *Studies on Hysteria* that unconscious forces could cause physical illnesses. This sounded preposterous to most of their peers. In 1890 America's most respected psychologist, Harvard professor William James, published a psychology textbook of 1,400 densely packed pages; he devoted only six of them to the unconscious, which he dismissed as "pure mythology." In another popular book James's colleague Hugo Munsterberg listed reasons for rejecting the concept and concluded that the unconscious simply did not exist: "There are therefore no unconscious psychic phenomena." Leading European psychologists agreed.[8]

Despite scorn from his profession's best-known authorities, Freud continued to apply his method, which he called "psychoanalysis," and to follow the evidence wherever it led. In the mid–1890s he realized that dreams opened what he called "a royal road" into the unconscious and began carefully documenting those of his patients as well as his own. In the fall of 1897, he began to write *The Interpretation of Dreams*, finishing the manuscript two years later. "It contains," he wrote long afterward, "even according to my present-day judgment, the most valuable of all the discoveries it has been my good fortune to make. Insight such as this falls to one's lot but once in a lifetime."[9] His Viennese publisher Franz Deuticke printed 600 copies and issued them on November 4, 1899 (with a title page dated 1900). Over the next two years only 228 copies were sold and a second edition wasn't needed for another decade. At least a dozen reviews appeared, generally polite but unenthusiastic.[10] The first of them quickly found its way to America.

This was "Wissenschaftliche Traumdeutung" ("The Scientific Interpretation of Dreams") by Carl Metzentin which was reprinted in the German-language newspaper *Der Deutsche Correspondent* in Baltimore on January 21, 1900.[11] The paper had been founded in 1841 by ex-patriate editor Friedrich Raine (1823–1893) to provide the growing German-American community with news from home and in 1900 had a weekly circulation of more than 15,000. The review of Freud had first been printed the previous month in the Berlin journal *Die Gegenwart*, a liberal weekly on literature, art, and current affairs. "The book has had one single review," Freud wrote when he saw it, "in the *Gegenwart*; as a critical evaluation it is empty and as a review it is inadequate. It is just a bad patchwork of my own fragments. However, I am willing to forgive everything because of the one word 'path-breaking.'"[12] The Baltimore reprint of this review appears to be the first notice of Freud's ideas in America outside the scientific or medical literature.

A second quickly followed when the *San Francisco Call* printed a brief account of the book in its magazine section on March 18, 1900.[13] This three-paragraph piece, "Mystery of Dreams Revealed," summarized Freud's argument in *The Interpretation of Dreams* without evaluating it. At the time, the *Call* was one of California's largest newspapers, with a circulation of about 62,000.[14] Although not as large and influential as it would become after William Randolph Hearst bought it, the *Call* was the first periodical to put Freud's ideas in front of the general public in the U.S.

Three weeks later Freud's first American book—using the term loosely—appeared in the form of a 16-page pamphlet filled with condensations and quotes from *The Interpretation of Dreams*. It was Freud's first separate publication in the U.S., issued without his knowledge or permission on April 5, 1900, by Benjamin Tucker (1854–1939), one of the best-known radicals in Victorian America.

Tucker grew up in Dartmouth, Massachusetts, in a Unitarian-Quaker family where questioning authority was taken for granted. As a teenager he rejected Christianity and embraced a variety of extremist causes. "I was a woman suffragist and emancipationist," he recalled of his teenage years, "a prohibitionist and of course a teetotaler, a free trader after having been a protectionist, a believer in an eight-hour law as an adequate solution of the labor problem, at least a doubter as to the sanctity of marriage, and without any doubt whatever as to the sanctity of democracy and majority rule." His parents wanted to send him to Harvard but he refused and only grudgingly agreed to enter M.I.T. which he quit in 1873 without graduating.[15] Instead he spent most of his time doing political work in Boston, where "that day was an exception when I did not pass in the street either Ralph Waldo Emerson or Wendell Phillips or Oliver Wendell Holmes or Charles Sumner or A. Bronson Alcott or Alcott's daughter Louisa."[16] His friend George Schumm described him in 1893 as "an all-round man— Atheist, Anarchist, Egoist, Free Lover—not, like so many reformers, radical in one direction and reactionary in another."[17]

In 1875 Tucker began publishing anarchist tracts and over the next four decades went on to print 80 titles by European and America authors. In 1881 he launched a polemical magazine called *Liberty* which soon became the leading anarchist periodical in the country. He was a radical libertarian, believing that "all the affairs of men should be managed by individuals or voluntary associations, and that the State should be abolished." He claimed to be "the first American—I may say the first

Anglo-Saxon—to start an avowedly Anarchistic newspaper printed in the English language. It is everywhere regarded as the pioneer and principal organ of modem individualist Anarchism." By the late 1880s *Liberty* was read by more than 1,000 subscribers worldwide.[18]

Tucker was a zealous defender of intellectual freedom. In *Liberty* he published every anarchist, socialist, or communist perspective, including those with which he vehemently disagreed. When one editor proposed shortening a book by condensing the arguments of his opponents, Tucker refused on the grounds that it would be unfair to them. When the 1881 edition of *Leaves of Grass* was banned in Boston, he wrote author Walt Whitman offering to "put the book on the market, advertised as the suppressed edition, and invite the authorities to dispute my right to do so." Whitman never forgot the gesture. "Tucker did brave things for *Leaves of Grass* when brave things were rare," the poet told his friend Horace Traubel. "I could not forget that.... I love him: he is plucky to the bone."[19]

Like many political journals, Tucker's *Liberty* was chronically short of cash. In 1899, after moving to New York, he thought that he might cover the costs of the magazine by publishing more books and embarked in search of investors. He found 125 shareholders across the East and Midwest, including "a plasterer, a surveyor, a dealer in ostrich feathers, some lawyers, a printer, several doctors, and some prominent people like Clarence Darrow and William Lloyd Garrison, Jr."[20] With their money he launched the Tucker Publishing Co. early in 1900 with a series of pamphlets called "The Balzac Library."

Tucker intended the pamphlet series to bring cutting-edge European ideas to American readers in an attractive, inexpensive format. Between February 19 and May 21, 1900, he printed short works by George Moore, August Strindberg, Guy de Maupassant, Vernon Lee, Knut Hamsun—and Sigmund Freud. This was a violation of their rights under the 1886 Berne Convention, but the United States had refused to sign that agreement and, under American copyright law at the time, books by foreign authors were only protected if they had been manufactured in the U.S. The Balzac Library included pamphlets on women's rights, imperialism, animal welfare, and militarism as well as literature. He described his readers as mostly lawyers, physicians, "a large number of journalists," "one or two college professors," "artisans of every sort," "farmers by the score," and "at least one policeman."[21]

Each booklet carried an Art Nouveau cover printed in reddish brown with a floral design. They were printed on cheap, acidic paper, staple-bound, and sold for three cents each (roughly equivalent to $1.00 today) or $10 for a subscription to the whole series. In the spring of 1900 Tucker issued a new title almost every day, 70 titles in 12 weeks. Number

29, published on April 5, was the 16-page pamphlet *What Are Dreams?*, which excerpted Freud's book published six months earlier in Vienna.

Freud's book was probably brought to Tucker's attention by his assistant, George Schumm (1856–1941). Schumm had grown up in Sauk City, Wisconsin, in that state's community of radical German "Forty-Eighters." As a young man he wandered the country, settling first in Chicago where he supported the Haymarket rioters in 1886, and then in Boston, where he became Tucker's chief ally. For two decades he served as printer, proof-reader, assistant editor, and general factotum for *Liberty*, as well as monitoring the German press for Tucker's readers.[22]

In that role Schumm likely noticed an anonymous review of *The Interpretation of Dreams* in the March 15, 1900, issue of *Die Grenzboten*, a well-established "Journal of Politics, Literature and Art" published in Leipzig.[23] The article was long and thorough, consisting almost entirely of summaries and quotations from Freud's book. It was probably translated by Shumm's life-partner Emma. A visitor to the *Liberty* office at the time recalled meeting "curly-haired, spectacled, little George Schumm, the proof-reader, enthusiastic and excitable, and Emma Schumm, his mate, thin, very shy and quiet, the German translator (free-union mates, these two, but in fact the most devoted monogamists I ever knew)."[24]

Her English version stuck closely to *The Interpretation of Dreams*. All but two of its 14 text pages contain condensations, summaries, or excerpts from the book. It described Freud's technique of free association and his concepts of the unconscious, instincts, and repression. It recounted three of Freud's dreams and the interpretations he gave of them. The anonymous German reviewer, while admitting reservations (he had mystical leanings about the soul and telepathy), gave a fair and reasonably accurate account of Freud's ideas in a small space.

What Are Dreams? vanished almost as quickly as dreams themselves. It was replaced the next day with number 30 in The Balzac Library, a short story about the conflict between reason and faith, and never reprinted. *Liberty*'s circulation had shrunk to only 600 by then, and it's likely that no more copies than that were printed.[25] Some would have been mailed to subscribers, others offered to the *Liberty* mailing list, and some sold on the street in New York. WorldCat, which lists more than 500 million titles held by over 15,000 libraries, records only two surviving copies.[26]

Tucker's hopes of becoming a successful book publisher were quickly dashed. George Schumm had to resign in May 1900 for a more reliable paycheck. In December Tucker Publishing Co. filed for bankruptcy, but he managed to keep *Liberty* afloat. In 1906, after inheriting $30,000, he opened The Unique Bookshop in Greenwich Village, hoping to sell enough radical literature to make ends meet and moving his editorial and printing operations to a building around the corner. When this was entirely consumed by fire in January 1908, Tucker finally gave up, took what remained of his savings, and with his life-partner moved to France, where it was cheaper to live. He died in Monaco in 1939.[27]

These 19th-century American publications by and about Freud made no impression at all on the nation's culture. A few Germans on the East Coast and a few curious readers in the Bay Area learned about Freud's dream theories in their newspapers. A few anarchists with ties to Tucker browsed his three-penny pamphlet and tossed it aside when the next one appeared. If any of them wanted to learn more about Freud, there was no way to do so. None of his books could be bought in an American bookstore and none had been translated into English. The mainstream press barely mentioned him again for another decade.[28] But among doctors and scientists, the seeds planted in the 1890s soon began to germinate.

2

Jelliffe's and White's Medical Monographs, 1908–1917

In the spring of 1900, while Benjamin Tucker was pirating Freud's work downtown, 33-year-old Smith Ely Jelliffe was two miles away at 111 Fifth Avenue editing the weekly *Medical News*. The *News,* which had printed Freud's first American articles in the early 1880s, monitored medical information published around the world and summarized it for American doctors. Jelliffe (1866–1945) had just joined its staff and was astonished at the chaos and confusion he found. "I recall one occasion early in my work there," he wrote many years later, "where Dr. Riddle Goffe, the editor, and Dr. Taylor, the office manager of Lea & Febiger, and Miss Nevins, the wiry, thin, underfed cigarette fiend and general copy and proof reader, were getting out a special number of the *Medical News* containing the report of the Congress of American Physicians [May 5, 1900]. Buttressed by dictionaries and directories, they took certain batches of proof and laboriously checked all the spelling and names of the contributors.... I knew how to spell, knew the names and the initials and home towns of all of the contributors by heart and it was with a slight trace of irony that I watched the pulling out of the dictionaries and the directories and their confused bemusings. The end result was that in about six months I was made editor and had the *News* running in an orderly fashion and on time."[1]

Few doctors ever read anything beyond the brief summaries that Jelliffe and his colleagues cranked out each week. Most of the 132,000 physicians in the U.S. in 1900 couldn't read other languages than English or easily travel to a large library, so they subscribed to American medical journals to keep up with recent research.[2] The most important of these for neurologists, "alienists," and others who worked with the mentally ill was the *Journal of Nervous and Mental Diseases* (hereafter *JNMD*). No other journal covered Freud's work more often at the turn-of-the-century. The only other periodical that American psychiatrists read regularly was *Alienist and Neurologist,* which appeared in St. Louis only four times a year and was, in the words of historian John Burnham, "a journal of low quality and strangely miscellaneous matter."[3]

Jelliffe also had a hand in producing the *JMND*, which he found equally chaotic. It was edited by Dr. Charles H. Brown and "for the ten days of the end of every month his house in West 45th Street was in a pandemonium, a going here and there, hunting for this or that proof, this or that ad, this or that bit to fill the magazine. A man of many admirable qualities, he was as capricious as the April weather and system knew him not. I was a godsend, since if I had any one quality, it was that of order and system." In October 1901 Dr. Brown died and Jelliffe bought *JMND* with a $2,500 loan from his father-in-law. He grew its circulation to 3,000 readers by 1910 and made it the leading journal in its field.[4]

By 1901 Jelliffe was editor of America's most widely read medical abstracting service (the *Medical News*) and publisher of its most important psychiatric journal (*JMND*), which made him the principal conduit for Freud's ideas at the turn of the century. A friend recalled that "his great attribute was zest. He had to drive right on, carried forward in time on the succeeding waves of every new idea—a powerful, vigorous, emotional man." He "devoted every afternoon throughout the week to laboratory, hospital, or clinical work" and edited the *JNMD* from his Manhattan home, where back issues piled up on steel shelves in the basement. He loved good food and drink, which accounts for his description of himself as "large and stout—5'10", 200 pounds, clean shaven, with a roundish face." Jelliffe was passionate about the theater and later enjoyed friendships with Hollywood celebrities such as John Barrymore and Helen Hayes. He admired Greenwich Village writers like Mabel Dodge and Max Eastman, some of whom were also his patients. Despite his professional stature and high-society connections, he was not above pretending to be Santa Claus at Christmas, climbing up on the roof, and shouting down the chimney to his children.[5]

When Jelliffe took over the *JMND* in 1901, he retained former editor Dr. William G. Spiller, "even more orderly and systematic than I, a much more meticulously accurate proof reader," to acquire and edit original articles, while he himself reviewed books and abstracted other publications from around the world. In any given year Jelliffe was likely to condense three dozen technical articles and review 10 or more medical books. His biographer estimated that over the course of his career Jelliffe shared nearly 1,000 medical texts this way, and emphasized the importance of this seeming drudgery:

Since most American physicians, even very good ones, did not in fact read foreign languages easily, if at all, Jelliffe came to serve as the agency through which many specialists and other physicians learned about the existence overseas of both experimental and clinical advances in neurology. It was in this way, along with what he did as translator and as coeditor of the Nervous and Mental Disease Monographs, that Jelliffe became in the United States the symbol as well as the effective mediator of knowledge of foreign medicine.[6]

His audience was peculiarly diverse. In 1900, American mental health professionals fell into several camps whose membership rarely overlapped. At one end of the spectrum were "arm-chair psychologists" like James and Munsterberg, lodged comfortably in university philosophy departments where they ruminated on the human soul as philosophers had done for centuries. On the other end were pragmatic managers of state-run insane asylums, often political appointees with no medical training at all who were trying to keep thousands of senile and chronically insane patients under control at the lowest cost to taxpayers. Between the two were neurologists dissecting brains in laboratories in search of the physical causes of mental illness, medically trained psychiatrists treating patients with hypnotism, suggestion, or primitive electric shock, and physicians recommending rest cures and special diets to depressed, anxious, or schizophrenic clients. Skirting the periphery was a smorgasbord of cranks, cultists, and con-men ranging from Christian Scientists to snake-oil salesmen.[7]

Shortly after finishing his medical degree in 1889, Jelliffe spent a year in Europe improving his medical skills and visiting museums in Vienna, Prague, Berlin, Rome, London, and Paris. It was the first of many regular trips to Europe to establish professional connections and bring back reports for his journals. In 1906 he spent six months in Munich; in 1907 he met Jung at a conference and visited the Burgholzli hospital in Zurich; he spent most of 1908–1909 in Paris and Berlin studying European approaches to mental illness. By 1909 he could count most of the world's leading neurologists and psychiatrists as colleagues, and they eagerly shared their research with him. A contemporary said that "his friends love him, his fellow workers admire him, and his opponents fear him."[8] Though not initially very sympathetic to psychoanalysis, he covered it in his journals with increasing frequency during the century's first decade. He mentioned it only in passing about once a year between 1901 and 1907, but after meeting Jung and Freud he published six substantial articles and a dozen shorter references in 1908–1909.[9]

A handful of American doctors read Jelliffe's notices of Freud, tracked down the original German publications, and tried to apply his methods. The earliest appears to have been Dr. James J. Putnam, who treated three patients with psychoanalysis in 1904 at Massachusetts General Hospital in Boston. In 1906 the *Journal of Abnormal Psychology* was founded there partly as a vehicle for psychoanalytic articles that weren't welcome in more traditional journals. Putnam's 1906 piece on his experiment at Mass General was the first paper on psychoanalytic technique to be published in the U.S.[10] In New York, Dr. Adolf Meyer, director of psychiatric programs in the New York state hospital system, began to apply Jung's psychoanalytic techniques in 1905. Over the next two years, his state-run asylums from New York City to Binghamton began experimenting with psychoanalysis and sharing their results in the *State Hospitals Bulletin*. When the New York Psychoanalytic Society was founded in 1911, 10 of its 15 original members worked for Meyer at his hospital on Ward's Island in the East River.[11]

Meanwhile in Washington, D.C., Dr. William A. White, director of St. Elizabeth's Hospital, also began applying Freud's methods. He and Jelliffe had met in the summer of 1896 when they were both practicing in Binghamton, N.Y., and had become best friends. Jelliffe's widow recalled that "he and Willy White were Damon and Pythias, I mean, like nothing I have ever seen. Those two men were the best friends that could ever be in that world! It was incredible what they meant to each other." White soon became co-publisher of *JMND* and Jelliffe later remarked that "White and I have written and published so many things together that I am not at all certain when I quote from one of them whether to say, 'White and Jelliffe,' or 'Jelliffe and White.'"[12]

Around the country a handful of other mental health professionals reported trying out Freud's methods. Some began travelling to Vienna or

Left: Dr. Smith Ely Jelliffe about 1909 (courtesy National Library of Medicine, HMD Collection Portrait no. 3781.2). *Right:* Dr. William A. White in 1909 (courtesy National Library of Medicine, Association of Military Surgeons of the United States records).

Zurich to learn the new techniques firsthand from Freud or Jung. One of these was Abraham Arden Brill (1874–1948), the "indomitable, irresistible uncompromising little doctor" who became Freud's first U.S. translator and literary agent.[13] Brill was remembered for his twinkling eyes, ready laughter, and cheerful disposition—unless he had to defend psychoanalysis, when "he became fervid, impetuous and impulsive, and thoughts seemed veritably to explode from his mind." Ernest Jones recalled meeting him in 1908: "Brill had emigrated alone to the United States from an eastern province of the Austro-Hungarian Empire at the tender age of fourteen, and had landed in New York with, I think, the sum of three dollars. He was the stuff of which so much of America has been made. He might have been called a rough diamond, but there was no doubt about the diamond.... And he had a heart of gold, as no one has better reason to know than myself." Mabel Dodge wrote of him, "I liked Brill immensely from the very first. One could have confidence in him, for his integrity was apparent at once."[14]

Brill, who did more than anyone else to bring Freud to Americans, was born March 12, 1874, in the city of Kańczuga in eastern Poland and emigrated in 1889, arriving in New York as a penniless teenager alone and unable to speak English. By sleeping on floors at night and doing odd jobs by day, he managed to put himself through New York University, graduating in 1901. His friend Clarence Oberndorf wrote that "occasionally Brill in a reminiscent mood would muse upon these days of hardship when he helped with chores about a saloon for the accommodation of sleeping there at night, taught mandolin and English to foreigners at twenty-five cents a lesson, and for a while slept on a mattress on the floor of the office of a physician-friend." In 1903, at the age of 29, he received his M.D. from Columbia and found work in Adolf Meyer's clinic.[15] "I was fortunate in being one among Dr. Meyer's first group of students at the Psychiatric Institute," Brill recalled long afterward, "where he gave us a thorough grounding in neuropathology and modern psychiatry in the form of lectures, clinics, and abstracts of the teachings of prominent psychiatrists of the German school." After four years under Meyer, Brill had saved enough money to study in Europe, and in the summer of 1907 he began an internship with Jung in Zurich.[16]

Jelliffe and White were in Europe that summer, too, and one of the things they discussed was how to get Freud's works past prudish American censorship laws. White recalled that "when Dr. Jelliffe and I were trying to get publishers in the United States to bring to the American medical profession some of the outstanding products of European thought, we failed completely, but we reached down into our own pockets and started a publishing business." They were already publishing *JMND* but decided to also issue books in a new *Nervous and Mental Disease Monograph Series.* It was run initially by Jelliffe in New York, though White was deeply involved in editorial decisions from Washington. Their first monograph was White's *Outlines of Psychiatry* (1907), which was followed over the next decade by 25 more titles, including three by Freud, two by Jung, and others by Adler, Rank, Stekel and other founders of psychoanalysis. The series was often in precarious financial straits; in the spring of 1916 they considered giving it up altogether and trying to sell it to Macmillan, Appleton, or Moffat, Yard and Co.[17]

When the *Monograph Series* launched, one reviewer wrote, "The editors, Drs. Jelliffe and White, announce that the series will consist of short monographs, translations, and minor text-books on subjects related to nervous and mental diseases." The writer was disappointed that White's inaugural volume was "published on poor paper and in a paper binding. It is worthy of a more stable structure."[18] They improved the paper quality, but titles continued to be bound in wrappers until 1917, when some copies of new titles began to be offered in paper-covered boards. "White's book was a great success," notes Jelliffe's biographer John Burnham, "and in numerous revised editions kept the Monograph Series profitable. Many of the other publications were highly technical and, for one reason or another, did not sell well in the limited medical/psychological fields."[19]

When Jelliffe and White returned to the U.S. in 1907, Brill stayed on in Zurich. On February 12, 1908, Jung wrote Freud that Brill "is most enthusiastic about the Breuer-Freud Studies. He wants me to ask you whether you would agree to a translation." In April Brill went down to Salzburg with Jung and Ernest Jones for the First Psychoanalytic Congress, where he met Freud for the first time. Brill and Jones returned to Vienna with Freud, who "was naturally interested in the spread of psycho-analytical work to America." When they discussed English translations, Freud agreed that Brill should translate his works for American readers: "It was during our first meeting that we agreed on the sequence in which I was to translate his works into English. I continued as his sole English translator until after the World War, when I voluntarily gave up the task."[20]

"When I returned from Zürich [in May 1908]," Brill recalled elsewhere, "I brought with me two manuscripts, Jung's *The Psychology of Dementia Praecox* and Freud's *Selected Papers on Hysteria*, the translations of which I made while at Burgholzli." But getting Freud's books into print proved problematic due to their explicit sexual content: "No American publisher was willing to take the risk of putting them out in this country." Brill soon crossed paths with Jelliffe, however, who suggested the translations be issued in the new *JNMD Monograph Series.* "I then met Jelliffe face-to-face for the first time," he recalled. "I always admired Jelliffe for his racy and learned reviews in the Journal and when I talked to him I was soon struck by his genial personality and versatile mind."[21] So plans were made for Jelliffe and White to publish Freud's first American book, *Selected Papers on Hysteria and Other Psychoneuroses*.

Brill faced three significant challenges as Freud's translator. First, he was not a native speaker of either German or English—sixty percent of his native region spoke Polish and the other 40 percent Ukrainian, and he'd picked up his English on the streets of New York's Lower East Side. Secondly, he wasn't yet well-versed in psychoanalysis: "When Jung, whom I first met at that clinic, asked, 'Did you read Freud's *Traumedeutung*?' I was somewhat puzzled by the title, but I acted as if I knew Freud quite well." Thirdly, Brill had significant doubts about his own ability. "I am really proud of the confidence which you are so kind as to place in me," he wrote to Freud when he got back to New York. "I shall endeavor to come up to your expectations, and hope to contribute my mite towards the propagation of your great works in America."[22]

These shortcomings led to awkward English expressions which were sharply criticized by Brill's colleagues and have drawn complaints ever since. Jones recalled being "horror-struck" when he saw the first drafts of Brill's translation of *Selected Papers on Hysteria*. They were "not only seriously inaccurate, with misunderstandings of the German text and ambiguous renderings that greatly impaired their value for scientific purposes, but were also couched in an undignified and colloquial form that was unworthy of Freud's style and gave a misleading impression of his personality." Brill later defended himself by explaining, "I made no effort to produce literary excellencies; I was only interested in conveying these new ideas into comprehensible English." A colleague recalled him saying, "I know there are plenty of mistakes in my translations, but put yourself in my place. When I started I had nothing to go by. It was up to me to decide how I should translate 'Verdrängung,' whether it should be called 'suppression' or 'repression,' and I worried about it a long time. So now all of you fellows are saved that trouble." Reviewers, however, generally praised his translations and their popularity testified to his success with readers.[23]

Brill began revising the manuscripts he'd drafted in Zurich earlier that year. "I am constantly working on your translations and will soon have some finished," he told Freud on October 23, 1908. A month later (November 18) he wrote asking for advice: "now and then I come across a term which I find very difficult to translate. I cannot get an appropriate English word or expression for *abreagieren* and its noun. I thought of 'reacting off' or 'off-reaction' but it sounds rather clumsy. I am now thinking of using the term 'ventilation' from the expression 'to give vent to one's feelings' but I am not at all pleased with it." He made similar requests for help in letters to his editor William White in Washington (they settled on the now-accepted "abreaction").[24]

Two months later, on January 10, 1909, Freud cautioned Brill about the hostile reception that was likely to greet the book: "You are a brave warrior. And you have to go through the 'ups and downs' of a fight. I like that you tend to be optimistic, but I think you face hard times. As sexuality comes to the fore in our teachings, you will find all sympathy deserted." A month later he replied to Brill's anxiety about the book's explicit sexual language: "It would be an undignified and unwise deed to hide sexuality—let's say: eroticism, that sounds finer—and thus to follow the example of the neurotics themselves. We can only impress if we stay true to ourselves, uncover the truth and treat audiences like we treat our sick ... as in Europe, some will attack us, but others will come to their senses and begin to examine whether we are not right." Privately, Freud expressed deeper doubts, telling Jung, "Jones and Brill write often, Jones's observations are shrewd and pessimistic, Brill sees everything through rose-colored spectacles. I am inclined to agree with Jones. I also think that once they discover the sexual core of our psychological theories they [American publishers] will drop us. Their prudery and their material dependence on the public are too great."[25]

Josef Breuer had given Brill permission to publish his contributions to the co-authored 1895 volume, but these were replaced in *Selected Papers* by more recent articles and essays by Freud. The first two chapters went to the printer on May 3, 1909, as Brill continued to translate the later ones. When he suggested including one last essay as the manuscript neared completion, Freud replied on May 25, 1909, "I am very touched by your great effort with the translation. I really think you're doing something very good with it. But why do you want to increase the work? Of course I wouldn't mind handing over the fragment. But shouldn't everything that we have selected from the studies and the first volume of the theory of neuroses suffice to fill a volume of 250 pages? In Vienna we already considered Papers (or Selected Papers) on Hysteria and Other Neuroses as a title." In July the printer was delayed by other work and in August Brill and White were still debating the book's title ("neuroses" or "psychoneuroses"), but by the end of the month the entire manuscript was at last in the hands of the printer. Brill accepted a 10 percent royalty which he passed on to Freud.[26]

As Freud prepared to attend the September 1909 twentieth anniversary conference at Clark University, he told Brill that he hoped the book would be ready in time to distribute at the meeting. Brill was at the dock to meet Freud on August 29 but the book was not. It was still held up at the printer. "The translation should be coming out in two weeks," Freud wrote to his family, but it actually took another month before his first American book appeared on September 30, by which time he had already sailed for home. Although Brill must have promptly shipped a copy to Vienna, it only reached the author in November. "The day after your letter," Freud wrote to Brill on December 1, "both copies of the translation finally arrived, one of which went to [co-author Josef] Breuer."[27]

Selected Papers on Hysteria and Other Psychoneuroses was the fourth volume in Jelliffe and White's *Monograph Series* and, like the others, was humble in appearance. The interior pages were printed on quality laid paper, but they were bound inside heavy, dark brown, acidic wrappers. Most surviving copies are owned by libraries that stripped these away when they rebound the book in hardcover, so few examples of the original wrappers exist. No records have been found that show how many were printed. Jelliffe's own copies were destroyed when his summer home burned in 1953, and it's possible that the records of the *Monograph Series* were destroyed then, too; none were found in his or in White's papers. Although *JNMD* had 3,000 subscribers in 1909, it's likely that only a few hundred copies of the book were printed since it had to be reprinted less than three years later.[28]

Over the next few months *Selected Papers* was listed dozens of times in medical journals as they announced new books, but it received only five reviews. These were all positive, praising Brill's translation and Jelliffe's and White's *Monograph Series* as well as highlighting the importance of Freud's ideas. "The editors have done their work well," wrote the *American Journal of the Medical Sciences*, "and the translator, A.A. Brill, still better, for anyone who has read the original can appreciate the difficulty of translation." The *Interstate Medical Journal* in St. Louis was the most laudatory, claiming that "a new and hitherto undreamed of territory has been opened up for psychical exploration."[29]

Freud was pleased, too, telling Brill on December 1, 1909, "I can no longer delay thanking you for this work.... I don't want to forget to add that the editor has long since fulfilled his obligations to Deuticke [Freud's Vienna publisher, who had licensed the American edition to Jelliffe]. D. sent me half of the fee (62.5 Kr = 12 1/2#). You probably didn't get rich from the translation either. Let us hope confidently that the book will contribute in other ways."[30]

The first edition* was followed in 1912 by a second that added two new

---

*I have used the word "edition" for all copies of a book printed from the same setting of type regardless of where, when, or how they were printed. An "impression" is all the copies of an edition printed at the same time and place (synonymous with a "printing"). An "issue" is all the copies of an impression intentionally published as a distinct unit, such as those in a special series with its own branding. "State" refers to all the copies of an impression that contain the same unintentional features such as a typographical error.

essays, "On Wild Psychoanalysis" and "The Future Chances of Psychoanalytic Therapy." Brill revised the text again for a third edition (1920) and added a new chapter, "The Testimony of Witnesses and Psychoanalysis." In the *Standard Edition*, James Strachey cites a fourth edition published in 1922 but WorldCat does not record it and no copy has been located. In 1952, the publishers of the Encyclopædia Britannica included the 1909 text in *The Major Works of Sigmund Freud*, volume 54 of their *Great Books of the Western World* series.[31]

When Brill inquired in 1934 about printing a complete edition of *Studien über Hysterie*, including Breuer's chapters as well as Freud's, William White replied that "'Selected Papers on Hysteria' has been out of print for several years and we do not contemplate reprinting it." Over the next two years they worked out contract details and in December 1936 issued 500 copies of the first English translation of Breuer and Freud's complete 1895 book (Nervous and Mental Disease Monograph Series no. 61). Brill paid all production costs, including $585 to print it, in return for 50 percent of the sales income. It was reprinted in 1937, 1947 and 1950, when it was licensed to Beacon Press in Boston for paperback and hardcover issues. In 1955 Brill's translation was superseded by Strachey's *Standard Edition* translation (in volume 2).[32]

Selected Papers on Hysteria did almost nothing to acquaint the general public with Freud's ideas. It wasn't sold in bookstores and was all but ignored by newspapers and magazines (Havelock Ellis praised it in *Popular Science Monthly*, the only mention outside of medical journals).[33] A growing number of doctors began to take notice of Freud, though, and through them their patients, colleagues, and friends heard his name. But his major works were still inaccessible to American readers unless they knew German and lived near a library large enough to have imported them.

Jelliffe and Brill often worked together at Columbia's Vanderbilt Clinic and, since they lived near one another on Manhattan's Upper West Side, would walk home together through Central Park. "After our clinics," he recalled, "three times a week Brill and I walked homewards together through the park and as formerly with Dr. White we argued and argued and he persisted and thus I became a convinced Freudian."[34]

In 1911 Jelliffe and White published Freud's second title in the Nervous and Mental Disease Monographs series. This was *Three Contributions to the Sexual Theory* (altered to "*The Theory of Sex*" in subsequent editions), first published in Vienna in 1905. In it Freud argued that the origin of neuroses and psychoses lay in unresolved sexual conflicts, that even infants and toddlers felt a wide range of sexual impulses—"the sexual impulse of the child really shows itself to be polymorphous perverse"—and that a healthy sex life was key to happiness and productivity. He claimed that bisexuality was universal, urged tolerance for homosexuality, and argued that parents should not lie to their children about sex.

These ideas were abhorrent to an America steeped in Victorian prudery and Puritan repression, and Freud was heartily denounced from all sides. "To many Americans," wrote historian Henry May, "such ideas as infant sexuality were not only wicked, but insane."[35] His graphic, matter-of-fact descriptions of a wide variety of sexual acts by people of all ages was particularly offensive to contemporary standards. "I have always found it hard to understand why Freud's views on sex roused so much opposition," Brill wrote later. "Freud did not enter that realm voluntarily but ... was led, step by step, to discover and explore the realm of infantile sexuality. This discovery was based entirely on empiric material. In probing for the origin of hysterical symptoms, in tracing them back as far as possible, even into childhood, Freud found physical and psychical activities of a definitely sexual nature in the earliest ages of childhood." Brill's editor, William White, found it easier to understand the opposition: "The nineteenth century believed in ignorance and silence. Psychoanalysis believed in neither."[36]

Brill had begun translating the book soon after he returned to the U.S. in the summer of 1908 and kept at it throughout the following year. "Brill spoke seven languages," Oberndorf recalled. "He possessed an amazing capacity for work, frequently sleeping only five or six hours, so that he found time not only for his writing and other interests but for long hours in his office as a private practitioner." Working from the second German edition of 1910, the only liberties Brill appears to have taken with the original text were to rewrite, compress, and occasionally omit Freud's footnotes. Compared to his major changes to Freud's other texts a few years later, these seem minor. As the manuscript approached completion, Brill or Jelliffe persuaded Harvard psychologist James J. Putnam to write an introduction. "I respect Brill and have written an *envoi* for his translation of the *Drei Abhandlungen*," Putnam told Ernest Jones after seeing the manuscript, "but he writes atrocious 'English' (if one must call it such)."[37]

The book was a natural choice for the *Monograph Series* since Jelliffe had begun "routinely pointing out in reviews and abstracts (in which editorial matter was not routine) the contributions of Freud and criticizing authors who failed to mention the psychoanalytic viewpoint."[38] Like other volumes in the series, *Three Contributions to the Sexual Theory* was bound in paper wrappers, priced $2.00, and probably issued in an edition of just a few hundred copies. Jelliffe applied for copyright on December 1, 1910, and the two required deposit copies were received December 6, but *Publishers Weekly* didn't announce it until February 4, 1911.

The first printing sufficed until 1916, when the title was changed to *Three Contributions to the Theory of Sex* and a reprint issued billing itself as the "Second Enlarged and Revised Edition." This added Freud's two-page 1914 introduction and contained a much-expanded index, but otherwise it was nearly identical to the first printing. Over the next 15 years the book was reprinted three more times, with minor changes. A 1918 reprint called itself the "Third Revised Edition" although the text was virtually the same as the two preceding ones. A 1920 issue labelled "Second Edition, Second Reprinting" on its title page contained a slightly revised and expanded index but no major changes to the text. After that, demand for the book began to fall off. A stray royalty report in the Brill Papers, the only one for *Three Contributions* that appears to survive, shows only 138 copies sold during the year 1925. In 1930 a new revision, calling itself the "Fourth Edition," appeared with a new introduction by Brill and the text revised and reset to follow the 1924 German edition. In 1933 White told Brill that it this was "still selling quite steadily." All these issues were available in plain paper wrappers or in brown paper-covered boards printed in black. They were superseded in 1953 by James Strachey's translation in volume 7 of the *Standard Edition* as *Three Essays on Sexuality*.[39]

Although it breaks the chronological sequence, this is the most appropriate place to discuss the last of Freud's books in Jelliffe and White's *Monograph Series*.

Although they were enthusiastic about psychoanalysis, Jelliffe and White were also willing to promote other approaches. They continued to publish the work of Alfred Adler and Carl Jung after he broke with them, which alienated Freud. Brill reported in 1913 that "Jelliffe is a very ardent worker for psychoanalysis, but of course he is thoroughly Jung." Freud disapproved of him even more strongly for reprinting articles from European journals without compensation. When in 1913 White and Jelliffe founded the first English-language journal devoted to psychoanalysis, *The Psychoanalytic Review*, Freud refused to write for it. "The way in which the *Review* makes up for this deficiency with translations," he wrote to White, referring to reprinting of European authors, "may be commercially justifiable, what with the lack of copyright in America, but strikes me as unseemly. I find it difficult to regard the *Review* as anything other than a competitor.... This judgment of the *Review* is further supported by Jelliffe's intimacy with Jung, who in spite of his presidency has never lifted a finger for the International Association or its organs, but only pursued his own aggrandizement." He told Brill that "Jelliffe, in fact, is one of the worst American businessmen, translate: crooks, Columbus has discovered."[40]

By 1914 Freud's movement was fracturing, with different approaches all calling themselves "psychoanalysis" and unqualified amateurs opening private practices. Early that year he wrote a long essay on *The History of the Psycho-analytic Movement* to explain his ideas and their origins. After it appeared in Austria, Jones suggested to Jelliffe that he should publish it in the *Psychoanalytic Review* and recommended that *JNMD* editorial assistant Charles R. Payne translate it. When Brill learned this he was furious since Freud had appointed *him* official translator. "I have done my best to put the matter right with him," Jones wrote to Freud, "but he is what we call 'touchy.'" Freud replied, "Naturally Brill was suspicious and Jelliffe a liar as always.... On the whole, it does not matter to me where the translation appears and who does it, as long as it does get done. Naturally, I never wanted to encroach on Brill, and as a result left every decision to him."[41]

In the end, Brill did translate the long essay and in November 1915 Jelliffe and White accepted it not only for their journal but for the *Monograph Series*. Brill returned corrected galleys in March 1916, but White did not want to print the book until the text had been published in the *Psychoanalytic Review*. "The Freud article will begin to run in the next number of the review," White wrote Brill on May 9. "I had not clearly in mind that we were going to monograph it, but if you understood it and want it that way we can get it into the monograph form I hope early in the winter."[42]

In fact, *The History of the Psycho-analytic Movement* did not appear until the October 1916 issue. It then went into production as a monograph, with page proofs arriving at Christmas, but the book was not published until mid–February 1917, as number 25 in the *Monograph Series*.[43] It was bound in paper wrappers (some copies were issued in brown paper over boards) with the front cover dated 1916, since Jelliffe and White had hoped to get it out before the end of the year. The title page bears the correct date of 1917. It contains a six-page advertising catalog in the back promoting all the titles in the series as well as *The Psychoanalytic Review*. It was not reissued separately but was anthologized in Brill's 1938 Modern Library Giant collection, *The Basic Writings of Sigmund Freud*. Strachey's translation appeared in volume 14 of the Standard Edition in 1957, Collier included it in their 10-volume paperback set *Collected Papers of Sigmund Freud* in 1963, and a separate paperback version was issued by Bantam Books the same year.

Between 1900 and 1920, Jelliffe played a critical role in disseminating Freud's ideas to the American medical community. As editor of the *Medical News* from 1900 to 1908, he made sure that Freud's German publications were abstracted and publicized on this side of the Atlantic. As an editor and publisher of *JMND* for half-a-century, he printed longer articles, reported on foreign research, and reviewed every new book about psychoanalysis. By founding the *JMND Monograph Series* in 1907, he

S.E. Jelliffe's bookplate, designed by Anne Jouard (1896–1978) (author's collection).

and White made available Freudian books that no other American publisher would touch. And by starting *The Psychoanalytic Review* in 1913 they guaranteed an outlet for the growing number of reports by doctors applying Freud's methods. Jelliffe's efforts may not have reached the American masses, but they were one of the main channels through which Freud's ideas flowed to mental health professionals. He and Freud eventually smoothed over their differences and had a warm collegial relationship during the 1920s and 1930s.

Jelliffe's role as bibliographic mediator fueled his love of book collecting. This bookplate drawn by Anne Jouard (1896–1978) shows him pleasantly overwhelmed by a cascade of books. Over the decades he amassed a personal library of more than 20,000 volumes that contained not just medicine and science but also works by nature writers Henry Thoreau and John Burroughs, the great 19th-century British novelists and historians, classic Greek dramatists, and German romantic poets. In the early 1940s, he sold most of the psychiatric titles to the Hartford Neuropsychiatric Institute (now the Institute of Living) in Hartford, Conn. He kept about 2,000 volumes, including his own copies of the complete *Monograph Series* and his working copies of his own books. These were all destroyed when his summer home burned in 1953 but a number of other books from his library eventually reached the antiquarian book trade.[44]

Throughout their careers, Jelliffe and White remained eclectic in their therapeutic approaches, White as superintendent of St. Elizabeths Hospital in Washington, D.C., 1903–1937, and Jelliffe in private practice. As a result, during the 1930s and 1940s they were ostracized by the orthodox Freudian community. Both, however, continued to see patients, write, and publish nearly until they died, White in 1937 and Jelliffe in 1945.[45]

3

Freud's Lectures at Clark University, 1909

Freud's ideas had been circulating among physicians for several years before he stepped to the podium at Clark University in September 1909. So much has been written about the Clark conference, and in such detail, that I'll provide only enough background to explain how his third American book grew out of it. Readers interested in other aspects of Freud's famous U.S. visit can easily consult other sources.[1]

Clark was tiny in 1909—only 16 faculty members and 91 graduate students—but President G. Stanley Hall had raised about $300,000 in today's dollars to commemorate its twentieth anniversary. Hall was one of the country's best-known psychologists, editor of the *American Journal of Psychology* and author of a ground-breaking study of adolescence. He also popularized the metaphor of the mind as iceberg, our normal waking consciousness being dwarfed by the inaccessible but more powerful unconscious: "The mistake of ego-theorists is akin to that of those who thought icebergs were best studied from above the surface and were moved by winds, when in fact about nine-tenths of their mass is submerged, and they follow the deeper and more constant oceanic currents, often in the teeth of gales."[2] He had praised Freud in his book, taught him in classes, and was proud to have him as the conference's principal speaker.

Brill met Freud at the dock on August 29, 1909, and guided him, Carl Jung, and Sandor Ferenczi around New York City for a week before they headed north to Worcester, Massachusetts. During the initial week of celebrations in July, Hall had opened the campus to the public for 47 lectures given by experts on child welfare and other social topics. During the concluding week in September, 136 lectures were given by leading scholars in the humanities and sciences, including Ernest Rutherford, the father of nuclear physics, who'd just won the Nobel Prize, Franz Boas, the creator of modern anthropology, and six psychologists including Jung and Freud.

The opening ceremony was attended by 175 people; probably no more than 200 attended the lectures.[3]

From Tuesday, September 7, through Saturday, September 11, Freud spoke extemporaneously in German at 11:00 a.m. His talks were probably attended by 100–150 people, including reporters who summarized them for newspapers in Worcester, Springfield, and Boston (helped by English-language press releases coordinated by Hall). Near the front sat Emma Goldman, who was touring New England at the time to give talks on anarchism. Back in 1896 she'd attended Freud's Vienna University lectures and found that "his simplicity and earnestness and the brilliance of his mind combined to give one the feeling of being led out of a dark cellar into broad daylight." At Clark 13 years later she "was deeply impressed by the lucidity of his mind and the simplicity of his delivery. Among the array of professors, looking stiff and important in their university caps and gowns, Sigmund Freud, in ordinary attire, unassuming, almost shrinking, stood out like a giant among pygmies."[4] Also in the audience at times were James J. Putnam and William James from Boston, Adolf Meyer and A.A. Brill from New York, William A. White from Washington, and Ernest Jones from Toronto, as well as Jung and Ferenzci from Europe. S.E. Jelliffe was in Paris, so did not attend.[5]

During his daily lectures Freud talked off the top of his head about his research and its theoretical underpinnings. Before leaving for home, he promised Hall that he would write out the lectures afterward for publication in the *American Journal of Psychology*. Hall agreed to also print them in a separately published book that would include all the speakers' lectures and asked to have Freud's manuscript by Christmas. Freud sent the first three essays by that deadline but could only deliver the last two in January 1910. Hall assigned one of his graduate students, Harry Chase, to translate them and, after revising Chase's work, Freud approved the final text.[6] The English translation appeared in the April 1910 issue of Hall's quarterly *American Journal of Psychology* alongside Jung's talk on the word association method.[7]

The separate book printing didn't appear until late autumn. The 250-page collection was printed on heavy laid paper by Worcester printer Oliver B. Wood during the fall of 1910 from the same setting of type as the *Journal* (Freud's name is misspelled "Frued" in the running head on the final two pages of both). It was bound in light blue stiff paper wrappers that were usually discarded when the book was bound by libraries. As its frontispiece, the pamphlet included a now-famous photograph of 42 conference participants standing on the steps of the Clark library, where the lectures were given. The number of copies printed is not known, but the edition was surely small. The *American Journal of Psychology* had only 500

Clark University, September 1909. Front row, from left: Freud, G. Stanley Hall, Carl Jung. Back row, from left: A.A. Brill, Ernest Jones, Sandor Ferenczi (Library of Congress, Manuscript Division, Sigmund Freud Papers, *Subject File, Clark University, Worcester, Mass., photographs, 1904 to 1909*).

subscribers at the time and only about 300 people had attended the final ceremony of the conference, at which honorary degrees were conferred. The print run of the follow-up volume was probably somewhere between the two. Freud was among the first to receive a copy. "Lectures to celebrate the 20th year came from Worcester yesterday as a special publication," he wrote to Brill on November 6, 1910. Clark's own copies were accessioned in November and Harvard didn't receive its copy as a gift until December.[8]

   Although Freud's Clark lectures were in many ways an ideal introduction to his work for laypeople, they didn't reach a wide audience for more than a decade. In 1910, like Jelliffe's and White's monograph series, they were read mainly by professionals. They weren't printed again until 1924 when they were included in *An Outline of Psychoanalysis*, edited by the Boston psychoanalyst James Van Teslaar for Boni and Liveright's Modern Library; this remained in print until 1955 and may have ultimately reached 100,000 readers (see Chapter 12). Their first separate publication in America was a paperback issued by Henry Regnery in 1949. Regnery had contracted to publish the 54-volume *Great Books of the Western World* series for the Encyclopædia Britannica and as the hardcover series was being produced, he printed a number of its shorter works in advance. His paperback edition of Freud's Clark Lectures remained in print for several decades, some paperback issues bearing the imprint of his Gateway Editions. When the Great Books debuted in 1952, volume 54, *The Major Works of Sigmund Freud*, included the Clark lectures; it sold 35,000–50,000 sets per year for decades and totaled a million copies by 1990. Freud's five Clark lectures were also included in two 1957 American reprints of the Hogarth Press anthology *A General Selection from the Works of Sigmund Freud*; the first was a hardcover from Liveright Publishing Co. and the second a paperback from Doubleday's Anchor Books. Finally, in 1957 the lectures were included in volume 11 of the *Standard Edition*, retitled "Five Lectures on Psycho-Analysis" and translated by James Strachey.[9]

Like *Selected Papers on Hysteria*, Freud's Clark lectures did nothing to change the attitudes and understanding of the American public in 1910 because they only reached a tiny audience. They were informal, easy to read, and fast-paced, with touches of humor, but their explicit sexual references, especially the frank discussion of infantile sexuality in the fourth lecture, would have brought the censors down on any trade publisher who dared to print them. But with 500 copies going to physicians in Hall's *Journal* just a few months after his *Selected Papers* had appeared, Freud's ideas began to reach more deeply into the medical community. Younger physicians, especially, began to discuss his theories and experiment with his methods.

As they became better known, Freud's ideas met with more resistance. Most American physicians were skeptical or even hostile to his work, preferring to believe that mental illness was inherited or produced by as-yet-undiscovered physical causes. Freud's claims that obsessions, phobias, and other neuroses had sexual origins was deeply offensive to contemporary values. In the spring of 1910, New York neurologist Joseph Collins condemned psychoanalysis as "pornographic stories about pure virgins." A speaker at the American Psychological Association meeting in Baltimore denounced the "mad epidemic of Freudism now invading America."[10] There was no epidemic. Few Americans had heard of Freud in 1910 and the fledgling psychoanalytic groups in New York and Boston were so tiny that they met in their members' living rooms. But that was about to change.

4

The Mainstream Press
Discovers Freud, 1910–1912

As soon as the Clark conference ended, President G. Stanley Hall dashed off a summary of it for the *Nation*, a liberal New York weekly with 8,000 readers.[1] This was only the second article to discuss Freud's work outside professional medical journals:

> One of the most attractive of the eminent foreign savants who came to this country expressly to attend the celebration was Sigmund Freud of Vienna. Far too little is known in America of either the man or his work ... partly because so much that he taught was new and revolutionary, he has until lately had but scant recognition; and because he attempts to do justice to sex in his scheme, he was for years socially ostracized. Happily, however, he is now coming to his own and a growing circle of very vigorous young men in all civilized countries are giving him due recognition and working out his ideas.

He also acknowledged that "most of those who gathered together were themselves professors, who lectured to each other in turn." This prompts the question, how did Freud's ideas escape the confines of academia to take root in the minds of the general public?[2]

The mainstream press largely ignored the Clark conference. The *Boston Evening Transcript* reported on it each day and even printed a two-column interview with Freud on September 11 in which he described his goals, methods, and conclusions. But that paper only reached about 1,250 readers in greater Boston. Neither the *New York Times* nor any other major newspaper or periodical in the nation gave space that month to Freud and his work.[3]

But over the next 18 months, nine serious articles on Freud or psychoanalysis appeared in popular newspapers and magazines. *Current Literature*, the *New York Times*, and *Scientific American* each carried two, and *American Magazine*, *Century*, *McClure's* and *Popular Science* each printed one. *Publishers Weekly*, the industry journal read by virtually every bookseller in the country, reflected this burst of interest. Though it had mentioned Freud or psychoanalysis only twice between 1900 and 1907, it printed five references in 1908, six in 1909, and then 25 between 1910 and 1912.[4] In 1910 Freud began to emerge from behind ivy-covered walls.

This was due largely to the proselytizing of Ernest Jones and A.A. Brill after the Clark conference. "I must have given some twenty papers or addresses before various American societies in that time," Jones recalled in his autobiography. "My sister used to refer to these numerous visits to the United States as 'raids over the border' [because he was based in Toronto]. These visits took me mostly to Washington (three times), Baltimore (four times), and the relatively near range of Chicago, Boston, New York, etc." Brill stayed closer to home in New York City where he lectured "literally dozens of times ... as soon as I became known as an exponent of Freud [in May 1910], I was actually swamped with invitations to speak." The pair also flooded the professional literature with Freudian ideas, publishing at least 15 articles in medical journals during the single year 1910. Freud thanked them for their efforts, writing in 1914 that "for the further spread of this movement Brill and Jones deserve the greatest credit: in their writings they drew their countrymen's attention with unremitting assiduity to the easily observable fundamental facts of everyday life, of dreams and neurosis. Brill has contributed still further to this effect by his medical practice and by his translations of my works, and Jones by his instructive lectures and by his skill in debate at congresses in America."[5]

Brill was an especially effective propagandist. A colleague said that he pitied anyone who started an argument with Brill, who confessed later, "I knew how to dispose of my opponents by taking the starch out of them." His friend Clarence Oberndorf recalled that "Freud's postulates were and still are repugnant and threatening to most people and Brill's manner of presenting them was never softened by shading or vagueness. He unhesitatingly risked his reputation by confronting the most influential authorities in America in neurology and psychiatry with bald and bold statements of the role which repressed sexuality and sex perversion played in the genesis of neuroses and psychoses." Another colleague wrote,

> Picture, if you will, this stocky little bearded fellow passionately propounding, in a thick accent, Freud's ideas to anyone who would listen. What impressed me was his direct, forthright, I would say even blunt, approach bespeaking great moral and intellectual honesty and personal independence. Here was a man of great pride and self-esteem who bowed his head to no man.... At the drop of a hat he would vigorously debate the skeptics and scoffers over these new, and indeed in those days unsettling, scientific revelations.[6]

In November 1910 *American Magazine* reported that psychoanalysis was "being pressed vigorously by Freud and a rapidly increasing band of disciples, two of whom—Brill, of New York, and Ernest Jones, of Toronto, Canada—have been ably presenting it for the consideration of American psychologists and physicians." In November 1912, when Jung returned from a second American trip, he reported to Freud that "Brill has gone to a lot of trouble and is now reaping the reward of his labours. Altogether, the PA movement over there has enjoyed a tremendous upswing since we were last in America."[7]

Word spread to newsrooms and editorial offices, where scholarly papers presented at academic conferences were soon being repackaged by the mainstream media. During the 12 months between May 1910 and May 1911, popular magazines ran six substantial articles on psychoanalysis, putting Freud's ideas in front of more than a million American readers. Sometimes the same article appeared in two or three slightly different versions within a few weeks. This wave of popularization during 1910 and 1911 represents a turning point in Americans' awareness of Freud. How, precisely, did it happen? Who were the journalists that wrote these articles and the editors that commissioned or approved them? What audiences did they reach? What impact did they have?[8]

The first popular piece to follow Hall's conference wrap-up appeared in the Sunday magazine section of the *New York Times* on May 8, 1910. It was a long unsigned article on Brill, reprinting most of his paper "Dreams and Their Relations to the Neurosis" from the weekly *New York Medical Journal*. It summarized Freud's main concepts, describing the unconscious, repression, wish fulfillment, and latent and manifest dream content before recounting at length his own analysis of a patient's dream (a woman pursued by chickens). *Sunday Times* editor Alden March took Brill's account of Freud from the *Medical Journal* read by 20,000 doctors and put it in front of 600,000 curious laypeople.[9]

Equating circulation statistics or book sales with influence is obviously problematic. We can't know how many subscribers to a magazine saw any specific article, or how many buyers of a book actually read it. Homes are littered with books and magazines people intended to read but never did. And even among those who *do* read a specific article or book, we can't know how many embrace its views, how many reject them, and how many simply shrug their shoulders. Reading changes lives, but it's impossible to determine how many lives were changed from how many books were sold or how many people subscribed to a journal. At the same time, it's reasonable to assume that more minds were changed by an article reaching 600,000 people than one that reached only 6,000. A book bought by 5,000 people had more impact than one that sold only 500. We simply can't measure that impact in any precise, or even meaningful, way.

The *Sunday Times* editor who chose to print the article on Brill, Alden March (1869–1942), was not particularly interested in Freud or psychoanalysis. A colleague recalled that March "ensconced himself in a high-backed swivel chair in the news room, where each day he read telegrams and dispatches from special correspondents and news agencies.... He had read most of the classics and a large number of modern writers, until he began to find them too shallow for his liking." His father and two of his brothers were university professors and perhaps kept him abreast of

SIGMUND FREUD

Whose admirers claim that he has founded not only a new system

Unattributed photograph of Freud used in H. Addington Bruce, "Masters of the Mind" (*American Magazine*, November 1, 1910).

the latest intellectual developments.[10] To March, Freud's theories simply made good copy. His lead stories that week were about the coronation of George IV in London. He buried the Brill article on page 11, giving it a little less space than a nearby story on cannibals eating missionaries. But he opened a door: over the next two years, the *Times* would publish six more articles about Freud or psychoanalysis.

The longest piece in the 1910–1911 wave of articles was "Masters of the Mind: Remarkable Cures Effected by Four Great Experts Without the Aid of Drugs or Surgeons' Tools," which appeared in *American Magazine* on November 1, 1910.[11] Muckraking journalists Lincoln Steffens, Ida M. Tarbell, and some friends had bought this monthly in 1906 to attack the status quo and support Progressive reforms; it also carried human interest stories and popular fiction. In 1910 it had 287,000 subscribers and could be bought on newsstands all around the country.[12]

The author of the November 1910 piece was H. Addington Bruce (1874–1959), a Canadian-born science writer who published 63 articles and seven books between 1903 and 1918. He'd enrolled in 1906 as a graduate student in psychology at Harvard under William James and was a friend of Boston psychologists Morton Prince and Boris Sidis. He wrote about other scientific subjects, too, but quickly became an advocate for what was beginning to be called "the new psychology." The previous spring Bruce had written:

> The publication and ready sale, during the past few months, of an extraordinarily large number of books dealing with psychotherapy, or mental healing, has brought considerable embarrassment to those good souls who, in the pulpit, the physician's office, and the editorial sanctum, have been confidently predicting that the 'mind cure craze' would soon die out.... Lectures on psychotherapy are being given in medical schools, the subject is being gravely discussed in leading medical journals, and here and there doctors are adopting psychotherapeutic methods as systematic adjuncts in their practice of medicine.[13]

Bruce viewed this as a good thing, hoping that the "new psychology" might transform human behavior the same way that "new" physics, chemistry, and engineering had given birth to airplanes, automobiles, and electrical appliances. Unlike Freud, he was full of Progressive-era optimism about the perfectibility of human nature. He viewed the unconscious as a reservoir of untapped potential rather than a cesspool of untamed primitive instincts. Though he wrote about science, Bruce was not entirely scientific. He also believed in telepathy and psychic phenomena, and the year before writing his long article on psychoanalysis had published a book on ghost-hunting.[14]

"Masters of the Mind" was an 11-page essay in which Bruce reported at length on the work of Pierre Janet, Sidis, Prince, and Freud. The section headed "Freud's Method of Psycho-analysis" was an overview of *Selected Papers on Hysteria* and the Clark lectures. Bruce praised Freud but was skeptical of his claims about the sexual origins of neuroses: "Thus far, it must be said, no other leading psychopathologist has accepted this sweeping, audacious theory." But he praised Freud for "his psycho-analytic method of 'tapping the subconscious' [which] has resulted, like Dr. Sidis' method of hypnoidization, in placing a new and powerful instrument of diagnosis and therapy in the hands of the psychologically trained physician."[15]

Bruce's article was illustrated with sketches and photos of its subjects, including one "reproduced from a remarkable group photograph taken at the celebration of the twentieth anniversary of the opening of Clark University." It shows Hall flanked by Freud and Jung outside the university library with Brill, Jones, and Ferenzci standing behind them (see page 39). This photo, like the better-known image of 42 conference participants on the library steps, was taken by the Worcester studio of Schervee and Bushong. The larger photo taken on the steps had first been printed the previous month in Hall's privately issued edition of the Clark Lectures, but this smaller image had apparently never been published before. It was common for magazines to contact photography studios to request copies and permission, so probably Bruce or the staff at *American Magazine* reached out to Schervee and Bushong in order to use this now-famous image for the first time.[16]

Bruce's article was followed that winter by another popular piece that went through three printings in four months. "Medical Report from a New Psychological World" appeared as a three-page essay in the February 1, 1911, issue of *Current Literature.* This was a monthly miscellany of fiction, drama, poetry, news, and opinion that abbreviated content from other publications, similar to the slightly later *Reader's Digest*. It was read by 100,000 subscribers all over the country.[17] Its article, "Medical Report from a New Psychological World," was taken from the professional press. The original author, Dr. E.W. Scripture, "associate in psychiatry at Columbia University," had published a longer version of it in the *Medical Record* on December 24, 1910. Scripture's text began by describing Jung's work and acknowledging his dependence on Freud, before devoting three full pages to Freud's dream theory. *Current Literature* cut out the last third, leaving the article mostly about Jung. This truncated version was reprinted again in the *Scientific American Supplement* on April 15.[18]

Though unsigned, the article was almost certainly the work of *Current Literature*'s associate editor George S. Viereck (1884–1962), a close friend of Harvard psychology professor Hugo Muensterberg. Viereck was born in Germany, came to the U.S. as a child, graduated from the College of the City of New York in 1906, and gained national fame the next year as a poet. A friend remembered him as "badly dressed and generally 'gauche.' Within a short period he became a great dandy, foppish in his appearance.... He was extreme in his dress, wore velvet collars on his dinner coat etc. Anything to be different." Viereck's poems were followed in 1907 by a horror novel about vampires and then in 1910 by *Confessions of a Barbarian*, a book condemning the bad taste of Americans. A passionate lover of all things German, he opposed U.S. entry into World War I and 20 years later supported Hitler, spending most of World War II in prison. Throughout it all he remained unapologetic: "I do not question the sincerity of my foes. I merely analyze them with a knowledge gained from the study of Freud."[19]

Viereck studied Freud closely between 1900 and 1910 and embraced a Freudian view of human nature. "In the Harvard Psychological Laboratory," he recalled in 1910, "I once saw little white mice revolving in a circle, crazily, without pause, like dancing dervishes.... Even thus we, I sometimes fancy, obey not our own volition, but the monstrous caprice of an alien will. There is an irresistible—scientists would say compulsory—impulse that urges our pens and animates our chisels." During the 1920s he wrote two articles praising Freud and in 1927 published a long interview with him prefaced by the remark that Freud was "a cultural force to which we can assign a definite historical place in the evolution of civilization. Columbus, seeking merely a new passage to Cathay, discovered a continent. Freud, attempting to find a new method of mental therapeutics, discovered the submerged continent of man's mind." Freud broke with him after Viereck defended Hitler in the 1930s, saying, "I regret that you have debased yourself by siding with those wretched lies."[20]

In May 1911, Viereck shared a second article on Freud by reprinting part of a long and thorough piece by Harry W. Chase, Hall's student at Clark who had translated Freud's 1909 lectures. Chase (1883–1955) had finished his degree and landed a teaching job at the University of North Carolina. His nine-page article, "Freud's Theories of the Unconscious," in the April 1, 1911, issue of *Popular Science*, was a very clear summary of Freud's model of the mind, including the unconscious, the conscious mind, repression, sublimation, complexes, and dreams.[21]

Popular Science, where Chase's article first appeared, was quite eclectic. In addition to pieces on physics, botany, and astronomy, the April 1911 issue contained essays on economics, philosophy, and higher education. The magazine had been bought in 1900 by Columbia professor James M. Cattell (1860–1944) in order to bring science to a broad spectrum of readers. Cattell published other scientific journals, too, and was always on the lookout for fresh content. He was an old friend of G. Stanley Hall and had attended the Clark conference where he probably met Freud, Jung, Brill, Jones, and Chase, since members of the same disciplines ate and socialized together between lectures. Cattell was certainly no Freudian, however, writing in 1925 that "psychoanalysis is not so much a question of science as a matter of taste, Dr. Freud being an artist who lives in the fairyland of dreams among the ogres of perverted sex."[22]

Across town at *Current Opinion* (the new name of *Current Literature*), George Viereck apparently saw Chase's piece in Cattell's magazine and scooped it up for his monthly miscellany. He cut it nearly in half, condensing and rewriting it to fit into a smaller space. Although this mangled the original text, it also put Freud in front of 100,000 readers, compared to only 6,500 at *Popular Science*.[23]

If he ever saw Chase's article, Freud probably disapproved. "The dissertation that Chase sent me (he is the translator of the Worcester lectures)," he wrote to Brill in May 1911, "was not good. He doesn't understand the Ucs [unconscious] and sees it with the eyes of the Cw [conscious mind], as it is for many who only know it from the literature and don't know the phenomenon that we face every day [as therapists]."[24] Chase went on to have a very successful career, eventually moving from the classroom into administration and serving as president of the University of North Carolina, the University of Illinois, and New York University over the next several decades.[25]

After this burst of articles in the mainstream press between May 1910 and May 1911, Freud became a staple of journalists. More than a dozen other substantial articles appeared in popular magazines before the end of 1914 and over the next five years at least 35 more were published, far more than can be described here. But two pieces from this early period that deserve notice are "Dreams and Forgetting," published by Edwin T. Brewster in *McClure's* in the fall of 1912, and the Freudian detective stories of Arthur B. Reeve (1880–1936).[26]

Brewster (1866–1960) was born just after the Civil War and lived long enough to see the first satellites launched into space. For most of his career he taught science at Phillips Andover Academy outside Boston and moonlighted by writing mass-market science articles. He earned a master's degree in zoology at Harvard, started teaching in 1892, and began writing popular articles in 1901. He wrote for young people in books like *Natural Wonders Every Child Should Know* (1912) and *A Child's Guide to Living Things* (1913) but also produced articles for adults in major national magazines such as *Woman's Home Companion* and the *Nation*. Between 1909 and 1913 Brewster published 10 pieces in the phenomenally popular *McClure's*, including one about Freud's dream theory.[27] *McClure's* was the mouthpiece of the Progressive movement, but it also published fiction, drama, and poetry, was heavily illustrated with original art and photographs, and reached 450,000 subscribers around the country. Brewster's piece on Freud in the October 1, 1912, issue was the first to appear before such an enormous audience. It was sandwiched between a short story by Jeffery Farnol and a critique of presidential nominating conventions.

In "Dreams and Forgetting" Brewster was cautiously supportive of Freud, whom he called "probably the most discussed man in his field in the entire scientific world." After giving a sanitized overview of psychoanalytic theory that omitted all sexual references, he acknowledged Freud's opponents but asserted that, "in general, in spite of much opposition, expert opinion is swinging toward Freud's side." He went on to discuss Freud's dream theory, describing a case of Ernest Jones's at length, before turning to slips of the tongue, faulty memories, etc.: "this whole Freudian scheme of analyzing inhibitions, dreams, tricks of manner, failures of memory, queerness of all sorts, arose as a practical device for putting an end to the [patient's] disturbance." He concluded by discussing falling in love and how it is influenced by complexes unresolved since infancy: "perhaps matches are made in heaven. Perhaps, as the Freudians maintain, every person's conjugal fate turns on his parent of the opposite sex. Perhaps the whole thing is only a crazy dream of Dr. Sigmund Freud."[28] The article put a simplified version of Freud's ideas and techniques in front of almost half a million readers, four times as many as Viereck's *Current Opinion* and exponentially more than the medical journals edited by Jelliffe and Hall.

Another conduit for Freud's ideas before World War I was mystery writer Arthur Reeve, whose detective, Prof. Craig Kennedy, was sometimes called the American Sherlock Holmes. Kennedy used psychoanalysis to solve crimes, referring explicitly to unconscious drives, repression, and libidinal motives. He first appeared in August 1913 in *Cosmopolitan*, which was then a men's magazine. Since most of Reeve's short stories appeared later than the period under discussion here, they'll be considered below, in Chapter 6. It's simply worth noting now that while expositions of Freud's ideas were appearing in medical journals and popular monthlies, an explicitly Freudian detective was also solving fictional crimes for 800,000 readers in *Cosmopolitan*.[29]

Bruce (a journalist), March (a newspaper editor), Viereck (a student of the Boston analysts), Cattell (a friend of Hall), Brewster (a popular science writer), and Reeve (a mystery writer) were the bridge between professional specialists like Brill, Jones, Meyer, Jelliffe, and Putnam and the general public. They brought Freud's ideas to nearly two million readers between October 1910 and October 1912, when his books and articles had been seen by only a few hundred doctors.

Freud was not, however, immediately embraced by American readers. Given the prevailing moral code in the U.S. in 1911, many readers found his ideas obnoxious, especially his insistence on the "polymorphous perversity" of infants and children. Even in the medical professions Freud had many more detractors than supporters. He had his own explanation for their resistance: "They have forgotten their own infantile sexual activity under the pressure of education for civilization and do not care to be reminded now of the repressed material."[30] When Brill established the first psychoanalytic society in New York in 1911, he could find only 21 people willing to meet. When Jones organized the first national group three months later, only eight people joined. Over the next few years, membership in each group hovered between 20 and 30, many of whom failed to show up for meetings. In 1911 psychoanalysis in America was still more like a cult than a movement.[31]

5

George Brett Puts Freud
into Bookstores, 1913–1914

Freud's name in popular magazines undoubtedly caught the eye of book publisher George Brett at Macmillan in 1911. Brett "followed the practice common today," historian John Tebbel wrote, "of carefully scanning magazines and newspapers, where the first work of promising new writers might be found. He often observed that a publisher's function was 'to keep his ears to the ground and interpret through books the sounds that he hears.'" One of America's largest and best-known publishing houses, Macmillan then had nearly $2 million in annual sales and its books were distributed to booksellers in every major city and small town.[1]

After four articles on Freud appeared in the spring of 1911, Brett approached London publisher Swan Sonnenschein about jointly issuing an English-language edition of the *Interpretation of Dreams*. American publishers often partnered with a foreign company when a book's potential sales were unclear, so they could import printed sheets or bound copies rather than incur the expense of typesetting, printing, and binding a separate American edition. Unfortunately, this

George P. Brett, president of Macmillan, in 1913 (*The Independent*, November 20, 1913).

51

process meant that the book could not be protected by copyright in the U.S. The 1909 U.S. Copyright Law only protected works "printed from type set within the limits of the United States, either by hand or by the aid of any kind of typesetting machine, or from plates made within the limits of the United States from type set therein ... and the printing of the text and binding of the said book shall be performed within the limits of the United States." A decade later the lack of an American copyright for *The Interpretation of Dreams* would come back to haunt Freud.[2]

Swan Sonnenschein consulted Freud's Austrian publisher Franz Deuticke and then turned to British physician Eden Paul, son of the publisher Charles Kegan Paul, to make a translation. Paul recalled that "in 1909 or 1910 [sic] I was asked to translate Freud's *Traumdeutung*. Terms had been arranged, and the work was about to begin, when an injunction arrived from Vienna. The Austrian publishers had exceeded their rights in giving the authorization, and the author had independently made arrangements with an American translator." When Freud had caught wind of the proposal, he'd immediately intervened because he'd already promised all English translation rights to Brill. He suggested that Brill contact Macmillan in New York. By then Swan Sonnenschein had fallen on hard times and was being taken over by George Allen & Co., who became Macmillan's partner and Brill's main contact. Brett, Brill, and Allen went back forth about terms during the spring of 1912: the translation was to be done in New York and the editorial work in London, where copies for the American market would be printed and bound for Macmillan in addition to the British copies.[3]

Freud considered *The Interpretation of Dreams* his most significant work. "It contains," he wrote in 1931, "even according to my present-day judgment, the most valuable of all the discoveries it has been my good fortune to make. Insight such as this falls to one's lot but once in a lifetime." In 1908, when Brill had asked if he could translate it, Freud was skeptical: "it is unfortunately untranslatable and would have to be rewritten in each language." In a footnote to the 1909 German edition he wrote, "It is impossible as a rule to translate a dream into a foreign language and this is equally true, I fancy, of a book such as the present one." Brill tackled it anyway, acknowledging when the task was finished "the almost insurmountable difficulties in the translation." In 1930 Freud revised his footnote to include "Nevertheless, Dr. A.A. Brill of New York, and others after him, have succeeded in translating *The Interpretation of Dreams*."[4]

As soon as the contract was signed on May 7, 1912, Brill engaged one his patients, 26-year-old Alfred Kuttner (1886–1942), to help with the translation. Kuttner, a recent Harvard graduate, took the German edition with him when he headed into the Maine woods for the summer of 1912 with his best friend Walter Lippmann. In a solitary cabin 25 miles from the Quebec border, "Kuttner was putting into English theories that would transform the way people thought about the unconscious," Lippmann's biographer wrote, "while a few feet away Lippmann was trying to figure out why politics so often seemed contrary to human behavior and needs. Around the fire at night, as Kuttner explained what Freud meant by words like 'taboo' and 'sublimation,' Lippman glimpsed a new analytical tool." Kuttner would later help Brill with other translations, write his own articles about psychoanalysis, and become one of Freud's most faithful allies among the Greenwich Village avant-garde.[5]

Proofs went back and forth across the Atlantic during the fall and winter of 1912–1913, until in January, when most of the book was already printed, Allen discovered explicitly sexual passages near the end of the text. These discussed sexual development and erotic dreams in frank detail and raised the possibility that the publisher might be prosecuted under British obscenity laws. The solution to the problem, discussed below in Chapter 9 where the offending passages are examined, was for Allen to restrict British sales to the medical profession while Macmillan braved the U.S. censors. Allen may have been extra cautious since his company was in the midst of fiscal hardships and even went into receivership briefly in 1913; it was rescued when Stanley Unwin bought a controlling interest in August 1914. Allen's timidity frustrated Brill, who wrote on March 6, 1913, "to be frank I will say that I am disgusted with all these delays. If you have no desire to publish the book why waist [*sic*] time. All these minor details should have been attended to long ago."[6]

Allen initially printed three impressions (in March, May, and November 1913) which totaled 1,763 copies, of which 1,457 were sent to Macmillan with American title pages. Brett had originally agreed to import only 500 copies for America and reduced that to just 250 in June 1912, but in the end imported many more. This could have been at the urging of Allen, whose expectations of British sales were unexpectedly disappointed at the last minute when he discovered Freud's candid language about sex. When the book was finally published in April 1913, Allen told Brill "the first edition is practically exhausted, owing to the large number taken by the Macmillan Company."[7]

The 1,457 copies shipped to New York in April 1913 were bound in blue cloth printed in gold with an American title page and Macmillan's name on the spine. The first few copies contained an error on page 87 and an erratum sheet was pasted into them (see appendix for details). Brill complained about the quality of the index, which he also did later with other publishers, and Allen promised to improve it in future editions. Sixty copies were sent to the press for review or otherwise distributed for free, and only 246 copies were sold in Britain during 1913. These contained a note

George Allen & Co. balance sheet for *The Interpretation of Dreams*, December 31, 1913, sent to A.A. Brill (A.A. Brill Papers, Library of Congress, box 15).

pasted to the front free endpaper reading, "The sale of this book is limited to Members of the Medical, Scholastic, Legal, and Clerical professions." At the end of 1913, Allen sent Brill a royalty on the American sales of 35 pounds, or about $2,500 today, which Brill passed along to Freud in Vienna. By the time Freud died in 1939, the book had earned at least 900 pounds in America ($63,325 in 2022 dollars). It has never been out of print since Allen and Brett took a chance on it in 1913.[8]

The title page bore a motto from Virgil, "*Flectere si nequeo superos, Acheronta movebo*," commonly translated as "If I cannot deflect the will of heaven, then I shall move [the Acheron River in] hell." Freud later explained that it "was meant merely to emphasize the most important part in the dynamics of the dream. The wish rejected by the higher mental agencies (the repressed dream wish) stirs up the mental underworld (the unconscious) in order to get a hearing."[9]

Freud was not entirely happy with the translation and began to go through it "page by page with a view to suggesting corrections for a second edition. I have just gone through the first 100 pages." Between Kuttner's draft and Brill's reworking of it, the text contained what reviewer one reviewer called "English that is German, all too German, a diction in which literalness is mistaken for accuracy."[10] Brill's recasting of some of Freud's examples was particularly problematic. Translator James Strachey explained in 1953 the dilemma in handling "fairly frequent instances in which an interpretation depends entirely upon a pun."

> There are three methods of dealing with such situations. The translator can omit the dream entirely, or he can replace it by another parallel dream, whether derived from his own experience or fabricated ad hoc. These two methods have been the ones adopted in the main in the earlier translations of the book.... But there are serious objections to them. We must once more remember that we are dealing with a scientific classic. What we want to hear about are the examples chosen by Freud—not by someone else. Accordingly the present translator has adopted the pedantic and tiresome third alternative of keeping the original German pun and laboriously explaining it in a square bracket or footnote. Any amusement that might be got out of it completely evaporates in the process. But that, unfortunately, is a sacrifice that has to be made.[11]

The problem would surface even more dramatically the next year when Brill tried to turn *Psychopathology of Everyday Life* into English and again in 1916 with *Wit and Its Relation to the Unconscious*. Despite Freud's reservations and careful list of errors, no corrected American edition of *The Interpretation of Dreams* was published for two decades.

In the six months following its first publication, *The Interpretation of Dreams* was listed dozens of times in book trade bulletins and library newsletters but only a handful of reviews appeared in magazines outside of medical journals. They nevertheless put the book in front of more than 400,000 readers. The earliest one, an unsigned essay in the *Nation* on May 15, 1913, complained that Freud's "morbid tendency to over-emphasize the potency of erotic influences ... [led] him to improbable and revolting explanations." It incorrectly predicted that "the value of his practical work in relation to hysteria and kindred problems will be remembered long after his theory of dreams has been forgotten." Horace Kallen in the *Dial* was even harsher, accusing Freud of circular logic and ending by claiming "he selects his facts to suit his theory ... his total operation is one vast begging of the question." *Scientific American* and Cattell's *Science* were lukewarm, as was the *New York Times*, though the latter recommended that every student of psychology should read it. J.P. Kerfoot was the most enthusiastic, in *Life*, predicting that "before the snow flies, *The Interpretation of Dreams* may be found at the head of the weekly list of non-fiction demands in such scattered literary centres as Montclair, New Jersey, and Montezuma, New Mexico."[12]

That was an exaggeration, of course, but the *Interpretation of Dreams* remained one of Freud's popular American books. Allen printed 11 impressions in England between April 1913 and February 1927, with Brett usually importing shipments of 250 copies at a time to keep pace with the American demand. Their correspondence and Brill's papers record 7,623 copies sold in the U.S. between 1913 and 1929; no records survive, however, for five of those 17 years so the actual total was perhaps closer to 10,000 copies. Starting with the impression of December 1915, both publishers' names were typically included at the foot of the title page and only the binding distinguishes them. London copies had Allen's name at the foot of the spine rather than Macmillan's and were covered in gray rather than dark blue cloth.[13]

In the summer of 1929 Brill proposed to Stanley Unwin that a second English edition be prepared from the latest German edition then appearing in Vienna. Unwin agreed and Brill retranslated the whole book, but Unwin held up producing it for two years in order to sell his remaining stock of the previous edition. He also enlisted an unnamed English editor to polish Brill's revised text. When Brill saw these edits in May 1932, he responded with pages of corrections to errors that had been introduced, delaying publication still further. When the final proofs reached him in November 1932, he was dissatisfied with the index and demanded still more changes. Unwin agreed to make them but wrote back in exasperation, "I find that we have upwards of 150 orders outstanding for the new edition and the booksellers have already got to that stage of restiveness that some of them are cancelling their orders, so that it is my opinion, and I think you will agree with me, that any further delay is likely to do the book more harm than the appearance of some possible defect in the Index, though for that matter I see no reason why there should be any defects after all the care that has been lavished on it!"[14]

Despite the date on its title page, the 1932 Allen & Unwin balance sheet shows that no copies of the second edition were actually printed that year. Brill received his first copy on March 1, 1933, and wrote to Unwin, "I am very pleased with it. It looks a little sombre on its face but its interior is in every way perfect." Brill's revised second edition was reprinted five times through 1950. He also included it in the 1938 Modern Library anthology, *Basic Writings of Sigmund Freud*, where he cut Freud's 80-page opening literature review down to five pages (see Chapter 12). This truncated text was kept in print as a separate Modern Library volume from 1950 until 1985. In 1952, the Encyclopædia Britannica included it in *The Major Works of Sigmund Freud*, volume 54 of their *Great Books of the Western World* series, which sold 35–50,000 sets per year for decades and totaled a million copies overall. Brill's 1932 translation consequently became the most widely read version in the U.S. In 1953 the *Standard Edition* translation by James Strachey eclipsed Brill's as the preferred English text. It was published in hardcover in 1955 by Basic Books and in paperback in 1961 from John Wiley & Sons Science Edition brand.[15]

The Interpretation of Dreams was not only a monumental intellectual achievement when it appeared in Vienna in 1899, but a monumental physical one, too, at nearly 400 densely argued pages. The American edition was even more imposing at over 500 pages. Recognizing that the size of the book would intimidate many readers, Freud agreed to write a shorter version for a series of technical monographs called *Grenzfragen des Nerven-und Seelenlebens* published in Wiesbaden. This was not unlike Jelliffe and White's *JNMD Monograph Series* in New York, and his 40-page condensation appeared in Wiesbaden in 1901.[16]

A decade later, Ernest Jones thought this shorter book might appeal to English-speaking readers, too. He proposed the idea of translating it to his pupil and fellow-analyst M.D. Eder in the spring of 1911 and Freud approved it in July. This undercut Freud's 1908 pledge to let Brill handle all his English translation work, but Brill acquiesced and even took on the negotiations with American publishers anyway. Freud suggested Brill approach Swan Sonnenschein & Co. Ltd., who had just been bought by George Allen, but surviving records suggest that the talks did not go smoothly. Freud commiserated with Brill at the end of 1911, "I hope that these difficulties will not detain you for long."[17]

The translator, M.D. Eder (1865–1936), was one of the first psychoanalysts in Britain. He'd earned his medical degree in 1895 and then worked as a doctor in Latin America, North Africa, and impoverished working-class neighborhoods in England before meeting Ernest Jones. Described as "burly and strong" yet "kind, sardonic and sagacious," Eder began using psychoanalysis in his practice in 1908. In 1911, when he described the unconscious sexual origins of one patient's obsessions to a meeting of the British Medical Association, the entire audience stood up and walked out. He went into analysis with Jones in 1912 and visited Freud at the end of the year. Freud recalled that "one's heart warmed at the thought of him."[18]

When they met in Vienna in 1912, Freud and Eder probably discussed his progress on the translation of *On Dreams* and the difficulties Brill was having finding a publisher. Through his work with the Fabian Society, Eder had become good friends with George Bernard Shaw and H.G. Wells, both of whom had been published by William Heinemann. Heinemann had just branched out into medical books, so Brill and Eder turned to him when negotiations with Allen failed. Heinemann (1863–1920) had started his firm in 1890 and was in close touch with modern continental authors such as Ibsen and Maeterlinck; in England he published not only Wells and Shaw but also Henry James and Joseph Conrad.[19]

It was something of a departure, therefore, when in 1913 he purchased an established medical publisher, Rebman and Co., with a backlist of 100 titles in "Standard Medical, Surgical and Hygienic Works." Heinemann set up Rebman as a semi-independent division that issued books over the imprint "Heinemann (Rebman)" on their title pages. The division was run by Hugh Elliot who, undoubtedly looking for saleable new titles to float the new venture, may have been the person whom Eder or Brill approached.[20]

Meanwhile Frank Rebman (1852–1940), who'd founded the company bearing his name in 1893, had returned to the U.S. He was born in Germany but emigrated to Philadelphia, where he found work as a book traveler for medical textbook publishers. In the 1880s he moved to England and using funds borrowed from his father-in-law created a company to distribute American medical books in Britain. He gradually expanded into publishing his own new medical books as well, and was so successful that he restructured the company, sold out to Heinemann, and returned to the U.S. to head its small New York branch starting in 1903.[21]

On Dreams was finally published by Heinemann (Rebman) in London on May 14, 1914, three years after Jones had proposed the idea, with a long introduction by Scottish public health pioneer William Leslie Mackenzie. The American issue was announced in the *New York Times* on June 21 and the first review appeared on August 15 in the *Chicago Medical Recorder*; for unknown reasons, it was only listed in *Publishers Weekly* more than a year later. No U.S. copyright could be filed because the sheets were imported from England. There is no date anywhere on the American issue of the book, which has produced some confusion among booksellers and library catalogers. The number of copies issued is not known.

On Dreams is a book which, like the Clark lectures, could have been a fine introduction for laypeople but which instead went unnoticed because Rebman promoted it only to the medical profession and failed to secure any reviews at all in the mainstream press. There were nine reviews in the professional literature, most of which were lukewarm.[22] Some reviewers cautioned doctors that it could not replace the much longer treatment in *The Interpretation of Dreams*. Despite its begrudging tone, the *American Journal of Clinical Medicine* was more enthusiastic than many others: "It is, in fact, no exaggeration to say that [Freud's ideas] have given us the key to a rational ordering of the mental sphere, as truly as Darwin gave us the key to the ordering of the physical.... [*On Dreams*] is extremely interesting and suggestive, and evidently is feeling toward the truth. But it should be read with a very critical and discriminating mind."[23]

It was reprinted in 1915 and sold by Rebman bound in yellow or gold cloth just as World War I broke out and communications between America and England became precarious. Although a third London issue was published in 1924, no more copies were issued in the U.S. until W.W. Norton brought out James Strachey's translation in 1952; this was included in volume 5 when the *Standard Edition* appeared the next year. Popular editions proliferated after that, and it has since become what it might always have been, a convenient overview of Freud's theory of dreams and their significance.

Meanwhile, in 1913 Brill had shared with George Brett at Macmillan his manuscript translation of *Psychopathology of Everyday Life*, in which Freud explained how forgotten names, lost objects, and slips of the tongue are often caused by unconscious forces. Allen was interested in partnering with Macmillan a second time, but Brill had reservations about working with either of them again. "I am not very pleased with Allen for many reasons," he wrote to Freud. "He continually delayed the publication of the *Interpretation* although he promised to do it very soon after he received the manuscript ... the Macmillan company of New York asked me for the manuscript [of *Psychopathology*] and after keeping it for months they finally refused to publish it—saying that it would not pay. I suspected at the time that they wanted me to give it to Allen so that they should have no responsibility and yet handle the American edition as they did with the *Dreams*. I was naturally very angry at them for keeping the manuscript so long after asking me for it in the first place. So, in order not to give it to them, I purposely refused to give it to Allen."[24]

Brill had instead approached British publisher T. Fisher Unwin in November 1913. Fisher Unwin was recalled by an associate as "a lonely man who did not like loneliness. His sense of humour was only slightly developed. He could never understand how he antagonised people yet he was doing it all the time. He also developed irrational jealousies of members of his staff," which included his nephew Stanley Unwin. After several years of bad treatment, Stanley resigned and started a competing firm in August 1914 by buying out George Allen and forming Allen & Unwin. His uncle Fisher responded with predictable hostility and their feud lasted for years.[25]

Brill sent a proposal and draft manuscript to Fisher Unwin on November 8, 1913, and the next month heard back that they were eager to publish *Psychopathology* in England. "I have no objection to your placing the book in America through an American publisher," Brill replied. "The book is in great demand here and any publisher will be willing to give it out." He was surprised, though, when Macmillan picked up the U.S. rights since they had previously turned him down. Despite the success of *The Interpretation of Dreams*, Macmillan was still hesitant to risk the costs of producing an American edition from scratch and preferred to partner with Fisher Unwin by having the book printed and bound in England.[26]

"I was busy this whole month [March? 1914]," Brill wrote to Freud, "reading the proof sheets of the *Psychopathologie* and writing an introduction and index. The introduction is very brief. I thought that it would be appropriate to give an account of the coming into existence of the *Psychopathologie* and of what it treats. I am quite pleased with the translation and I am sure that you will be satisfied."[27]

Translating the book had been unusually difficult. In the introduction Brill wrote that "while the original text was strictly followed, linguistic difficulties often made it necessary to modify or substitute some of the author's cases by examples comprehensible to the English-speaking reader." This was his way of glossing over major changes that he made to Freud's text by substituting American expressions and anecdotes in place of the original German ones. James Strachey summarized what Brill did in 1953:

> he omitted every example which involved terms that could not be rendered into English and inserted a certain number of examples of his own which illustrated similar points to the omitted ones. This was no doubt an entirely justifiable procedure in the circumstances. At the date at which Brill made his version, Freud's work was almost unknown in English-speaking countries, and it was important not to put up unnecessary obstacles to the circulation of this book which had been designed by Freud himself expressly for the general reader. How well Brill succeeded in this aim is shown by the fact that by 1935 sixteen printings of his translation had been issued, and many more were to follow. His own examples, too, were for the most part excellent and two or three of them were in fact included by Freud in later editions of the German original.[28]

"Strictly speaking," Brill confessed to Fisher Unwin, "it is more than a translation, as I myself have written about one fourth of the book. It is impossible to translate everything in the original so that Prof. Freud gave me permission to omit whatever was useless and substitute it by my own materials." Freud also confirmed that he'd authorized Brill to make changes as he saw fit, and even used some of Brill's substitutions in revised German editions that followed. Historian John Burnham, who investigated Bill's omissions and mistranslations in detail, generously concluded, "who can say that better translations would have aroused more interest in psychoanalysis in this early period?"[29]

Proofs and a new introduction went back and forth across the Atlantic that spring and on May 19, 1914, Unwin told Brill, "Your book is now practically ready and we shall publish it on June 3." Brill wrote Freud on June 7, "By this time you have received the *Psychopathology of Everyday Life* which I hope you will like better than the *Interpretation*."[30] Fisher Unwin printed the sheets of the American issue in England and supplied them to Macmillan in New York, where the book appeared in early August. The first American issue was bound in bluish-gray cloth stamped in gold; later impressions were bound in gray or red. Over the years, British copies were generally bound in shades of red and printed in gold or black on their spines and covers with "T. Fisher Unwin" at the foot of the spine.

The first review, in the *Nation* on September 24, was the most negative, criticizing Freud for being "willing to go to unwarranted lengths in his efforts to bring the facts of observation into line with his theories" and lamenting that "his tendency to look for erotic influences constantly warps his judgment." Most were neutral, like Kuttner's full-page article in the *New York Times Sunday Magazine*, accompanied by a large portrait of Freud. Kuttner opened with a long amusing anecdote of his own before recounting some from the book and introducing others from literature. He then reproduced several more of Freud's and Brill's, but never assessed the book's methods or argument, describing it without judging it. Kuttner's piece was reprinted in Dallas and Galveston, Texas, a few weeks later. The *St. Louis Dispatch* published the most positive review of all: "Once you start reading it you can not let go until you have reached the last page. When you have closed the book you are sorry that there is not more of it." The *Boston Evening Transcript* said that "it commands the reader's interest in the beginning, and is sure to hold it to the end," concluding, "the book is as entertaining as it is useful, and will be valuable not only to the physician and professional psychologist, but to pastors, parents and social workers." Four of the eight reviews appeared in newspapers and magazines far from East Coast centers of culture, a sign that as early as 1914 editors around the country had begun to think that Freud would interest their audiences.[31]

Fisher Unwin and his successor Ernest Benn reprinted *Psychopathology of Everyday Life* 16 times between 1914 and 1935. Although it was a shorter and easier book than *The Interpretation of Dreams*, it did not sell as well. By the end of the 1920s approximately 5,000 had been sold in the U.S. (roughly half as many as *The Interpretation of Dreams*). Annual balance sheets show that 400–500 sold annually until 1923, when the number dropped to about 250 per year. By 1930 demand had entirely ceased, and in 1937 Brill had to order one from London to use it in compiling *Basic Writings* because, as he wrote to Ernest Benn, "it is a funny thing that one cannot find a single copy of this book in New York City." Under the original contract with Fisher Unwin and after 1926 with Ernest Benn, Brill received a 10 percent royalty which he forwarded to Freud in Vienna. By 1929, these payments had totaled more than 210 pounds or about $900 (roughly $13,000 today) since the book's publication.[32]

In 1938 a second edition, the first in paperback, was published by Penguin Books in England (v + 218 pages); this was sold in both countries after Penguin opened an American branch in 1939. In 1948 Penguin spun off this U.S. subsidiary as an independent corporation called New American Library of World Literature, which issued a third edition of *Psychopathology of Everyday Life* in 1951 under its non-fiction "Mentor Books" brand (159 pages); this went through at least five printings by 1960. Alan Tyson's translation eclipsed all of these when it was published as volume 6 of the *Standard Edition* in 1960.[33]

In 1913–1914 George Brett responded to emerging public interest in Freud by publishing trade editions of his two most important books. Brill, meanwhile, continued to push Freud's ideas to professionals by writing the first American book about them, a 337-page volume titled *Psychanalysis [sic]—Its Theories and Practical Application*, which appeared in December 1912 from medical publisher W.B. Saunders in Philadelphia. The first printing was immediately exhausted and a second impression was required just five months later, in May 1913. Brill continued to publish revised and enlarged editions for the next decade as interest in Freud rapidly grew.

6

Freud Among
the Bohemians,
1914–1918

America's growing fascination with Freud and psychoanalysis is reflected in the number of articles and books that appeared in the decade following the 1909 Clark conference. The table below shows the number of results returned from searches on the terms "Freud" and "psychoanalysis" (with and without a hyphen) in five full-text databases covering the years 1909–1918.[1] But first, a note of caution. Bibliometric analysis of this sort is always suspect—faulty OCR leads to inaccurate results, the selection of publications included in any database is inevitably limited and biased, English is privileged over other languages, database editors define scope in varying ways, and writers in earlier generations used different terms than we do today, to name but a few flaws in this approach. Bibliometric

	Index Medicus	Readers Guide	Full-text Newspapers	Publishers Weekly
1909	5	0	5	0
1910	9	4	0	7
1911	31	13	41	15
1912	51	4	28	25
1913	48	4	22	19
1914	58	3	13	13
1915	46	13	36	9
1916	27	7	69	32
1917	30	12	50	26
1918	23	2	86	32

Uses of "Freud" or "psychoanalysis" in five full-text databases, 1909–1918.

analysis therefore can never capture the whole truth but only reveal broad patterns, can never *prove* but only suggest. In this case, however, the trend is unmistakable.

In graphic format:

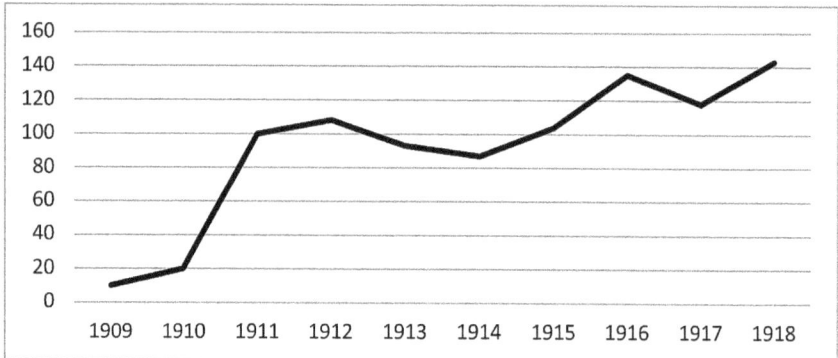

Uses of "Freud" or "psychoanalysis" in five full-text databases, 1909–1918.

The burst of interest that occurred in 1910–1912 while Brill and Jones were on the road proselytizing was followed by a temporary decline until Macmillan published Freud's first two trade books in 1913–1914, after which another rise took place. The brief drop in published references during 1917 corresponds to the peak of anti–German prejudice that followed America's entry into World War I (see Chapter 9). Interest then picked up again after the war and soared in the early 1920s before dropping off again in the middle of the decade.

Many earlier writers have repeated the mistaken notion that Freud's ideas spread across America because Greenwich Village radicals encountered him first through Brill or Jelliffe, eagerly sought out his books, and then shared his theories with the rest of the country. This error was apparently first advanced in a 1947 article whose author argued that "professional journals serve as the first vehicle for the introduction of new systems of thought. So-called 'high-brow' magazines next took up the discussion, followed by popularized versions in magazines with a wider circulation."[2]

But as we saw above, the truth is more complicated. Between 1910 and 1912, daily newspapers and mass-market magazines carried popularized versions of Freud's ideas to nearly two million readers who lived not only in New York but as far afield as San Francisco, St. Louis, and Galveston. Between 1912 and 1917 another 40 articles appeared, the majority written not by avant-garde intellectuals but by professional journalists with no connection to the Village counterculture. Starting in 1914, a handful of articles by Village radicals *were* published in "high-brow" magazines and these were read by opinion-makers around the nation, people whom we would call "influencers" today. But by then Freud's first two books had already sold thousands of copies and been reviewed 20 times for half a million readers as far away as Missouri, Kentucky, Texas, Utah, and California. This had happened before many well-known Greenwich Village intellectuals had even moved to New York.[3]

Though avant-garde writers in the Village were not responsible for Freud's nationwide popularity, they nevertheless played a role in the dissemination of his ideas that's worth teasing out of the larger context. In 1910, Greenwich Village was populated almost entirely by working-class Italian and Irish immigrants whose landlords were trying to "clean up" the decaying neighborhood so they could charge higher rents. Neither the working-class Catholic tenants nor the upper-crust landlords welcomed the influx of young painters, writers, craftspeople, and other artists who began moving into boarding houses and converted stables near Washington Square (the analogy with Haight-Ashbury in the mid–1960s is inescapable).[4]

By 1912, hundreds of outcast intellectuals advocating socialism, women's rights, sexual freedom, trade unions, birth control, and other causes had joined the poets and painters in Greenwich Village. They represented a shift in the national mood which, in the words of historian Nathan G. Hale, was "reflected by the appearance of pragmatism in philosophy, by the growth of socialism, by the revolt against political machines, by the rebellious assertiveness of labor groups like the I.W.W., by the parades and demands of the suffragettes." These new values were expressed politically as Progressive reforms, in cultural life by jazz and the blues, realism in fiction, imagist poetry, and abstract art. They "wore orange neckties, flannel shirts; the women bobbed their hair, favored batik skirts, and, like Emma Goldman, smoked cigarettes in public."[5] They rejected hollow Victorian pretensions and hypocritical platitudes in a quest for authenticity. Freud promised insights into truths that lay beneath the falsehoods on which this new generation been raised, and the avant-garde rapidly seized his ideas as a stake to drive through the heart of the old order.[6]

Who, specifically, introduced Freud to Greenwich Village? Emma Goldman appears to have been the first of the Villagers to cite Freud. She had initially encountered him in Vienna in 1895 and heard him lecture at Clark in 1909. She was living in the East Village in 1910 when she wrote, "Freud believes that the intellectual inferiority of so many women is due to the inhibition of thought imposed upon them for the purposes of sexual repression." That spring, 20-year-old Walter Lippmann was attending weekly seminars with William James at Harvard and he probably heard about Freud there. On May 8, 1910, an article on Brill and Freud filled a two-page spread in the *New York Times*, after which Brill said people "came to me from everywhere wanting to know about it." Those possibly included Lippman's friend Alfred Kuttner who, after graduating from Harvard in 1908, had returned to New York and become one of Brill's first patients.[7]

The classic Greenwich Village memoirs make no mention of Freud until 1912, when Lippmann and Kuttner shared the cabin in the Maine woods described in the previous chapter. They stayed up late into the night discussing psychoanalysis. "I have been studying it with a great deal of enthusiasm for several months now," Lippman wrote after they returned, "and I feel about it as men might have felt about *The Origin of Species*! ... The dream interpretations, the book on wit, the aesthetics, the child psychology, do for the first time in any psychology I know furnish a picture of human nature in the act, so to speak, of creating and expressing the character."[8]

At the end of 1912 Mabel Dodge (1879–1962) returned to the U.S. after living several years in Europe.* She'd first heard about Freud in the spring of 1911 while visiting her friends Leo and Gertrude Stein in Paris. When she returned to America she took an apartment two blocks off Washington Square at 23 Fifth Avenue where she hosted a famous gathering moderated by Lippmann at which Brill explained psychoanalysis to the assembled Villagers for the first time.[9] Another early Freudian was Max Eastman (1883–1969). In 1913, troubled by his turbulent sex life, he consulted Dr. Beatrice Hinkle. She'd studied with Jung in Zurich and referred him to Jelliffe for analysis. In the fall of 1913 Floyd Dell (1887–1969) moved to Greenwich Village from Chicago, having already read everything by Freud he could get his hands on. He remembered that "there must have been at that date, a half dozen or more people in the Liberal Club who knew a good deal about psychoanalysis, and a score or so more who were familiar enough with the terms to use them in badinage."[10] That is, Dell thought that late in 1913 only about 25 Village residents were especially interested in Freud. By then more than a million readers nationwide would have seen the articles on him in *McClure's*, *American Magazine*, and *Cosmopolitan*, which had published fiction about Arthur Reeve's Freudian detective (see below).

The Liberal Club to which Dell referred had recently relocated from midtown to 135 Macdougal Street in the Village. Calling itself "A Social

---

*Dodge's surname changed several times with her various marriages. I've used the form by which she became famous during her Greenwich Village years. Most sources cite her under her final married name, Luhan.

Center for Those Interested in New Ideas," in 1913 its regulars included Goldman, Dell, Eastman, Lippman, Eugene O'Neill, John Reed, Theodore Dreiser, Sherwood Anderson, Edna St Vincent Millay, and Lincoln Steffens. The Club offered public lectures on women's rights, anarchism, nudism, science, eugenics, birth control, prostitution, and modern art. I.W.W. leader Big Bill Haywood, poet Vachel Lindsay, muckraker Upton Sinclair, birth control advocate Margaret Sanger, and anarchist agitator Alexander Berkman all spoke there, some coming straight from jail to the podium. Its basement housed the immensely popular Polly's Restaurant, where anarchist activist Hippolyte Havel (1871–1950) waited on tables and washed dishes.[11]

Next door, Albert and Charles Boni opened the Washington Square Book Shop in 1913, cutting a hole in the wall so Club members and customers could easily pass back and forth. "It was through this book shop," recalled theater designer Bobby Jones, "that the works of Dr. Sigmund Freud, Lord Dunsany and Old Doctor [William J.] Robinson filtered into the thought currents of the age." Jones claimed that "the blame for Psychoanalysis rests squarely upon the shoulders of Moritz Jagendorf" who purportedly encouraged the Boni brothers to stock books by Freud.

Jagendorf (1888–1981) was an anarchist theater producer deeply involved in the radical Ferrer Center at the Modern School on St. Marks Place. Like the Liberal Club, the Modern School offered lectures on socialism, sexual freedom, literature, women's rights, psychoanalysis, and modern art but it also held adult education classes, ran a childcare center, and produced concerts and plays.[12]

In addition to institutions like the Liberal Club and the Modern School, Mabel Dodge's apartment became a popular venue for sharing new ideas. "It was there and thus," Lincoln Steffens recalled, "that

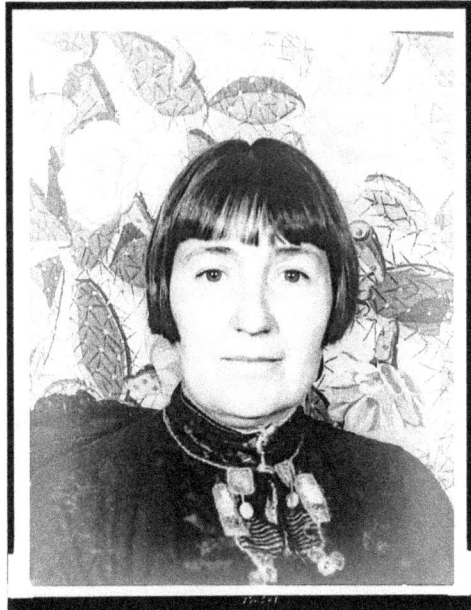

Mabel Dodge (1879–1962) in 1934 (Library of Congress, Prints & Photographs Division, Carl Van Vechten Collection, LC-USZ62-106861).

some of us first heard of psychoanalysis and the new psychology of Freud and Jung, which in several discussions, one led by Walter Lippmann, introduced us to the idea that the minds of men were distorted by unconscious suppressions, often quite irresponsible and incapable of reasoning or learning."[13] Brill recalled a famous evening where he first explained Freud's ideas:

> Another interesting group before whom I spoke during the winter of 1913 was at Mabel Dodge's salon. The person who invited me to speak there was a young man named Walter Lippmann, a recent Harvard graduate working with Lincoln Steffens. There I met radicals, litterateurs, artists, and philosophers, some of whom have influenced the trends of our times in no small way. Lippmann's first work contains many quotations from Freud. My talk aroused a very interesting and lively discussion, and the questions I was asked there by such people as John Collier, Sam Lewisohn, Bill Hayward, and others equally distinguished, were quite different from those posed by medical men.

Dodge remembered, "We had him [Brill] come down and talk to us one of the Evenings and several guests got up and left, they were so incensed at his assertions about unconscious behavior and its give-aways. Although I had invited Dr. Sachs to come on the Psychoanalytic Evening, he repudiated my invitation with the tone of an admiral who has been invited to tea on an enemy submarine. He said he was not at all in sympathy with the subject or with the manner of presenting it to the public, and, he added, he considered the subject a dangerous one for me."[14]

It's important to remember, though, that this wave of interest among New York's bohemian set was a small part of a general trend. Between 1913 and 1918, 43 articles on Freud or psychoanalysis were published in 18 popular magazines that reached 6.8 million people (not counting brief book reviews and Dodge's biweekly self-help columns, which will be examined below).[15] Greenwich Village authors wrote only nine of the 43 and reached only about 20 percent of the total readership (1,481,500). Thirty-four of the 45 were written by professional journalists with little or no connection to Greenwich Village; these reached 80 percent of the possible readers (5,357,457). The first American book about Freud, Brill's *Psychanalysis* [sic], *Its Theories and Practical Application,* went into its second edition in 1914 and three influential Freudian books came out the next year (James J. Putnam's *Human Motives,* Edwin Holt's *The Freudian Wish,* and Isador Coriat's *The Meaning of Dreams*); none of these authors were among the Greenwich Village avant-garde. Exponentially more Americans discovered Freud through mainstream book publishers or *Ladies Home Journal* than through *The Masses* or the Boni brothers' bookshop.

The first articles about Freud by the Village intelligentsia came from Harvard friends Kuttner and Lippman. Nearly a full page long and featuring a large portrait of Freud, Kuttner's review of *Psychopathology of Everyday Life* in the *New York Times* in October 1914 (circulation 192,000) was impossible to overlook. It used more than a dozen anecdotes to illustrate and praise Freud's explanations for slips of the tongue, lost objects, and forgotten obligations. Kuttner followed it a month later with a "Note on Forgetting" in the *New Republic* (circulation 15,000) in which he briefly explored Freud's claim that "the mind has an inveterate tendency to forget the disagreeable" by burying it in the unconscious. He emphasized that in this respect the minds of the "normal person" and of the mentally ill differ only in degree. The next spring, Kuttner also wrote a scathing letter to the editor excoriating a reviewer for rejecting Freud's emphasis on the role of sexual impulses: "We should not think much of a scientist who congratulated Darwin on his vast accumulation of facts but deplored his apparent obsession about making everything evolve." The next month Lippman also compared Freud to Darwin but went even further: "In Freud I believe we have a man of much the same quality, for the theories that have grown from his clinic in Vienna have always flowered in endless ways. From anthropology through education to social organization, from literary criticism to the studies of religions and philosophies, the effect of Freud is already felt. He has set up a reverberation in human thought and conduct of which few as yet dare to predict the consequences."[16]

Max Eastman took the Village perspective on Freud to the masses in a pair of articles published in the summer of 1915 in *Everybody's Magazine* (nationwide circulation 600,000) for which he was paid $1,000. The two articles totaled 19 double-column pages on "the amazing new science of psycho-analysis." They were illustrated with portraits of Freud, Jung, Hall, Brill, Jelliffe, and White, as well as sketches of scenes in which people forgot names, mis-spoke, and made similar unconscious mistakes. Eastman or his editor opened by sarcastically imitating the language of patent medicine ads: "Do you suffer from headaches, nausea, 'neuralgia,' paralysis, or any other mysterious bodily disorder for which your physician can discover no bodily cause? It may be that your trouble is a mental cancer which can be dissected out by this new method, and leave you sound and free and energetic." Eastman went on to describe the research of the six psychologists, summarizing their findings and detailing their methods but ignoring the sexual origins of neuroses, the polymorphous perversity of infants, and other controversial concepts. His two articles provided a lengthy, popularized, upbeat, and sanitized appraisal that would have intrigued half a million curious laypeople around the nation.[17]

But even Eastman's watered-down, optimistic account of Freud didn't reach as many readers as articles by professional journalists for whom Freud was just one topic among many. H. Addington Bruce, who'd written one of the first mainstream assessments of psychoanalysis back in 1910, published two more in 1913 and 1915 with a combined readership of 800,000. "Stammering and Its Cure" described Brill's treatment of a stutterer by psychotherapy rather than surgery. "Fears of Childhood" focused on the ways that early traumas lay behind adult phobias and how psychoanalysts addressed them: "Their latest pronouncements are indeed unusual and have an important bearing on the treatment of a number of adult mental derangements. This article gives in popular form the results of this very recent and profound psycho-analytic research."[18]

Another mainstream journalist whose readership dwarfed that of the Greenwich Village little magazines was San Francisco–based Peter Clark MacFarlane (1871–1924), whose two-part article "Diagnosis by Dreams" appeared in *Good Housekeeping* in the spring of 1915 (circulation 350,000). MacFarlane had been a railroad worker, Protestant minister, and actor before taking up journalism around 1910. His stories and articles were soon appearing in mass-market magazines such as *Collier's* and the *Saturday Evening Post* and his novels were serialized in Hearst newspapers. His stories were known for their uncompromising, realistic characters and focus on moral conflict; they were in many ways forerunners of the hard-boiled detective stories of the 1930s. Macfarlane, facing a terminal illness, calmly shot himself in the head outside the door of the San Francisco City Morgue in 1924.[19]

Unlike the Village bohemians, in 1915 Macfarlane was a household name all across America. The first of his two articles recast Freud's ideas in lay language and retold stories of miraculous cures from published case histories. His praise was extravagant: "The system is called psycho-analysis—soul analysis, that is—meaning by soul the whole stream of mind-life, conscious and unconscious. It is so new that its founder, Sigmund Freud, an Austrian Jew, still lives and pursues his studies and his practice in the city of Vienna." Macfarlane's second article described Freud's principal theories carefully, including infantile sexuality, the sexual origin of neurosis, and explanations of fundamental concepts like libido, repression, and sublimation. He used idealized versions of case histories or fictionalized examples and, as in the first article, these were heavily illustrated with original drawings and sketches and colorful captions.[20]

The editor at *Good Housekeeping* who bought Bruce and Macfarlane's long articles on psychoanalysis was 36-year-old William Frederick Bigelow (1879–1966). Bigelow was the opposite of avant-garde—a Methodist, Republican, and Prohibitionist—but he published articles supporting women's rights and sex education and denouncing child labor, advocated Progressive reforms like pensions for widowed mothers, and demanded honesty in advertising. He was appointed editor of *Good Housekeeping* in

1913 after Hearst bought the magazine and he grew its readership to more than a million by the mid–1920s. Bigelow's editorials make no mention of Freud or psychoanalysis and it seems likely that, having observed the rise of interest in Freud during previous stints as editor of *Cosmopolitan* and *Hearst's Magazine*, he simply welcomed articles on the topic by two of his regular contributors.[21]

No article about Freud published during these years reached more people than John Toohey's "How We All Reveal Our Soul Secrets" in *Ladies' Home Journal* (circulation 1.5 million). Toohey (1879–1946) was on the verge of abandoning journalism for a successful career as a Broadway press agent. He is best remembered today for launching the famous Round Table group at the Algonquin Club, where he gave the *New Yorker* magazine its name at a luncheon in 1925. He'd already written for newspapers in Washington and New York when he placed his popular account of Freud's theories in *Ladies Home Journal* in the fall of 1917.[22]

Toohey's 2,500-word piece opened with hypothetical examples of slips of the tongue before crediting the discovery of their importance to Freud and outlining key psychoanalytic concepts in lay language:

> Briefly stated, the Freudian psychology rests upon the theory of "repression." He and his followers believe that there is a chamber of the mind, which they call the "unconscious," which is the repository for an enormous amount of undesirable psychic material which has been "repressed" from consciousness because of our cultural development. Here are stored away all the primitive impulses which are so active in childhood, but which are curbed and checked by the process of education. Here are housed many of the unrealized wishes of our lives, all the desires which came to us in the years that have gone and which we "crowded out of thought," as the saying goes, because they did not harmonize with our religious, our ethical or our cultural notions. Here, too, are the memories of many of the disagreeable and painful experiences of our lives, the things we "just couldn't bear to think about."

Toohey went on to cite examples from his own life, anecdotes shared by colleagues, and examples published by Freud and Jones. Although never explicitly referring to *Psychopathology of Everyday Life*, he shared its main points in language that any literate person could grasp. "Truly, we all reveal our real personalities when we do not think or realize that we are doing so. Fortunately, very few of us have to pass the scrutinizing inspection of a psychological detective."[23]

The editor who printed Toohey's piece, Edward Bok (1863–1930), was about to retire after running *Ladies Home Journal* for nearly three decades. He had no sympathy for Freud's ideas: he urged regular church attendance, opposed women's suffrage and equal rights, believed that poverty strengthened character, denounced sexy new dances, and patriotically supported the war. Toohey's article might have been commissioned by Bok's managing editor, Karl Edwin Harriman (1875–1935), who had previously edited a literary magazine in Chicago and went on to produce a pulp magazine that specialized in true crime and science fiction. Harriman had ties to the younger generation of realist writers, including Stephen Crane and Upton Sinclair, and presumably was in closer touch than Bok with modern trends like psychoanalysis.[24]

During the autumn of 1917, when Toohey's piece appeared in *Ladies Home Journal*, Mabel Dodge's advice columns were running in Hearst newspapers. Like her 1913 salon event with Brill, they have been celebrated as a turning point in the dissemination of psychoanalysis. But few of those who made this claim appear to have actually read them, because her texts reveal a different story. None of Dodge's 27 articles mentioned Freud's name or used the word "psychoanalysis." Fewer than a third mentioned basic Freudian concepts such as the unconscious, repression, instincts, or transference. Dodge never discussed Freud's dream theory, the sexual origin of neuroses, or the psychosexual stages of child development. Instead, the majority of her short articles simply contained generic self-help advice like the "Dear Abby" columns of later decades.

Dodge was a patient of Brill's in 1917 when he suggested she take up writing. By then she'd been married three times, borne a fourth man's child, taken several lovers of both sexes, and tried to kill herself three times. She was already famous for her beauty, eccentricity, wealth, charisma, and for patronizing modern painters, writers, playwrights, and radical causes. Her friends included Gertrude Stein, Pablo Picasso, Alfred Stieglitz, Georgia O'Keeffe, Lincoln Steffens, John Reed, Carl Van Vechten, and D.H. Lawrence. She was also a lifelong friend of the most powerful journalist in America, Arthur Brisbane (1864–1936), Hearst's chief lieutenant.[25]

Dodge and Brisbane had grown up in the same social circle in Buffalo, where her father was the city's richest banker and Brisbane's was a prominent writer. Their Gilded Age childhoods featured live-in servants, riding lessons, private schools, and tours to Europe. In 1912, when Dodge returned to New York after renovating a fifteenth-century villa near Florence, Brisbane reached out to her from his office at the center of the Hearst empire to welcome her home. Five years later, when Brill suggested she take up some creative work, Dodge approached him. "I had asked Arthur Brisbane for work on the *Journal*," she recalled, "and since he had been insisting for fifteen years that I was a writer (perhaps because he himself was one!) he could not very well refuse me a chance to be one." After meeting in his office on July 15, 1917, he hired her to write one or two columns a week on any topic of her choosing. "Don't think of your own little group of people when you write," Brisbane insisted, "but think of the woman making up the beds in the hotel, or the woman working in the store, or the mother raising a family of children." He reminded her that this was "an easy start on the best page of the paper with the biggest circulation in the United States."[26]

Writing soon became one of Dodge's main pleasures. "These little *feuilletons* of mine took me an hour or so to write and they amused me very much. I held my public in my mind, the shop-girls and young clerks who, Arthur said, read the *New York Journal*, and I wrote down for them all I learned about psychoanalysis and about myself, and anything else that came along. The editors immediately boomed them and advertised them in black letters two inches high: 'Mabel Dodge Writes About Mother Love!' 'Mabel Dodge Asks Do You Work for a Living?' The city editor's captions were always embarrassing! They were syndicated in every Hearst paper in the United States." At the time, the Hearst empire included 15 dailies in eight cities, with a combined circulation just under two million. Local editors chose when and where to run her columns and adjusted the text and headlines to suit their needs.[27]

Dodge's pieces were only a few paragraphs long. Their light and chatty tone was meant to resonate with working- and middle-class women whose lives had been turned upside-down by new expectations, new technology, and new freedoms. Many of the columns were not about personal problems at all: "Mabel Dodge Writes on Old Time Quilts" and "Mabel Dodge Writes About More Light in the Home" are just two examples. Her most explicitly Freudian piece ran the week of November 24, 1917, under the heading, "Mabel Dodge Writes About the Unconscious." She called it "the vast submerged part of us. It is, to our conscious selves, as the depth of the lake is to its own surface.... Here lie the instincts—the instinct of reproduction, the instinct of self-preservation, the instinct to develop and grow.... Here in our past lies our future—waiting, waiting the magical awakening ... the Unconscious is the true fairyland. The place of marvels and wonders. Watch yourself; you will see glimpses of it from time to time." That advice ran beside editorials advocating more war workers and protesting automobile taxes, a pair of anti–German political cartoons, two gossip columns, a note on parenting, and a large portrait of a switchboard operator with a plea to be more considerate during phone calls.[28]

About half of Dodge's columns illustrated concepts common to all therapeutic approaches without being explicitly Freudian. For example, "The men who have not really grown up are the ones who have never been able to relinquish the mother-comforts and the ease of life that mothers give. These men may be observed all along the line of regression, stuck in various stages of immaturity—in varying degrees of shirking

THE CRAIG KENNEDY SERIES

THE
DREAM DOCTOR

BY
ARTHUR B. REEVE

FRONTISPIECE BY
WILL FOSTER

HARPER & BROTHERS·PUBLISHERS
NEW YORK AND LONDON

responsibility. They cannot get away from their mothers.... These are the failures! The stay-at-homes! They have never made that essential escape from the mother that is necessary for producing and achieving." Others silently applied generic psychological ideas to modern circumstances. In "Mabel Dodge Talks of Women Who Seek Masters" she wrote, "Their idea of man is the idea of the father, and they go through life trying to recover the childish past, so as to perpetuate their golden age.... When will women be able to let go the father's hand and learn to look forward?" And many were simply inspirational: "If you are doing something you believe in— go ahead and do it. Make a plan and carry it out.... Don't wonder whether people are critical of you or your achievements. If you have something to do, it needs all your attention.... Give the whole of yourself to what is ahead of you, to what you want to bring to light."[29] Entering two million homes twice a week, Dodge's articles certainly made many American women more reflective and introspective, but they didn't necessarily make them better-informed about Freud.

A more explicit presentation of Freud's views that reached millions of readers came in the detective stories of Arthur B. Reeve (1880–1936) whose protagonist, Prof. Craig Kennedy, relied on psychoanalysis to solve crimes. These appeared between 1913 and 1918 in *Cosmopolitan*, then a men's magazine like modern *Esquire*, and were later collected into books. Reeve's editor introduced the first story in August 1913 by asking, "Do you dream? Have you ever heard of Dr. Sigmund Freud, of Vienna? Do you know what he is doing? In the following story, Craig Kennedy solves a baffling murder mystery by searching the soul—by analyzing, according to Dr. Freud's theories, the dreams—of one of the innocent characters in the tragedy."[30]

In the climax of this story, Prof. Kennedy spends two full pages explaining Freud's theories and how he used them to solve the murder: "It is as though we had two streams of thought, one of which we allow to flow freely, the other of which we are constantly repressing, pushing back into the subconscious, or unconscious.... Freud says that as soon as you enter the intimate life of a patient you begin to find sex in some form. In fact, the best indication of abnormality would be its absence. Sex is one of the strongest of human impulses, yet the one subjected to the greatest repression." He then connects the dreams of one character to murderous actions by her lover.[31]

Reeve's detective Prof. Kennedy made overt use of psychoanalysis like this in only three stories, but references to Freudian ideas are sprinkled throughout his tales, which were read in 800,000 homes every month in

Opposite page: **Arthur Reeve's fictional Freudian detective, Professor Craig Kennedy, 1914 (University of California Libraries via archive.org).**

Cosmopolitan. In her 2004 dissertation, Jessamyn Hatcher demonstrates how Reeve's fiction was aimed at middle-class men with white collar jobs in businesses like banking, insurance, and sales (as well as book publishing) and helped make psychoanalytic concepts commonplace among literate Americans. One wonders if Freud, who read Agatha Christie and Dorothy Sayers for pleasure, ever encountered Prof. Kennedy.[32]

The success of mass-market articles like these meant that a watered-down, over-simplified, and usually sanitized version of Freud's ideas swept the nation. In Greenwich Village, "every Tom, Dick, and Harry in those days was misinterpreting and misapplying the general rules underlying analysis." Playwright Susan Glaspell recalled, "You could not go out to buy a bun without hearing of someone's complex" and her friend Edna Kenton remembered that "Washington Square and its many radiating little streets bloomed into a jungle of misunderstood theory and misapplied terms." Kuttner lamented that in 1916 "an informal canvas revealed that approximately five hundred individuals were quite willing to psychoanalyze patients in the city of New York alone, whereas there were probably not more than six properly qualified medical practitioners in the whole State. Advertisements offered to teach the psychoanalytic technique by mail and instructors in chiropractic included it in their curriculum." The problem of unqualified practitioners, disaffected former pupils, and blatant charlatans prompted Freud to write the essay "Wild Psycho-Analysis" urging readers to be wary of consulting anyone who had not studied personally with him.[33]

Freud's nephew Edward Bernays recalled that about 1920, one New York bookstore stocked 200 titles dealing directly or indirectly with psychoanalysis. A Macy's department store ad asked in September 1922, "How much do you know about this new science—psychoanalysis. The whole subject has been so clearly and simply set forth by recent writers that everyone can now grasp it. There are books for beginners, mere outlines that are but introductory to more technical volumes, yet written by masters, including the great Freud." It offered for sale *How to Psycho-Analyse Yourself,* by Joseph Ralph of Long Beach, California, and three titles by lay analyst and notorious plagiarist "A. Trydon"—André Tridon, who will be discussed in Chapter 11.[34]

The unfortunate result of this wave of popularization was that, in the words of one historian, the common reader was "apt to acquire nothing beyond a smattering of jargon which makes him think he knows something about psychoanalysis when he has only a new set of words for his ignorance." On the brighter side, a growing number of mental health professionals began to equip themselves with new tools. By 1917, as Peter Clark MacFarlane noted, specialists were "pioneering in this wonderful kind of therapy in nearly every great city of America."[35]

Dr. William Robinson, Crusader and Crank, 1915

The boom in all things Freudian is reflected in the Ngram chart below. It displays the frequency with which the word "psychoanalysis" (with or without a hyphen) appeared on the pages of 25 million books, magazines, and newspapers that have been digitized by Google. It's subject to the same flaws and vulnerabilities as all bibliometric analysis, outlined above, but the trend is nevertheless obvious:

A bump occurred in 1913–1914 after Macmillan published *The Interpretation of Dreams* and *Psychopathology of Everyday Life* and a smaller

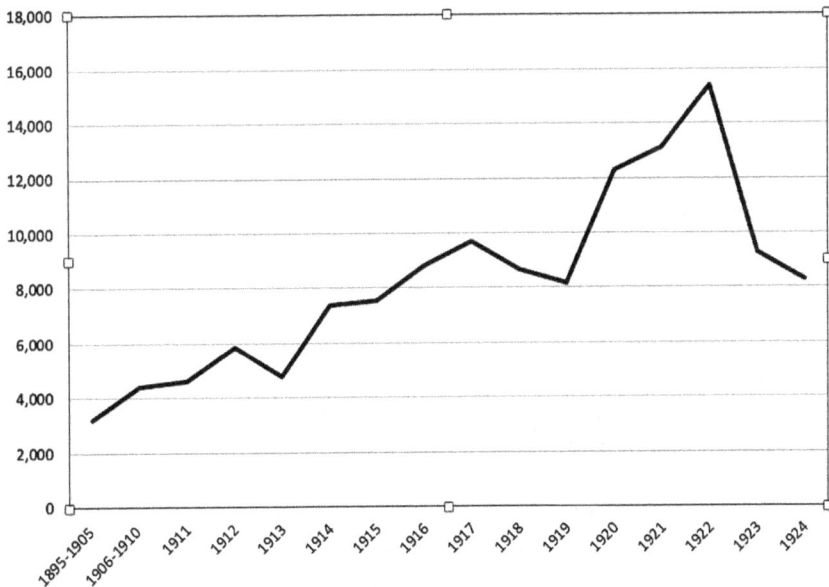

Uses of the term "psychoanalysis," 1895–1924, retrieved by a Google Ngram search.

one between 1915 and 1917 during the wave of articles discussed in the previous chapter. The drop in 1917–1918 reflects anti–German prejudice after the U.S. entered World War I (see Chapter 9). The most dramatic leap occurred during the three years 1919–1922 when, according to World-Cat, 88 different books on psychoanalysis were published in the U.S. The decline starting in 1923 marks the saturation of public interest and its shift to new trends, something noted by publishers and booksellers. At the end of the 1920s Freud's visibility and popularity rose once again.

The upsurge in discussions of psychoanalysis between 1910 and 1920 happened during a time of chaos in American medicine. Folk remedies used for centuries still survived, augmented by patent medicines and questionable new approaches like psychic research, Christian Science, and the Emmanuel Movement (a blend of religious counseling and group therapy which resembled Alcoholics Anonymous). At the other end of the spectrum, university-trained physicians attempted to discover the physical causes of mental illness, dissecting nerve tissue and measuring craniums. Most of them suspected that psychological problems were hereditary, caused by genetic material that deteriorated over generations. Comparatively few mental health professionals were more interested in helping patients than in explaining and classifying them; they prescribed hypnosis, diets, primitive electric shock, and rest cures without much success. The chronically mentally ill in asylums endured the same horrors they'd known for centuries.[1]

During these years many Progressive reformers who fought poverty, prostitution, and sexually transmitted diseases also endorsed the eugenics movement, whose goals were encapsulated in the title of Dr. William Robinson's popular book, *Fewer and Better Babies*. They campaigned for birth control, which required better knowledge of sexual anatomy and techniques of contraception. A medical sub-discipline called "sexology" therefore grew up, its publications precariously balanced between edification and titillation. All these movements attacked the prevailing Victorian prudery by speaking explicitly about sex, calling down the wrath of prosecutors intent on suppressing vice. Books were denounced, challenged or confiscated, and their publishers were dragged into court, including four of Freud's.[2]

Near the center of this whirlwind was headstrong New York doctor William J. Robinson (1867–1936)—"an impossible man to get along with," in the words of a good friend—who pirated one of Freud's classic essays and sold it without permission for more than 20 years.[3]

Robinson was born December 8, 1867, in Staro-Konstantinov, Ukraine, to an Orthodox Jewish family named Rabinowitz. He quickly lost his faith: "at the age of nine I was a convinced, conscious freethinker and made myself obnoxious to my religious relatives and friends by trying to convince them that their beliefs were but insane delusions." After leaving home at age 12, "I visited a number of cities, dwelt in various countries, gained a smattering of several languages, studied diligently whenever I had a chance, gave lessons whenever I could get pupils, and even for a few weeks supported myself by the labour of my hands. I came into close contact with poverty, suffering, and oppression. I became intimately acquainted with the joyless and sunless life of the people. It was during this period that my character was fashioned, and my outlook on the world formed." As a teenager in Odessa

Dr. William J. Robinson, ca. 1915 (*Medical Review of Reviews*, February 1936).

in the 1880s he worked with the revolutionary underground, more than once escaping arrest, imprisonment, and Siberian exile. A native German speaker, he also learned Russian, French, and Latin, in which he and fellow-activists passed messages that hoodwinked the police. After several close calls, Robinson and his young wife escaped to New York in 1887.[4]

Three years later he qualified as a pharmacist and in 1893 earned his M.D. at New York University, opening a private practice the same year. To augment his income, Robinson taught chemistry and pharmacology to medical students preparing for the Pharmacy Board exam. Business was so brisk that in 1889 he opened the Board of Pharmacy Institute, charging $50–75 per student. Four textbooks he wrote were soon adopted elsewhere, and the income from his medical practice, textbook sales, and teaching enabled Robinson to live in comfort for the first time. "Father was a prosperous physician," his son Victor later recalled, noting that he grew up "in a bourgeois household of comfort and culture. I never walked the streets looking for a job (never had a job of any kind); never was hungry (except between meals)." In 1905 Robinson bought a large brownstone at 12 Mt. Morris Park West, across the street from what is now Marcus Garvey Park in Harlem, where the household included himself, his wife, their three children, an Austrian maid, and a Black servant from the Caribbean.[5]

The success of Robinson's various ventures enabled him to abandon general practice in favor of specializing in reproductive health, an unusual choice during an era in which sex could not be talked about publicly. "For over twenty years, namely since the very beginning of my medical practice [in 1893]," he wrote in 1915, "I have been convinced of the very great importance, I might say of the life-and-death importance, of the knowledge of preventing conception, of avoiding undesired pregnancy." But to lecture about birth control or send information about it through the mails was illegal: "there was not a publication, either medical or lay, that could be induced to touch the subject however mildly, however gingerly. Any discussion of it, either pro or con, was in the literal sense of the word, taboo. It was considered indecent, obscene to refer to it." This was even true of medical schools: "When I was a young man, there were medical colleges in the United States at which no reference to venereal diseases was made in the curriculum. The matter was regarded as 'improper,' as unworthy the attention of a respectable physician!" His leaflet *Why and How the Poor Should Not Have Children* (which described condoms, cervical caps, diaphragms, suppositories, and douches) reputedly circulated to millions of eager readers. Emma Goldman and her companion Ben Reitman were jailed in New York, Ohio, and Oregon for distributing it at their speeches.[6]

To address widespread ignorance and challenge the puritanical status quo, Robinson launched a journal in 1903 called the *Medico-Pharmaceutical Critic and Guide*, followed in 1907 with another titled the *American Journal of Urology*. Their purpose was to combat the silence of doctors about sexuality and contraception, though they often embraced other topics as well. "I started the 'Critic and Guide' as a safety valve," he wrote in 1915, "to relieve the internal pressure within me. I had so much to say, and I wanted to say it in my own way. At that time there was no periodical ripe enough either for my ideas or for my way of expressing them. I had to start one of my own! I have been editor of several other journals, and there you will not find the personal pronoun even once. They are purely scientific publications. In them, I can be as impersonal, as 'respectable,' and as dull, as any editor in America. But in the 'Critic and Guide,' which is my own personal mouthpiece, I prefer to be otherwise. I prefer to be myself."[7]

Its monthly issues were liberally sprinkled with Robinson's radical politics, his editorials advocating women's rights, pacifism, economic justice, and sexual freedom. "Let There Be Light!" the *Critic and Guide* declared on its masthead, describing itself as "A Journal of Individuality. A Free Lance in the Noblest Sense of the Word. No 'policy' except the policy of Truth, Honesty and Fairness. No padding. No dead Matter. All Frauds and Humbugs fearlessly Exposed."[8]

In January 1910, Robinson also took over publishing the *Medical Review of Reviews*, whose purpose was to survey the world's medical literature and aggregate citations into its *Index Medicus,* cited at the start of the previous chapter.[9] He delegated editorial responsibilities to his son Fred. In December 1912, 21-year-old Edward Bernays "boarded the recently electrified Ninth Avenue elevated and by chance sat down next to Fred Robinson, a schoolmate whom I had not seen since 1904."

> Fred was helping his father, a physician, publish books, pamphlets and a monthly, the *Critic and Guide*, that protested the prevalent sex prudery... "My father just gave me a gift of two monthly medical magazines," Fred told me, "the *Medical Review of Reviews* and the *Dietetic and Hygienic Gazette*." The *Review* was edited by Ira S. Wile, a highly respected pediatrician. "I'm proud of its *Index Medicus*," said Fred. "It's a bibliography of the world's medical periodical literature that is more comprehensive than the A.M.A. *Journal's*. The *Gazette* appeals to physicians' interest in dietetics and hygiene." He added casually, as though he were offering me a stick of gum, "Ed, how'd you like to help me run the *Review* and the *Gazette*? You'll get twenty-five dollars a week." ... My job was to edit the *Gazette* and assist in production, circulation, promotion and advertising solicitation for both magazines.... I wrote enthusiastic editorials on the importance of a daily bath, at a time when the Saturday-night bath was still traditional.[10]

Bernays soon tired of medical journalism, however, and travelled to Europe, where he vacationed with his cousin Anna Freud and his uncle Sigmund. He was a nephew of Freud on both sides—his mother was Freud's sister and his father was the brother of Freud's wife.

Besides editing two journals, Robinson also published more than 40 books between 1909 and 1919. They included technical works on sexually transmitted diseases, dermatology, eugenics, and birth control by European and American doctors, including, of course, Robinson himself. His 1915 book *Fewer and Better Babies, or, the Limitation of Offspring by the Prevention of Conception* (further subtitled *the Enormous Benefits of the Practice to Individual, Society and the Race*) became a minor classic and went through dozens of printings during his lifetime. He also published books by Havelock Ellis, Wilhelm Stekel, and Marie Stopes, whose marriage manual led to his arrest on obscenity charges.[11]

In the May 1910 *Critic and Guide* Robinson summarized an article by Brill on Freud's dream theory, and from that point on he kept a close eye on Freud's work. "I consider Freud one of the world's geniuses," he later wrote. "He will be and he deserves to be immortal. His contributions to the subject of infantile sexuality, the light he has thrown on the hidden springs of human conduct, etc., are imperishable. But it is utterly impossible for me to swallow the whole Freudian philosophy."[12] Five years later he announced in the *Critic and Guide* that "we have on hand a large number of articles by some of the greatest living European sexologists, and their publication will commence with the October issue [of his *American Journal of Urology*]." These included Freud's essay "Die 'Kultuerlle' Sexualmoral und dei Moderne Nervositaat" which had first appeared in German in 1908. In it Freud argues that modern civilization depends upon repression and rechanneling of sexual energy, which causes widespread anxiety, neurosis, and unhappiness that prompted him to wonder "whether our 'civilized' sexual morality is worth the sacrifice which it imposes on us."[13]

Robinson called the essay "a very important article by Prof. Sigmund Freud of Vienna" and printed a translation—without consulting or compensating the author—in the next issue of the *American Journal of Urology*, omitting its first 10 paragraphs and changing the first word of its title. *Publishers Weekly* later claimed the translation had been made by popularizer and plagiarist André Tridon.[14]

A few weeks later Robinson reissued it as a 16-page pamphlet titled *Modern Sexual Morality and Modern Nervousness*. Though he claimed copyright in his own name on the cover, no copyright application was filed in Washington. The number of copies printed is not known, but it was a flimsy production and only one copy has survived (at the Library of Congress). The insides of both covers contained advertisements for Robinson's other publications. The pamphlet issue was from the same setting of type as in the *American Journal of Urology*, with the lines shifted slightly and new page numbers inserted to accommodate the pamphlet format.[15]

Brill caught wind of the piracy and asked Freud about it in October 1915. "I have nothing to do with the translation of the article," Freud wrote back. "Nobody asked me." He then drafted an open letter to the American Medical Association objecting to the piracy: "I have learned that a Dr. William J. Robinson is publishing English translations of my work that has appeared in German. Although the existing laws do not prohibit this, I hope that I will have your approval when I protest against this material and scientific damage. I do not know Dr Robinson and I cannot guarantee the reliability of his translation. The only one I have given permission to translate my work into English is Dr. A.A. Brill in New York."[16]

Freud's protest did nothing to deter Robinson, who included the pamphlet in a display ad in December 1917, calling it "the greatest single essay Prof. Freud ever wrote. Contains more 'meat,' more thought provoking ideas than many a big book. All amateur sexologists ought to be forced to read this fine essay. Price, Twenty-five cents."[17] In June 1920 he published the text in the *Critic and Guide*, preceded by this note:

> Freud's Best Essay. The editor considers Freud's essay on the relationship of sexual abstinence and nervous diseases, printed in this issue, the best thing Freud has ever done, without any qualifications. It is free from cabalistic jargon; deals with no fanciful hypothesis or untenable theories; it discusses facts the validity of which every earnest and unbiased investigator must recognize. A study of this essay should be obligatory on all teachers, jurists, physicians, clergymen, and last but not least, parents. I published this essay in the *American Journal of Urology and Sexology* five years ago but that issue was exhausted as soon as published. And it is in compliance with numerous requests that I am reprinting it in the *Critic and Guide*.[18]

Two years later Robinson announced a new edition in *Publishers Weekly*, on September 23, 1922. In November he advertised it in *Survey Graphic* with other books coming from the Cosmopolis Press, 257 West 71st Street, a firm with whom he entered a short-lived partnership. No copies of either 1922 printing have been found. When another finally came out in 1923, the text had been entirely reset. It was printed on 48 pages (including six pages of advertisements at the end), priced at 50 cents, and bore the *Critic and Guide* imprint. As with the first edition of 1915, only a single copy of this 1923 edition is known to exist today.[19]

In 1931 Robinson pirated Freud's essay a third time. He'd dedicated his 1930 book *If I Were God* to Joseph and Fay Lewis, proprietors of the Eugenics Publishing Company, for being "valiant fighters in the battle against soul-corroding superstition and baneful ignorance." Lewis had been prosecuted for publishing one of Robinson's earlier books and the two became good friends.[20] The Lewis' Eugenics Publishing Co. published Freud's essay in 1931 as a pamphlet with a new introduction by Robinson that read, in part, "whether one accepts Freud's teachings in total or rejects a great part of them as unsubstantiated and untenable, one must admit that his influence on modern thought has been tremendous, incalculable—and *on the whole* beneficial…. That psychoanalysis has been exploited by charlatans and ignorant laymen for their own benefit and to the detriment of their victims is not to be laid at the door of its founder. Of all Freud's writings—and their number is enormous—the writer considers the present essay the most important—the most important barring none." This 1931 edition was printed on cheap acidic paper and sold for $1.00; some copies were bound in paper-covered boards. The Library of Congress Copyright Office received a deposit copy on April 13, 1931, with a list of Robinson's books on page [49] and no advertisements on page [50]; this is presumed to be the earliest issue since others contain updated advertisements on those pages. It seems likely that Joseph Lewis kept the type standing and ran off impressions with new ads and variant bindings as demand warranted. Seven years later, in 1938, Eugenics Publishing issued it again, this time as a slender hardcover. Both 1930s printings closely followed Robinson's second edition of 1923 (six preliminary pages, 37 pages of text, and four pages of advertisements) and are the only versions met with today.[21]

As the preceding quotations show, Robinson was by no means a strict Freudian. "Freud's name will live forever," he admitted.

> The foundations of his philosophy are permanent. Some of his ideas may now safely be declared to be imperishable truths. He has put a new, more correct valuation on human sexuality. He has given us an insight into the motives and mainsprings of human conduct which we did not possess before, or which we sensed only vaguely. The greater is the pity, that with what is true in Freudism there is mixed so much that is false, so much that is bizarre, ridiculous. In fact, when we read some of the writings of Freud's disciples, we cannot help being in doubt as to the sanity of their authors.[22]

Those American disciples thought even less of Robinson. When Freud inquired about New York analysts in 1919, Jones and Brill denounced one of them for "associating with a rather questionable crowd, W.J. Robinson, a Russian Jew of the Bolshevik type who is editing the 'Critic and Guide' and similar stuff, a most unscrupulous person."[23]

Robinson wrote in 1927 that all his life he'd possessed "a profound (perhaps morbidly intense) sympathy for the oppressed and downtrodden; and a fierce indignation towards all forms of injustice and cruelty." So when the U.S. entered World War I in 1917, he launched an anti-war monthly called *A Voice in the Wilderness* to protest militarism, conscription, and war-profiteering. But before he could mail the first issue to subscribers, all copies were seized by the U.S. Post Office and he was arrested under the Espionage Act for "obstruction of recruiting and enlistment." After paying $5,000 bail, Robinson fought back until the government dropped the case after the war ended.[24]

But a year later New York authorities prosecuted him for publishing Marie Stopes' "obscene" book, *Married Love*. Robinson faced up to a year in prison and a fine of $1,000 but was let off with paying $250 when the case was settled a year later. Harassed by government officials, accused of treason by federal authorities, sued for libel by his critics, despised by quacks he'd exposed, and denounced by the medical establishment for transgressing the limits of decency, Robinson left America for Europe, where he spent much of the 1920s. He eventually returned and resumed his crusade for sex education, birth control, freedom of the press, and other radical causes until dying from a sudden heart attack in 1936.[25]

8

Moffat, Yard and Co. Capitalize on the "New Psychology," 1915–1918

"Book publishing was dominated by stuffy old firms," Edward Bernays recalled, "who treated the business as if it were the practice of a sacred rite. The Macmillan Company, Doubleday, Harper's, Scribner's, E.P. Dutton, Henry Holt & Company and G.P. Putnam's were run like conservative banking houses." These family-owned companies were pillars of conventional society, their taste and their values steeped in Victorian propriety. Their affluent, Anglo-Saxon, and Protestant directors locked arms against the Greenwich Village radicals and young Jewish upstarts who were entering the profession but opened doors for fledgling entrepreneurs of their own class and kind. These included William Moffat (1865–1946) and Robert Yard (1861–1945), who published five of Freud's books during World War I.[1]

Moffat and Yard attended Princeton together in the early 1880s, married each other's sisters, and joined the ranks of Scribner's where they soon rose into management. When they reached their early thirties, they raised $100,000 and started their own publishing house, Moffat, Yard and Co. in 1905. They produced lavish coffee-table books, a best-seller about the Russo-Japanese War, and a children's series called the "Mother Lets Us Books," which opened with *When Mother Lets Us Cook*. Yard became a well-known figure in publishing, especially after he wrote a book about the industry in 1913. Within a few years their firm had a backlist of 300 titles.[2]

In 1908 Moffat and Yard brought in 43-year-old Joseph H. Coit (1865–1930), who'd just abandoned teaching at the elite St. Paul's School. Historian August Heckscher wrote of him, "bluff rather than bright, he was drawn from that strain of the Coit family which had produced businessmen and stockbrokers—except that the younger Joseph lacked the innate ability to make money." Coit, who was nicknamed Bull "for his robust insensitivity," took over day-to-day management of the company after Yard became editor of *The Century* in 1911 and Moffat of *The Mentor* in 1913; in 1916 he was named president. A competitor said of Moffat Yard under his leadership that "the only trouble with them was that they were too high-toned; they would not truckle to a debased taste, nor publish anything that was not intrinsically worthy."[3]

Coit began to publish books on psychology as soon as he joined Moffat Yard, starting in May 1908 with an account of the Emmanuel Movement by its founders. St. Paul's was an Episcopal school and Coit's father and brothers were Episcopal priests, so he may have learned about this quasi-religious therapy through ecclesiastical connections. In an April 1908 advertisement for the book, Moffat Yard claimed that "thousands of inquiries are coming to us by mail and telephone." That fall they brought out two more psychology books: *Personality in Education* by Coit's brother-in-law and fellow St. Paul's teacher James P. Conover and *The Riddle of Personality* by journalist H. Addington Bruce, whom we met above. From 1908 to 1915 Coit published at least one psychology title each year, including works by William James and Havelock Ellis.[4]

As Freud's visibility rose in the mass media, Coit turned psychoanalysis into one of the firm's top priorities. Between 1916 and 1918 they published five books by Freud and three about him, as well as works by Jung and Adler. In 1917 *Publishers Weekly* reported that "Moffat, Yard and Company, following their success in the field of psychoanalysis, have brought out this spring three additions to their rapidly increasing line of books on the new developments in this science." In August 1918 the *New Republic* commented, "By providing translations, as well as by favoring original American contributions, this firm has acquired an excellent list of psychological studies…. The material is now available in English for much more than a haphazard investigation of 'the unconscious.' It is a difficult work for any publisher to have undertaken, and a most creditable one, and the way is prepared for introducing general arterial drainage into the mind of man."[5]

The first of Freud's works to come from Moffat Yard were *Wit and Its Relation to the Unconscious* and *Leonardo da Vinci,* which were issued simultaneously in late September 1916 in translations by Brill. Brill had been working on an English version of *Wit* for at least three years. He was well into it by the end of 1913 and on January 14, 1914, wrote Freud, "Wit is practically finished—all I have to do is substitute examples, etc., while Totem u. Tabu I expect to have ready very shortly. I have a patient, a young writer, [Alfred Kuttner] who is helping me on it and as he knows German I expect to have it ready very soon."[6]

But Brill found himself delayed by a major translation difficulty similar to that he'd faced with *Psychopathology of Everyday Life*. The book is about jokes, puns, plays on words, and witticisms, and Freud had used dozens of German examples that simply weren't funny or even comprehensible in English. Confronting this problem in 1953, James Strachey wrote that "there are two methods one or other of which has usually been adopted in dealing with such intractable examples—either to drop them out altogether or to replace them by examples of the translator's own." Brill opted for the second and spent months searching for jokes in English that would work with American readers. "I have plenty of materials when it comes to dreams and psychopathology but I have to hunt for witticisms that would fit in with your thoughts and do justice to your own," he wrote Freud in October 1914. "That accounts for the tardiness." In the introduction he acknowledged the help of Horatio Winslow, a former editor at *The Masses*, "who has read the manuscript and has given me valuable suggestions in the choice of expressions and in the selection of substitutes for those witticisms that could not be translated." His manuscript was finally ready at the start of 1916.[7]

Meanwhile, Moffat Yard had decided to try selling books directly to customers through the mail via subscriptions. Coit approached his old St. Paul's classmate Robert Appleton (1865–1945) to carry out this experiment. Appleton had begun his career at the publishing house started by his grandfather, which had sold books by subscription for years, and he accepted Coit's offer to produce a 12-volume subscription series called "The Library of Modern Thought."[8]

In February 1916 Brill submitted the manuscript of *Wit* to Moffat Yard and Appleton accepted it, saying, "It seems to me that the book would fit in nicely in the 'Library of Modern Thought,' which will be sold (I believe I explained to you) on the subscription plan through agents." Brill insisted that their contract include three conditions: a separate trade issue to be published as well as the subscription-only one, Freud must always head the list in advertisements for the Library of Modern Thought, and a 10 percent royalty had to be paid on both trade and subscription copies. "From personal knowledge I can assert that hundreds of people are anxiously awaiting the appearance of *Wit*," he assured Appleton. Coit responded offering 15 cents per copy on the subscription issue rather than a percentage-based royalty because it was more expensive to produce; Brill accepted and the contract was signed on March 31, with publication planned for early fall. "For years," Brill assured Coit on March 26, "I have been referring to it in my own works, and in Prof. Freud's translations, and I have no doubt that every person who is interested in Prof. Freud's works will read this book."[9]

As *Wit* moved into production that summer, Brill carefully defended

Robert Appleton (seated left), Joseph Coit (seated right), and two other crew members at St. Paul's School, 1882 (Willis G.C. Kimball, "First Halcyon Crew 1882," St. Paul's School, Ohrstrom Library Digital Archives).

Freud's interests. He urged that Fisher Unwin be approached about a British edition, since they'd inquired about the book two years earlier; Coit followed up and later supplied sheets to them. When Brill noticed that Jung's name was listed ahead of Freud's on the letterhead of the Library of Modern Thought, he protested: "If you will refer to my letter of March 2nd you will see that as one of my terms for your publication of 'Wit' I asked that Prof. Freud's book should head the list of the library. As you accepted my terms (see your letter of March 23rd) I naturally expect you to follow your agreement. This may seem a matter of insignificance but it is of greater importance than you may think." Finally, when Appleton expressed concern about the term "libido" being used differently by Freud and Jung in their books for the Library of Modern Thought, Brill replied, "there is a marked controversy over that term between the Freudian school and Jung and his followers. We Freudians maintain that Jung's idea of libido is practically meaningless.... The Freudian meaning of the word for practical purpose may be translated as 'craving.'"[10]

Proofs were ready for correction in May, the book moved through the press over the summer, and on September 30 Coit sent Brill his complimentary author's copies and began to fill orders. It was advertised in *Publishers Weekly* that fall alongside Jung's *Analytical Psychology*, a juxtaposition that would surely have infuriated Freud if he'd seen it. The trade issue was bound in grayish blue cloth stamped on the spine in gold. It was reprinted in November 1917 with the spine stamped in black rather than gold. The number of copies in each impression is not known.[11]

Three months later, in December 1916, T. Fisher Unwin brought out a London issue of the American sheets bound in blue cloth stamped in gold on its spine and front cover. Another English issue appeared from Kegan Paul, Trench, Trubner & Co. which the British Library dated 1922, though no date appears on the book. When Moffat Yard was bought by Dodd Mead and Co. in 1924, they reported that a total of 1,465 copies had been sold to date; just 79 had been sold in 1923 and they still had 300 in stock. It's impossible to determine how these figures were divided across the five issues published over the previous seven years (U.S. trade and its 1917 reprint, Library of Modern Thought, and two London issues). A fifth issue was published by Dodd Mead, undated but possibly 1932 when they reprinted Freud's *Leonardo da Vinci*. This was bound in orange cloth with a paper spine label. Brill also included the text in the Modern Library's *Basic Writings of Sigmund Freud* in 1938, where it reached more than 300,000 readers (see Chapter 12). In 1960 Brill's translation was finally superseded by James Strachey's in volume 8 of the *Standard Edition*, under the title *Jokes and Their Relation to the Unconscious*.[12]

In the fall of 1916, while the trade edition was being sold and reviewed, Robert Appleton was busy assembling the Library of Modern Thought. His initial announcement in October 1916 said it would be "a comprehensive collection of volumes on psychology, philosophy, sociology, Christianity and allied subjects," to include works by Freud, Jung, Adler, Munsterberg, and Coriat, among others. It took Appleton nine months to have them all printed and uniformly bound in red cloth stamped in gold on their spines.[13]

As the 12 volumes began to arrive from the binder in June 1917, Appleton advertised in a national magazine for salespeople willing to go door-to-door: "Agents needed to represent this new and unique Library for the first time in all cities—Rare opportunity for School Teachers during the summer." He also requested photographs of Freud and Brill to use in "the specimen book" (salesman's dummy). The door-to-door campaign may have faltered, however, since in September 1917 the set was made available to customers through the mail at a discounted price of $19. The Library of Modern Thought issue of *Wit and Its Relation to the Unconscious* appeared in late summer or early fall of 1917 bound in red cloth stamped in gold, with the series title at the head of its spine. It contains a frontispiece photograph of Freud not found in the trade issue published 12 months earlier but is otherwise identical, being bound up from the same sheets printed in 1916 and dated 1916 on its title page.[14]

By the time it appeared in the fall of 1917, the Library of Modern Thought had been undermined by circumstances beyond anyone's control. The U.S. declared war on Germany in the summer of 1917 and launched an aggressive anti–German propaganda campaign at home. German names of foods, schools, and towns were changed, and suspected German sympathizers were attacked in their homes. Half the authors in the Library of Modern Thought had Germanic names and, as William Moffat told Brill in May 1918, "the eyes of the public grow very stern at the mere sight of a German book or a book of German origin." Customers had stopped buying them and bookstores were returning copies of Freud's works. The wave of anti–German prejudice apparently killed the Library of Modern Thought as a subscription series.[15]

Appleton and Coit then tried to unload the sets however they could. "WHAT DO YOU KNOW ABOUT YOURSELF?" asked a May 1918 ad. "The Master Minds in Modern Thought—The Greatest Thinkers of Today are at Your Command." It claimed that during the past year, "the publishers of 'The Library of Modern Thought' has [sic] already printed several large editions. There are just three hundred sets, of twelve volumes each, left." All 12 volumes could be purchased for $21, with just $5.00 down. A November 1918 ad in a St. Louis magazine claimed the series "will keep you abreast with the present day intellectual struggle with the unknown." Readers were encouraged to write for "a specially prepared and exceptionally interesting brochure on the new psychology." But nothing seemed to work, and the rarity of surviving copies suggest that few sets were actually sold.[16]

Advertisement for Moffat, Yard & Co.'s "Library of Modern Thought" (*Current Opinion*, June 1917).

Wit and Its Relation to the Unconscious was a serious work which, like *Psychopathology of Everyday Life*, attempted to explain how hidden forces influence the lives of ordinary people. The four other books by Freud that Moffat Yard brought out were very different. They were speculative essays, shorter and more exploratory, which attempted to apply the findings of psychoanalysis to art, literature, anthropology, and current events. By 1910 Freud had connected the recurring fantasies and dreams of his patients to specific personality traits and behaviors. Patterns had emerged. He wondered what might be discovered if he applied this new knowledge to the dreams recorded in da Vinci's private notebooks. His book-length essay, *Leonardo da Vinci, A Psychosexual Study of an Infantile Reminiscence*, was an experiment which examined the effect of early childhood experiences on Leonardo's later artistic and scientific work. Freud had written the book quickly and published it in the spring of 1910.

No evidence exists showing when Brill began to translate it because much of the correspondence between Freud and Brill during the war years does not survive. He sent the completed manuscript to Robert Appleton on May 24, 1916, with a warning that *Leonardo* contained sexually explicit passages: "I doubt whether the pamphlet can be given out to the general public without some sort of an admonition, such as 'Sold Only to Savants' etc., because of the nature of its content." But Moffat Yard pushed it quickly through the press and it appeared on the same day as *Wit*, September 30, 1916, bound in dark green cloth printed in gold; the number of copies is not known. Three years later it was challenged in court for obscenity (see Chapter 9), after which Moffat Yard agreed to raise its price to $5.00 to put it beyond the reach of casual buyers. This undoubtedly helped limit its sale to only 1,310 copies over seven years.[17]

When Brill's translation appeared, it was disparaged by Harvard professor James J. Putnam. "His Leonardo (translated by Brill) is out," Putnam wrote to Ernest Jones on November 12, 1916, "as of course you know. I am sorry to say the translation seems to me extremely poor, mainly to be sure from the literary standpoint. It seems to me a serious misfortune that Freud, whose writings and style, which though fine are sometimes hard to master, should have been presented so inadequately to his English-speaking public. I am somewhat surprised that Brill himself, who is conscientious, should not have seen this. However, so it is." Jones was even harsher: "I was deeply shocked time and again to see punctuation as illiterate as that of a servant girl's, with expressions of a similar order."[18]

Jones nevertheless worked with Kegan Paul, Trench, Trubner & Co. to bring out a London edition. In a foreword he explained that it was "designed to meet the English demand for the book, which cannot be advantageously supplied by the importation of copies of the American edition, on account of the very high price ($5) at which that edition is issued." Working with Moffat Yard they printed a cheaper issue in January 1922 by using a new method called the Minul process which reproduced the 1916 edition photographically. The work was done by printer Otto Elsner of Berlin who produced a particularly unattractive book with broken letters, inconsistent inking, and other blemishes that must have annoyed Jones at least as much as Brill's flawed English. Some copies of this were also sold by Moffat Yard with their own title page, undated but presumably issued in early 1922 bound in brown cloth with black spine lettering. These 1922 issues do not include any of the new footnotes or edits Freud inserted in the 1919 German edition but are simply facsimiles of the original 1916 New York text.[19]

In 1931 Kegan Paul proposed to issue it again, using the London printer Butler and Tanner, and Dodd Mead agreed to take copies for the American market. When Frank Dodd informed Brill, he replied on August 24, "I am delighted to hear that you are to give out a new edition of Freud's Leonardo Da Vinci ... for the book deserves better treatment than it has hitherto received.... I will write an Introduction which will deal with the points I brought out in Court" (when the book was challenged in 1919). Dodd imported an unknown number of copies of this British reprint in 1932 (paginated viii + 130 pages, like the first issue) but did not use Brill's lengthy introduction or reissue the book when copies were exhausted.[20]

In 1947 Random House published a true second edition, entirely reset (paginated 1–121), including for the first time Brill's long introduction dated February 1947. There were two issues, a Basic Book Club issue of 500 copies bound in dark blue cloth with gilt-stamped black panels on spine and cover (identified "First Printing" on its title page verso) and a general trade issue bound in burgundy cloth with black panels. The Basic Book Club had been started in 1945 to provide its members with one book on psychoanalysis every month; it evolved into the trade publisher Basic Books (see Epilogue). In the fall of 1955 Modern Library published the third edition of *Leonardo* (xxxviii + 122 pages) as number P11 in their short-lived paperback series. Alfred Knopf re-issued this in its Vintage line in 1961, after being acquired by Random House. These were all eclipsed in 1957 by Alan Tyson's translation for the *Standard Edition* (volume 11).[21]

In September 1917, exactly a year after their first two Freud titles, Moffat Yard published an unsanctioned edition of *Delusion and Dream: An Interpretation in the Light of Psychoanalysis of Gradiva, a Novel.* Freud had written this essay in the summer of 1906, applying the insights of psychoanalysis to a popular 1903 novel by Wilhelm Jensen about the delusions of an archaeologist with repressed memories. Moffat Yard's English version was not translated by Brill but rather by G. Stanley Hall's student Helen Downey, who presented the text of Jensen's novel alongside Freud's essay.

When Brill discovered this unauthorized translation, he immediately wrote to William Moffat:

> I was greatly surprised to hear that you were going to give out a translation of one of Prof. Freud's smaller works under the title of "Delusions and Dreams." I am convinced that I have told Mr. Coit and yourself on former occasions that I am Prof. Freud's sole English translator. I have a number of documents from Professor Freud in which he states very clearly that I am the only one who he authorizes to translate his works into the English language.... I have not the slightest doubt that the person who offered you this translation did not receive any permission from Prof. Freud to translate it and under the circumstances I do not think that any ethical publisher should take the work.... I know that legally anyone has a right, now a days, to take a German work and translate it into English but I assure you that I will do my utmost through my own efforts and through my friends in the scientific world to discredit such an action. I feel it my duty as a friend of professor Freud to take that attitude.[22]

William Moffat replied at once, blaming the mistake on confusion following the unexpected departure of Joseph Coit: "I am very much distressed over the whole matter.... Mr. Coit was called to [military] service early in July.... I assumed charge of matters in the office at once, and gathered up the loose strings as best I could." Brill replied, "there's only one way of giving Prof. Freud and me a fair deal, and that is to withdraw 'Delusion and Dream' from the market. I shall soon give out an authorized translation of this book under its correct title. I have had the translation ready for at least a few years, but have not published it because Prof. Freud preferred to have his more important works appear first." He also threatened to stop offering Moffat translations of Freud's future books, of which he claimed to have six in hand, if they didn't comply.[23]

The confusion over *Delusion and Dream* began when G. Stanley Hall attempted to help his student Helen Downey find a publisher for her translation. He was unaware that Freud had given Brill exclusive rights and had had translations of other short works made by other students. He approached Moffat Yard, who'd investigated *Gradiva*'s copyright status and agreed to publish it. After talking with Hall twice that fall, Brill calmed down, writing to Appleton on November 17, 1917, "I wish to say that after you left me, I did a lot of thinking, and decided that neither you nor Moffat, Yard and Company were to blame for what has happened, and that under the circumstances I would like to continue the same relations as before." Freud also came to accept it: "There never was any doubt in my mind," he wrote to Downey five years later, "that you and Dr. St. Hall acted with the best of intentions and best of faith…. American publisher are, as I know from other experiences, a dangerous breed."[24]

As with *Leonardo*, there was no simultaneous British issue of *Delusion and Dream*, but four years later, in 1922, Allen and Unwin licensed the rights and printed the first London edition. Copies of this were imported by Moffat Yard, bound in blue cloth. When Moffat Yard sold out to Dodd Mead in 1924, they reported a total of 1,363 copies sold to date. In 1927 Dodd Mead licensed it to the *New Republic*, who brought out an entirely reset edition of 2,000 copies in paper wrappers for $1.00. Called "Dollar Books," titles in this early paperback series were at first available only to subscribers, though they were eventually sold in bookstores and proved immensely popular even during the Depression. In 1956 Beacon Press brought out a new paperback edition (undated) with stiff paper covers. This was the last to appear until James Strachey's translation in volume 9 of the *Standard Edition* in 1959. All the American printings omitted a 1912 postscript by Freud in which he defended the use of psychoanalysis to investigate "the material of impressions and memories from which the author has built the work, and the methods and processes by which he has converted this material into a work of art."[25]

Freud's fourth Moffat Yard book, *Reflections on War and Death*, appeared in April 1918, though he'd written it during the spring of 1915 just eight months after war broke out. In it he discussed why people repress thoughts about death and how the coming of war forces such thoughts and feelings into the open. After the essay appeared in German, Brill set to work translating it with the help of Alfred Kuttner but didn't deliver the manuscript until the winter of 1917–1918. He was correcting proofs in early February 1918 and, given his recent experience with *Delusion and Dream*, insisted it be copyrighted in Freud's name. The book appeared that month as a small volume bound in red cloth, printed in white on the cover and spine, with Kuttner credited alongside Brill as translator. The number of copies printed is not known.[26]

A reset second edition of 500 copies was issued four years later bound in red cloth stamped in gold with a light blue dust jacket printed in black. This second edition had slightly different pagination and was issued under the one-word title, *Reflections*; only 423 copies had been sold by January 1924. A new translation by E. Colburn Mayne was included in volume 4 of Freud's 1925 *Collected Papers* published in London by the Hogarth Press and reprinted in John Rickman's 1939 anthology of Freud's political essays, *Civilisation, War and Death*, published in London but also distributed in the U.S. In 1952, the Encyclopædia Britannica included it in *The Major Works of Sigmund Freud*, volume 54 of their *Great Books of the Western World* series, which sold 35,000–50,000 sets per year for decades and totaled a million copies overall. Mayne's translation was slightly revised when published in 1957 in volume 14 of the *Standard Edition*.[27]

The last of Freud's books to be published by Moffat Yard was *Totem and Taboo, Resemblances between the Psychic Lives of Savages and Neurotics*, which appeared at the end of May 1918. A more ambitious work than the three shorter essays just described, it attempts to apply the insights of psychoanalysis to human evolution, the origin of social life, and the birth of religion.

On November 17, 1917, in his letter smoothing over the *Delusion and Dream* controversy, Brill wrote to Robert Appleton, "Pursuant to our telephone conversation, I sent you under separate cover the manuscript of Totem & Taboo, which you will receive in due time." Appleton began reading it immediately and sent back a contract a few days later. "Of course," Appleton cautioned, "we find that German names as authors of books have some effect on the sale of same, but we believe that this book in the long run will win out." Before signing the contract Brill insisted that Moffat Yard commit to publishing everything by Freud, that they formally copyright his American books, and that they agree never to publish translations by anyone else. The first provision, of course, was more than any publisher could promise but Moffat Yard agreed to move ahead with *Totem and Taboo* and a volume of case studies (never published).[28]

In February and March 1918 *Publishers Weekly* announced it as a forthcoming spring title and Appleton sent an advance copy to Brill on April 19. "Of course the condition of the war makes the sale of the books somewhat slow," he cautioned in his cover letter, "and in this case due to the fact that Freud is an Austrian the sale will no doubt be affected somewhat. At any rate I hope you will be satisfied with the book as it appears." Copyright was formally secured on May 24 and copies were in buyers' hands before the end of the month. The book was bound in blue cloth stamped in gold on the spine; when reprinted in 1919, this was altered to gray cloth printed in black.

Six years later Moffat Yard reported that only 1,567 copies of *Totem and Taboo* had been sold to date, and during 1923 only 118 had sold. As with *Delusion and Dream*, a completely reset edition of 2,000 copies was published by the *New Republic* in 1927 in paper wrappers for their "Dollar Books" series; it was reprinted in 1931. During the rest of the 1920s sales were very modest, just 412 copies of the trade edition and 1,794 copies of the *New Republic* paperbound edition. In 1938 Penguin issued it as a blue and white Pelican title with a stiff paper wrapper. In its licensing negotiations with Dodd Mead, Penguin said they expected at least 50,000 copies would be sold between Britain and America. That year Brill included it in Modern Library's *Basic Writings of Sigmund Freud*, where it eventually reached 345,000 readers. Knopf licensed it for a Vintage paperback edition in 1946 and Modern Library included it in their short-lived paperback series in 1960. James Strachey's translation was published in *Standard Edition* volume 13 in 1955.[29] *Totem and Taboo* was the last book by Freud that Moffat, Yard and Company produced.

Joseph Coit and his partners had nothing in common with the Greenwich Village avant-garde or crusading Dr. William Robinson who were also promoting Freud's ideas during these years. The Village radicals were aggressively trying to overturn the Victorian status quo ("the old ways were about over," Mabel Dodge wrote, "and the new ways all to create") and Freud was a powerful weapon in their sexual and cultural revolution. Robinson was a left-wing idealist challenging privilege and prudery in order to improve the lives of the poor and ignorant; he, too, saw a powerful ally in Freud. But Coit and his partners at Moffat Yard were Ivy League bluebloods who identified with the old guard and happily accepted its privileges. They patriotically supported the war while Dr. Robinson and Max Eastman were arrested and charged with treason for opposing it.[30]

There were also ethnic and class differences between Moffat Yard and Freud's other proponents. Robinson was a Jew who had fought the czar's secret police, arrived in New York as a refugee, and pulled himself out of the gutter by his bootstraps. Many of the most influential Greenwich Village writers were also Jewish, as were Freud's publishers Albert and Charles Boni and Horace Liveright. Yard, Moffat, Coit, and Appleton, on the other hand, were WASP conservatives. After attending elite private schools and Ivy League colleges, they walked through open doors into an unabashedly antisemitic publishing industry. Robinson lived and practiced in Harlem, then populated by working-class Eastern European Jews and Italian immigrants. Coit and his partners took the train each morning from suburban Connecticut or New Jersey, or lived in fashionable mid-town Manhattan. They were not idealists or revolutionaries campaigning for a better world but simply businessmen who saw the Freudian trend as a chance to turn a profit.

Joseph Coit never recovered from the death of his only son in the trenches of France; he abandoned publishing in 1917, retired from a lackluster business career a decade later, and died in Newport, R.I., in 1930. William Moffat edited the *Mentor* for 17 years until retiring in 1929; he died in a Manhattan hotel in 1946. Robert Yard left publishing in 1915 to help promote the newly established U.S. National Parks Service; he was a founder of the Wilderness Society in 1935 and served as its president and permanent secretary until his death in 1945. Robert Appleton retired from publishing in 1925, after the Moffat Yard partners sold the business to Dodd Mead. He went on to campaign for clean government and helped bring down the Tammany Hall machine in 1933.[31]

9

Freud Among the Censors

Two months before Freud stepped to the podium at Clark University in 1909, Anthony Comstock delivered a very different message from the same stage.

Comstock (1844–1915) had been invited to speak at the first session of Clark's 20th anniversary celebrations in July (Freud spoke at the second, in September). He told his audience about the work of his New York Society for the Suppression of Vice in a rambling lecture that revolved around a single theme: "the Spirit of Evil is ever active in crowding through eye and ear materials which he can use to the destruction of the soul." Comstock said there was "nothing more beautiful than the innocence of childhood. There is nothing on earth more sacred than woman. And if the highest and most sacred things can be hunted out for the purposes of debauchery of mind, or body, or soul, then there is reason why every Christian man and woman should stand up straight, and look this devil in the face, and strike from the shoulder." Comstock reported that during the last six months alone his society had seized more than three tons of dirty books, magazines, pictures, and other pernicious materials, made 67 arrests, and sent more than 90 cases to court. The audience erupted in multiple rounds of applause.[1]

The leading historian of the era summarized its prevailing sexual morality this way: "Sexual intercourse in marriage was a sacred duty, romantic love the most beautiful thing in life, and sexual lust evil. Since women, except the depraved few, were naturally pure, it was best that they have jurisdiction over the whole field of sexual relations. The duty of men was to make every effort to grow up pure, and especially to avoid the debilitating dangers that arose from evil thoughts. The crown of the whole civilization was the American family, with the father supreme in the economic sphere but the mother, freer and more respected than the women of other countries, in special charge of morals."[2]

Comstock had had a successful career. Fifty years earlier, prostitutes conducted their business openly on the streets of America's cities. Cheap pornography, sensational crime fiction, and salacious picture postcards were displayed on newsstands. Aphrodisiacs and sex toys were advertised and sold to both men and women. Dance halls, gambling dens, and brothels did a bustling business, catering to a new market of single men drawn to urban middle-class jobs like clerking and sales. To save these men from the dangerous temptations of the metropolis, the Young Men's Christian Association (Y.M.C.A.) was founded in 1852; it grew rapidly after the Civil War as veterans flooded into cities.[3]

In the spring of 1873, Comstock and wealthy Y.M.C.A. backers pushed through a federal law making it illegal to manufacture or distribute any "obscene, lewd, lascivious, indecent, filthy, or vile article, matter, thing, device, or substance … for any indecent or immoral use." The new law explicitly named "any obscene book, pamphlet, paper, writing, advertisement, circular, print, picture, drawing or other representation, figure or image" as well as sex toys, medicines, contraceptive devices, and abortion aids. In 1900, newly invented machines that showed moving pictures of naked women were added to the list. The law made it illegal to transport these objects through the mail, import them into the U.S., or assist anyone else in distributing them, and it empowered local authorities to issue warrants, conduct searches, and seize private property if any citizen lodged a complaint. Perpetrators were subject to a fine of up to $2,000 and imprisonment for up to five years.[4]

This "Comstock law" remained on the books, essentially unchanged, for nearly a century. As soon it passed, the New York Society for the Suppression of Vice accelerated its puritan crusade; under Comstock's aggressive leadership it thrived for four decades. Shortly after speaking at Clark, he died, handing the reins to John S. Sumner (1876–1971). Sumner claimed in 1930 that over its lifetime

John S. Sumner, executive director of the New York Society for the Suppression of Vice, ca. 1915 (Library of Congress, Prints & Photographs Division, George Grantham Bain Collection, LC-DIG-ggbain-20042).

the Society had "caused 5,055 prosecutions and has been instrumental in removing from circulation more than 75 tons of book matter, more than 3¼ million pictures and postcards, more than 23,000 photo negatives and films, nearly 32,000 plates for printing books, nearly 4,000,000 pieces of advertising matter, almost ½ million articles of indecent use and millions of miscellaneous articles of a harmful character." A less-quantifiable side-effect was self-censorship, as publishers sanitized manuscripts before publication or turned down those that might open them to prosecution. Some even shared submissions with Sumner before publication to make sure they wouldn't be harassed afterward.[5]

The values that fueled Comstock's "suppression of vice" were initially shared by the majority of his peers. The country's 300-year-old Puritan tradition elevated matters of the soul over those of the flesh, denouncing bodily functions as impure and corrupt. On top of this legacy was layered a Victorian ideal of womanhood as innocent, chaste, refined, and modest, and a standard of politeness that insisted on propriety, decorum, and silence about sex. Fear of the "evils" of city life also played a role: supporters of censorship often overlapped with reformers committed to stopping the "white slave trade," nativists wanting to restrict immigration, and Prohibitionists battling alcohol.[6]

Bigotry played a role, too, since the most vocal defenders of purity were white Anglo-Saxon Protestants and their targets were usually Eastern European Jews and Irish or Italian Catholics. In 1909, twice as many Jews and Catholics were prosecuted under the Comstock law as Protestants. The publishing industry in America had always been exclusively Christian (mainly Protestant) and resented the ambitions of the "goddamn Jews!" (as one bookseller phrased it) who entered the industry in the 1910s. Bennett Cerf recalled that Freud's publisher Horace Liveright "was deeply resented by the established publishers. They hated him; they even hated Alfred Knopf and B.W. Huebsch, who had started at about the same time. There had never been a Jew before in American publishing…. Suddenly there had burst forth on the scene some bright young Jews who were upsetting all the old tenets of the publishing business—and the flashiest of all was certainly Liveright." After World War I public opinion started to shift, readers began to condemn the self-appointed guardians of morality, and Liveright became one of a handful of publishers leading the fight against censorship.[7]

One consequence of Victorian "civilized sexual morality" (as Freud phrased it) was that sex simply was not talked about. Freud was only half-joking when he told an audience in 1917 that, "first and foremost, what is sexual is something improper, something one ought not to talk about." The "facts of life" were kept from children, especially girls. Mabel

Dodge, who came of age in the 1890s, wrote later about the shock of her first orgasm: "I had never heard of that gentle transformation that is, in sensation, as though the nerves expressed themselves in the manner of silent, fiery fountains falling on black velvet.... No one had ever told me about this definite, so definite and surprising thing. And I had never read of it." Horace Liveright recalled a friend telling him about 1908 that she'd become pregnant from kissing. "'When two people kiss each other as much as [Paul] and I have for the last two months,'" he remembered her saying, "what else could happen?" "Ridiculous as it may sound in 1934," he recalled, "it took me hours to delicately convince Magda that there was nothing to worry about." In this society-wide silent conspiracy, publications about sex, birth control, and sexually transmitted diseases were driven underground. When *Ladies Home Journal* advocated better education about sexually transmitted diseases in 1906, 75,000 readers cancelled their subscriptions. By universal consent, young women were kept ignorant about the most basic facts of their own biology, with predictably tragic results for millions.[8]

"In this battle," historian Henry May wrote, "and in the whole war that was opening, both sides were serious. To the intellectuals, censors were nasty and cruel old men, inflicting on others their own frustrations, denying to America the possibility of free and joyous self-expression. To some of the conservatives in the prewar years, a strange flood of filth was welling up from mysterious sources. Erotic plays and books, divorce, free love, lascivious dances, birth control were menacing not only American culture but the possibility of moral restraint, the sheet-anchor of any and all civilization."[9]

Freud, of course, insisted not only that sex should be talked about but that repressing sexual energy too severely produced mental and physical illness. His publications, therefore, were obvious targets for the upholders of the Victorian status quo. A copy of the *Interpretation of Dreams* at Harvard was shelved in a locked case with a sticker reading "Not to Be Removed from This Room." Publishers were skittish about issuing his writings, too, and his first censorship challenge came not from Comstock or Sumner but from George Allen and Co. while printing *The Interpretation of Dreams.*

As the book was in production early in 1913, William Allen came across passages that he feared might result in prosecution under England's equivalent of the Comstock law. "In your chapter on the 'Material of Dreams,'" he wrote to Brill on January 9, 1913, "especially the matter on pages 245–259, our attention has been drawn to some of the instances you give as being unsuitable for general publication, and we are wondering whether you could slightly modify or omit some of the examples, so as to make them less out of place for a volume intended originally for general publication…. Even with these alterations we should probably have to limit the sale to members of the Medical and Legal professions." (English censorship laws made exceptions for medical and legal publications.)[10]

The offensive passages are not identified more specifically, but in the chapter Allen cited Freud discussed menstruation, the breaking of a condom, the phallic symbolism of candles, unmarried sex between two servants, homo-erotic attraction between two schoolboys, a childhood memory of seeing a woman's genitals, urinating in front of his parents in their bedroom, a boil that once grew on his scrotum, men's dreams of having sex with their mothers, homosexual bondage, and witnessing one's parents having sex. These led to his conclusion that "the more one is occupied with the solution of dreams, the more willing one must become to acknowledge that the majority of the dreams of adults treat of sexual material and give expression to erotic wishes."[11] Footnotes added by Brill to the English translation contained similar references, including explicit ones to childhood erections, masturbation, and ejaculation.

Allen also proposed the cuts to Freud, who found the idea "shameful." But at the same time, he told Brill, "I don't want to frustrate your work or discourage the publisher from further undertakings. That's why I agreed in principle and added the condition, 'as far as you agree.' I couldn't help it as his suggestions weren't more specific. Now decide as you please and defend the rest like a lion." In his reply to Allen, Brill agreed to significant deletions: "If you can omit the following without disfiguring the book you may do so, otherwise publish it as it is. I have enclosed in pencil mark the parts to be omitted. As you will see I omitted one sentence on p. 246, a part and footnote of page 247, about half of page 248, and beginning with paragraph 'I shall now etc p. 249 leave out the rest of that page, and pages 250, 251, 252, 253, 254, 255, 256 & 257 to the line 'I conclude with the dream of a chemist.'"[12]

But with most of the book already printed and its publication date fast approaching, such large-scale changes were impossible for Allen to implement, so the London issue was sold with a slip pasted to the front free endpaper reading, "Publisher's Note. The sale of this book is limited to Members of the Medical, Scholastic, Legal, and Clerical professions."[13] This crushed any prospect of large sales in England that Allen may have had when he accepted the manuscript from Brill a year earlier.

Luckily, sales in New York, where Macmillan was bolder, made up the lost revenue. More than 80 percent of copies printed during the first year were sold in New York; less than 250 copies were sold in England, where the book was hardly noticed outside the medical press. On April 7, 1913, Allen wrote to Brill, "You will by now have received your copies. You will note that we were not able to make any deletion from the text, and as the first edition is practically exhausted, owing to the large number taken by Macmillan Company, we doubt whether it would be worthwhile to make any change if the book is reprinted."[14]

Brill's next encounter with censorship stemmed not from moral objections but political ones. After the U.S. entered World War I in the summer of 1917, the U.S. government mounted an aggressive propaganda campaign and outlawed actions that discouraged new recruits from enlisting. Anti-German prejudice and government repression flourished. Robert Appleton at Moffat Yard told Brill on November 22, 1917, that sales of books by authors with German-sounding names were declining. Brill protested that Freud's two books issued by Macmillan were selling better than ever and tried to get Appleton to commit to a volume of Freud's case studies. He added, "within a few weeks I will give you a very interesting work called 'Little Hans,' an analysis of a phobia of a five year old boy, and a few others." On November 27 he explained the other texts were case studies of Little Dora, "a case of Compulsion Neurosis," and "Psychoanalytic Observations of a case of Paranoia" totaling about 480 typed pages.[15]

Appleton agreed in principle to publish the case histories but became ever more cautious as anti–German sentiment grew. By the spring of 1918, when Brill suggested making the case studies less odious by changing the title from "Little Hans" to "Little John," William Moffat thanked him for the idea but backed away from publishing more Freud. He pointed out that the proposed title change

> does not rid it of its character as a translation from the German of a work by a well-known German. The eyes of the public grow very stern at the mere sight of a German book or a book of German origin.... One dealer in New York sent back, with some show of indignation, the copies that his buyer had purchased of Freud's 'Reflections Upon War and Death...' The trade revolts at the name of a German author. This affects the whole situation as far as Freud's books are concerned—as you may well imagine. I am now in a very serious quandary about the subject. I am almost of a mind to take some names—like Munsterberg and others—out of our Fall Catalogue.... Altogether, it seems wise to hold back on this sort of publication.[16]

Another Moffat Yard title by Freud incurred the wrath of Sumner's Society for the Suppression of Vice in 1919, ending up in court for violating the obscenity law. In the fall of 1916 they published Freud's *Leonardo da Vinci*, originally issued in Vienna in 1910. When Brill sent the manuscript to Moffat Yard on May 24, 1916, he cautioned them that it "might not be given out to the general public without some sort of an admonition" due to its frank treatment of sexual matters. The passages he worried about contained evidence of Leonardo's homosexuality and an explicit account of oral sex. In the book Freud warned that the idea Leonardo could have been gay was more than the self-appointed defenders of morality could bear: "They smooth over the traces of his life's struggles with internal and external resistances, and they tolerate in him no vestige of human weakness or imperfection ... they thereby sacrifice truth to an illusion, and for the sake of their infantile phantasies abandon the opportunity of penetrating the most fascinating secrets of human nature."[17]

But calling one of western civilization's great heroes gay was mild compared to Freud's frank descriptions of sex. After showing how one of Leonardo's earliest memories expressed a preoccupation with oral sex, Freud claimed that "the inclination to take a man's sexual organ into the mouth and suck at it, which in respectable society is considered a loathsome sexual perversion, is nevertheless found with great frequency among women of to-day—and of earlier times as well, as ancient sculptures show—, and in the state of being in love it appears completely to lose its repulsive character."[18]

This was too much for the American publishing establishment, and as Brill predicted, just six weeks after the book came out his editor at Moffat Yard reported "some of the dealers will not display the book at all, because of certain literal translations. Pages 39 and 40 are the passages in question. Of course, it would be most unfortunate to have any censor or society get after us as publishers of the book." Brill replied, "If you will refer to my letter of May 24 in which I offered you the manuscript of *Leonardo* you will note that I anticipated exactly what is happening. Since that time I have written to you and have spoken to Mr. Appleton about this very matter. I do not know what we can do.... I was always aware that *Leonardo da Vinci* will [*sic*] not be a book that can be offered to the general reader. I think it is a great mistake to have given it out together with *Wit* without adding something to warn the reader or to protect yourselves."[19]

Despite the publisher's and booksellers' anxiety, *Leonardo* flew under the radar until March 1919, when an anonymous letter-writer complained about it to Sumner's Society for the Suppression of Vice. "Read same and found it objectionable," the Society's monthly report says, "and March 12 obtained summons and search warrant." An agent of the Society visited Moffat Yard's office on Union Square, bought a copy from an innocent clerk named Ruth Rose, handed her a summons to appear in court, and seized all 36 copies of the book on hand. A hearing was held before Magistrate Charles E. Simms on April 23, 1919, at which the judge proposed

- "that [in] any further edition of said book published by the firm of Moffat, Yard and Co., alterations and omissions in the text thereof shall be made as per attached 'changes suggested,'

- "that any copies of the said book sold to a dealer shall be sold in a sealed wrapper on the outside of which shall appear prominently: 'This Book is for the Exclusive Use of Physicians and Medical Students and is not to be Sold or Delivered to any other Person,'
- "That no copies of said book shall be sold at retail by Moffat, Yard and Co., except that each copy of said book sold shall contain a serial number;
- "That no copy of said book shall be sold by said Moffat, Yard and Co., except upon receipt by them, through the retailer or other seller, of a letter from a customer showing his right to receive and possess said book,
- "That 36 copies of set book taken on search warrant in this proceeding shall be disposed of according to the direction of the district attorney of New York County."

The proposed "alterations and omissions in the text" included deleting or translating into Latin passages on pages 14, 28, 39–41, 52, 54, 56–59, and 77. The judge instructed the two parties to solve the problem together along the lines he proposed. Three weeks later the impounded volumes were returned to Moffat Yard with warning slips inserted into them by the Society.[20]

Brill later recalled the events this way: "after the book had been out for a number of years, (it sold well at $1.25 a copy), somebody in the Southwest objected to it on the grounds of immorality. It was brought to court by the Sumner Society and we defended it. I talked for a number of hours and impressed the judge with the great value that the book has for parents, teachers, etc. The judge thereupon would not condemn the book, but told the Sumner Society to come to some agreement with the publishers, so as not to make the book accessible to every Tom, Dick and Harry. Whereupon they agreed to charge $5.00 for it." Brill also described the proceedings in a lost letter to Freud, who acknowledged being "very amused by the Leonardo adventure in its quite American coloring."[21] When a new edition was printed in 1922 it still contained the offensive passages (in English, not Latin) with no warning to readers, but was priced at $5.00 and only advertised in medical journals. By 1924, when Moffat, Yard and Co. went out of business, *Leonardo* had sold only 1,310 copies in all.[22]

Freud's last run-in with the censors during these years involved a book for which he merely supplied part of a brief preface. On July 11, 1922, Sumner showed up in person at the offices of Thomas Seltzer and seized 722 copies of books that he declared obscene, including *A Young Girl's Diary* with a preface by Freud. Seltzer (1875–1943) was an uncle of Charles and Albert Boni and had partnered with them in founding the

Modern Library in 1917. An immigrant Russian journalist, Seltzer was a friend of Maxim Gorky and co-founder and first editor of the *Masses*. He translated Gorky, Dostoevsky, Tolstoy, Chekhov, and Turgenev for the Modern Library and, after starting his own firm in 1920, he became the American publisher of D.H. Lawrence and Marcel Proust. "An apologist for the working class," wrote one biographer, "he was physically incapable of doing a day's work of manual labor. A socialist theorist addicted to endless glasses of Russian tea, cigarettes, and stimulating conversation, Seltzer was referred to as one of the intellectual giants of Greenwich Village."[23]

The anonymous *Diary* had first been published in Vienna in 1919 by psychoanalyst Hermine von Hug-Hellmuth (1871–1924), who printed in her introduction a letter from Freud praising it. "This diary is a gem," Freud wrote:

> Never before, I believe, has anything been written enabling us to see so clearly into the soul of a young girl, belonging to our social and cultural stratum, during the years of puberal development. We are shown how the sentiments pass from the simple egoism of childhood to attain maturity; how the relationships to parents and other members of the family first shape themselves, and how they gradually become more serious and more intimate; how friendships are formed and broken. We are shown the dawn of love, feeling out towards its first objects. Above all, we are shown how the mystery of the sexual life first presses itself vaguely on the attention, and then takes entire possession of the growing intelligence, so that the child suffers under the load of secret knowledge but gradually becomes enabled to shoulder the burden. Of all these things we have a description at once so charming, so serious, and so artless, that it cannot fail to be of supreme interest to educationists and psychologists. It is certainly incumbent on you to publish the diary. All students of my own writings will be grateful to you.[24]

The *Diary*'s authenticity was questioned from the start and its authorship is still debated. Many researchers now believe that it was probably written by Grete Lainer, an Austrian girl who became a nurse during World War I; others insist it was written by Hug-Hellmuth herself and that "Freud had allowed himself to be hoodwinked by a fraud that sprang directly from his doctrine."[25]

The diary describes a typical upper-class girlhood in Vienna during the early 20th century, with accounts of family, friends, school, vacations, and social life. The passages that probably offended Sumner describe her first menstrual flow, first sexual responses, a man exposing himself, seeing two naked neighbors make love, fears about sexually transmitted diseases, flirting with boys, and crushes on older men and women. By today's standards they're entirely innocuous, but a century ago most of those topics could not be discussed in public, especially by teenage girls. In England the book's sale was restricted to members of the medical, educational, and legal professions. In America it was seized and prosecuted.[26]

Sumner had all the copies impounded, including those already for sale at Brentano's bookstore, and a trial was scheduled for July 31, 1922. After hearing defense witnesses argue for the *Diary's* value and Sumner's attorney demand its destruction, Judge George W. Simpson dismissed all charges. "This is not my victory," Seltzer told the press, "it is the victory of the entire reading public.... Technically it was a case of the people *vs.* Thomas Seltzer. In reality it was a case of the people *vs.* Mr. Sumner."[27]

But Seltzer's was a Pyrrhic victory, since Sumner's attorney persuaded New York Supreme Court Justice John Ford to open a grand jury investigation into pornography that centered on Seltzer. The publisher parried with a series of legal delays, and during the skirmishing charges against Lawrence's *Women in Love* were dropped. In the spring of 1925, facing a lengthy trial which he could not afford, Seltzer withdrew *A Young Girl's Diary* from circulation and destroyed the plates from which it was printed. The David vs. Goliath battle had significantly drained his resources, and after having brought to American readers the novels of D.H. Lawrence and Marcel Proust, the plays of Anton Chekhov, and the poems of e.e. cummings, Thomas Seltzer Inc. folded early in 1926. By then the diary's probable author, Grete Lainer, had been killed at the front during World War I and its editor, psychoanalyst Hermine Hug-Hellmuth, had been murdered by her own nephew, who was also one of her patients.[28]

Decades would pass before the Society for the Suppression of Vice lost its power, Comstock laws were changed, and today's standards of intellectual freedom were established. As late as 1944 Sumner was still raiding bookstores and seizing books; in 1945 he added inter-racial dating and marijuana smoking to his list of indecent offenses. Crucial legal battles were fought over *Ulysses* (1933), *Howl* (1957), and *Lady Chatterley's Lover* (1959) before government censorship of "obscene" books in America ended. The birth of the Internet, the invention of self-publishing software, and the ubiquity of laptops, televisions, and cell phones made it impossible for governments or self-appointed censors to stem the tide of erotic content that we now take for granted.

10

Horace Liveright Bets on Freud, 1920–1924

It's hard to overstate how much America changed between 1909, when Freud's first book appeared, and 1920, when his best-selling one did. "I wonder how many people who have grown up during the eighteen nineties," reflected his publisher Horace Liveright (1883–1933), "and have lived through these last turbulent twenty-five years of the twentieth century, realize how tremendous, magnificent, stirring, pulsating, utterly changed is the world in which they have revolved." In 1920, cars and trucks drove on paved roads where a decade earlier horses had plodded through mud. Airplanes soared overhead and subways rattled underground. Refrigerators, vacuum cleaners, toasters, and telephones graced middle-class homes. Young people talked openly about sex. "My son of twenty-one and his young boy and girl companions," Liveright continued, "my daughter of eighteen and hers, are a race of spiritual and intellectual giants, compared with the girls and boys of thirty years ago." Their worldview was partly due to the spread of Freud's ideas, in which Liveright himself played a major role.[1]

During the winters of 1915–1916 and 1916–1917, Freud had given two series of lectures at the University of Vienna that summed up his lifework. He was 60 years old and at the height of his powers. In these lectures he attempted to explain to a general audience his main theories, where they came from, how they had evolved over time, and how objections to them could be met. During those same years, in New York, Charles and Albert Boni gave up their Greenwich Village bookshop to try their hand at publishing. When they failed, Albert sought practical business experience in a Manhattan advertising firm where he crossed paths with Horace Liveright. Boni was looking for funds to start a new publishing company and Liveright, a Wall Street bond trader, was looking for a place to invest new capital. In the summer of 1917, they formed the partnership of Boni and Liveright and launched the Modern Library series.[2]

Meanwhile Freud's nephew Edward Bernays quit working for Dr. William Robinson in order to become a successful Broadway press agent. In 1918 he was hired by the U.S. Committee on Public Information to write war propaganda, and the next year was sent to the Paris Peace Conference with the American delegation to help sell the Treaty of Versailles to Americans:

> I asked a member of our mission [Carl Byoir] who was leaving Paris to open postwar relations between Austria and the United States to take a box of cigars to my uncle at 19 Berggasse. On his return to Paris, my colleague reported on his warm reception and brought me, from my uncle, an inscribed copy of the Introductory Lectures in German, delivered at the University of Vienna between 1915 and 1917.... On my return to New York I opened an office as a consultant in public relations. I urged book publisher Horace Liveright, one of our clients, to publish Freud's book *A General Introduction to Psychoanalysis*. He consented. Freud was to receive fifteen percent royalty on a four-dollar volume. I cabled for authorization to translate and publish the volume; he cabled the authorization. In 1920 most publishers did no promotion. But Liveright, a maverick, would promote the book, I knew. He had engaged our firm for that then novel purpose.[3]

The first time he met Liveright, Bernays recalled, the publisher "discussed agitatedly his grandiose plans for his forthcoming list. I paid attention quietly, trying to size him up, but I found this difficult. He demonstrated in his conversation exuberance, faith in aggressive publishing, willingness to gamble and a flair for publicity. But his overpowering ego enveloped him to such an extent that I could not penetrate to the mainsprings of his action."[4]

Liveright was personally enthusiastic about Freud's book but his staff were "appalled at the notion of publishing what appeared to be a densely written German text about medical matters and predicted disaster for the undertaking." Liveright, however, was astute enough to suspect that the name of Freud might sell the book all by itself during America's honeymoon period with psychoanalysis. Besides, Bernays's family friend and future brother-in-law Leon Fleischman had just put up $30,000 to buy half the company, so Liveright was inclined to look favorably on the proposal.[5]

Bernays had just opened the office of Edward L. Bernays Publicity Direction with Fleischman's sister Doris, three blocks from Boni and Liveright on 48th Street. By the end of 1919 they had 10 full-time employees, and the contract with Liveright was their most important project. "People found it difficult to accept the idea that Doris was both my wife and my professional partner," Bernays recalled. "In 1922 a woman entering any profession other than nursing, teaching or social work was a novelty. And treating her as an equal in a profession was a source of even more

Doris Fleischman and Edward Bernays in August 1925 (*New York Daily News,***
August 8, 1925).**

wonderment." He told historian Scott Cutlip in 1959, "She has played an
equally important role with mine, except that her insight and judgment
are better than mine."[6]

Bernays naturally applied Freudian insights to his new profession.
Cutlip recalled, "When I asked if Freud's theories had influenced him,
Bernays replied, 'I would say very definitely yes to this question. Although
I do not qualify as a psychoanalyst, because I was brought up in a background of psychology and my uncle's methods, I have undoubtedly gotten
a lot of it by osmosis, and what I didn't get by osmosis, I got from reading his works.'" In 1928, when hired to persuade women it was acceptable
to smoke in public, Bernays told his client, "Let me consult an expert, Dr.
A.A. Brill, the psychoanalyst. He might give me the psychological basis for
a woman's desire to smoke, and maybe this will help me." Brill's advice led

to Bernays's famous "Torches of Freedom" marketing campaign; he even advised on mockups of Bernays's magazine ads.[7]

Liveright hired Bernays and Fleischman to market new books by the Greenwich Village writers that he'd begun to cultivate, such as Eugene O'Neill, Theodore Dreiser, John Reed, e.e. cummings, Djuna Barnes, and Dorothy Parker. He was also bringing out startling new work by ex-patriates Ezra Pound, T.S. Eliot, and Ernest Hemingway who had yet to find their American audiences. Bernays and Fleischman were ideally suited for the assignment. They counted among their own friends Mabel Dodge, Lincoln Steffens, Emma Goldman, Sara Teasdale, Scofield Thayer, and other Village intellectuals. They lived in a former stable at 4 Washington Mews. A little later, when they rented a brownstone around the corner, "hardly an evening passed without guests for and/or after dinner," Bernays remembered, usually "writers, publishers, musicians, artists, psychologists, doctors, scientists, uptown socialites, stock brokers, bankers, politicians and businessmen."[8] But their relationship with Liveright proved challenging.

Liveright, in the words of the company's production manager, Manuel Komroff, "was very careless with the truth. In fact he had an uncontrollable passion for verbal distortion. He felt compelled to lie, even when he knew it would be to his disadvantage. The truth, he believed, was only used by simpletons. It was too stark, too direct. It lacked embellishment and imagination. On top of this Liveright drank very heavily and had a passion for gambling." But he had virtues, too, "and one of his most outstanding virtues was his generosity. His generosity was impulsive; it was never planned. It came straight from his heart." Komroff wrote that Liveright also possessed immense charisma. His "eyes were sparkling and often took on a sudden twinkle that reflected some jest or mischievous prank. This twinkle remained with him all his life and contributed greatly to his hypnotic charm. Without it, his face was angular and homely. With it his face was almost handsome."[9]

Freud—a conservative Viennese doctor who lived by the clock and whose manner was called "restrained and ceremonious"—would have been shocked by the Boni and Liveright office. One staff member recalled it as "the Jazz Age in microcosm, with all its extremes of hysteria and of cynicism … the madness, the extravagance, the orgies, the empty bottles that occasionally littered the stairs in the morning and the parties that cut into office hours." Bennett Cerf, who joined the firm in the spring of 1923, remembered that "authors in the waiting room were often outnumbered by bootleggers…. One of the big executives had a bottle of whisky in every drawer of his desk, the top of which was piled inches high with weeks-old communications of the greatest importance." Komroff recalled Liveright once opening an envelope with a $30,000 check, cashing it, and dividing the money among his employees. "The staff was so well organized and so extremely happy in their work," Komroff went on, "that the business routine could carry on if no boss was present."[10]

Liveright spent money as fast as it came in, often faster. "The head bookkeeper," Cerf continued, "(the only real business man in the place, as he proved so convincingly by winding up at the last as the sole owner of the entire outfit) had to show a perpetual deficit in his daily reports to the president, because if there ever was a cash balance it was gone by nightfall.... Other publishers—particularly in London—were continually outraged by Liveright's methods, and amazed that he could continue in the wild, reckless manner that he pursued." On at least two occasions Bernays had to sue Liveright to pay Freud's royalties. "Horace had no sense of money; when he had cash, he often speculated in new ventures and was unable to meet current obligations," Bernays explained; "he thought my action in engaging an attorney to secure money due my uncle was natural and admirable."[11]

After Liveright accepted Freud's lectures, Bernays took charge of preparing them for the press. Thinking that an introduction by a well-known academic would be an asset, in August 1919 he approached G. Stanley Hall who happily agreed. "Finding a translator was more difficult," Bernays wrote later. It also caused the only serious estrangement that ever occurred between Freud and Brill.[12]

Brill recalled to Ernst Freud that after being named as sole English translator in 1908, "I devoted virtually every moment of my spare time to it for over ten years" but that "following World War I, I asked your father to get another English translator." Brill had jealously guarded his role and was offended when others trespassed on it, as Helen Downey and Charles Rockwell Payne had in 1917 (see above). So when Bernays approached his uncle about translating the lectures, Freud referred him to Brill. In an August or September 1919 letter (now lost), Brill complained to Freud and asked for help "to protect him from unauthorized" competitors. Freud told Jones, "I have received a letter from Brill!, a long, tender, crazy letter not mentioning a word about the money but explaining away the mystery of his behavior. It was all jealousy, hurt sensibility and the like. I will do my best to soothe him." To complicate matters, Jones insisted from London that his new International Psycho-Analytic Press should have sole translation rights, including the American ones. Under pressure from both Brill and Jones, on September 24, 1919, Freud cabled Bernays to stop work. But by then commitments had been made, translators already hired, and money spent. On October 5 Freud replied to Brill apologizing and accepting Brill's apparent resignation as translator (given in a letter now lost). A rapprochement soon occurred and the two remained loyal friends until Freud's death in 1939, but future English translations came from Jones and his colleagues in London, culminating three decades later in the *Standard Edition*.[13]

Bernays recalled that during the fall of 1919, "our little office went into a translation frenzy surrounded by a group of expert translators." He explained to Freud, "We entrusted it to the daughter of Professor Hoch, whom you may have heard of. She had received a Doctor's degree on the basis of her psychoanalytical studies. The book was revised by Cora Senner, who studied with you. A large amount of money was spent further in reading, rereading and generally going over the translation. Dr. Stanley Hall gave close attention to it in writing the preface." Bernays was referring to Susan Hoch Kubie (1896–1973), the daughter of Dr. August Hoch (1868–1919), director of the New York State Psychiatric Institute. She became a psychiatric social worker; in 1938, her husband Lawrence Kubie helped persuade the Nazis to release the Freud family. Cora Senner was probably Cora Senner Winkin, a Columbia University physician.[14]

Through the late summer and early fall of 1919, Bernays's team "attempted to make a translation which not only maintains the thought and style of the author with faithful accuracy, but which maintains also that same intimacy of touch with which the lecturer is leading his untrained audiences through the mazes of a very difficult and complicated subject." But when Freud saw the resulting translation-by-committee the next year, he was appalled. He wrote to Bernays on July 20, 1920, that

> I have noted a number of misprints and misunderstandings which I am listing and shall put at your disposal for a second edition. You may tell the translator (name not mentioned) that I understand the difficulties which exist in rendering errors and dreams into another language, but I do not consider that the expedient he used of inventing similar examples to be the correct method. Such inventions do an injustice to the author and deprive the presentation of its plausibility. The only proper thing to do would have been to substitute for the untranslatable examples of slips of the tongue, puns in dreams, etc., other examples based on his own analytical experience, and occasionally to annotate the German example. But then the translator would, of course, have had to be an analyst, as for instance Dr. Brill. I am afraid that the reviewers will not fail to emphasize this shortcoming.

Jones went further, complaining to Freud that the translation was "loose and rapidly done, full of vulgar Americanisms. You are made to speak in a very unworthy style, so that the reader must get an unfavorable impression of your personality." He commissioned an entirely new translation for the London edition.[15]

The text was finalized in the fall of 1919, only to have production delayed by a city-wide printers' strike that lasted through all of October and November. The manuscript was finally sent to the printer on December 18, 1919, the day after Bernays and Liveright signed a formal contract. This document called for an advance of $1,000 for translating and producing the manuscript (a cost which Bernays had already covered out of pocket) and gave Boni and Liveright exclusive rights to sell the book in the U.S., to produce a cheap edition of their own, and to lease the rights to reprint houses after five years; Bernays retained the copyright.[16]

While the *General Introduction* was being translated, vetted, typeset, and printed, Bernays had been energetically promoting it in the media. "Books were handled in the same way they had been published," he recalled, "for a select audience and not for a larger public. Book publishing was static in the content of its books and in its promotion when it should have been, of course, vibrant with ideas. But Liveright was to change all that."[17] Publishers had traditionally limited their marketing efforts to sending catalogs, review copies, and author biographies to a few well-known literary editors and purchasing quietly dignified advertisements in well-respected journals. Bernays argued in a March 1920 essay that they failed to clearly identify their target audiences, failed to strategically position books where that audience already focused its attention (such as editorial pages and gossip columns), and failed to link their books to current events that were likely to attract visibility.

"It was not until recently," Bernays wrote, "that another method was introduced to supplement and reinforce advertising—namely, propaganda and publicity, which proved such a powerful factor in the war … it popularizes its subject by promoting its news and special feature values thru [*sic*] press and periodical exploitation … it discovers and executes the tie-up between a commodity and that sector of the purchasing public which is most likely to be interested in it … it ferrets out and promotes every possible selling point to the widest and at the same time most appropriate possible market."[18]

So while the *General Introduction* was being manufactured, Doris Fleischman wrote a weekly Boni and Liveright circular that was sent directly to 300 bookstores around the country, beyond whom were more than 100 million potential book-buyers. She also sent a short text about each important Liveright title not only to reviewers at literary magazines but also to managing editors of daily newspapers who, grateful for the free content, ran it in New York, Providence, Buffalo, Detroit, Kansas City, and other cities. When Waldo Frank's *Our America* came out in the fall of 1919, Bernays provided exclusive 1,000- to 1,500-word features with titles like "Psychoanalyzing New York" and "Psychoanalyzing Chicago and the Middle West" that not only highlighted Frank's book but also foreshadowed

Freud's lectures. Liveright ran multiple attention-grabbing ads in trade journals several months ahead of its official publication date. These featured startling display fonts, abundant white space, and tongue-in-cheek prose.[19]

The book's title, *A General Introduction to Psychoanalysis*, was another successful marketing device. The German title had used the equivalent of the English word "Lectures." By replacing this pedantic term with the more welcoming "General Introduction," Bernays and Liveright side-stepped off-putting academic associations and made the book sound accessible to any curious layperson. So many advance orders flooded in that two printings were required before Freud's book even reached store shelves. Boni and Liveright account ledgers show that a total of 2,200 copies were printed before publication on June 30, 1920, when the first 1,250 copies were delivered to stores.[20]

These were bound in dark blue cloth printed in gold on the spine and front cover with a light blue dust jacket printed in black. Another 1,353 were bound and delivered in July, the same month that a third printing (of 2,000) was ordered. Other printings rapidly followed. Copies issued after 1925 are sometimes mistaken for the first impression because they are simply dated 1920 with the imprint "Horace Liveright Inc." on the title page. That company name, however, was only adopted in 1928 and was changed in 1932 to "Liveright Publishing Corporation Inc." Copies of the true first impression say "Boni and Liveright" on the title page and "Boni and Liveright" on its verso (see appendix for further details).[21]

According to the publisher's records, 5,689 copies of *A General Introduction* were sold in the first 12 months. In its first 10 years, it sold 19,925 copies. This far exceeded any of Freud's previous books, even *The Interpretation of Dreams* (ca. 6,400 in its first 10 years) and *Psychopathology of Everyday Life* (ca. 4,000 in its first 10 years). By the time the *Standard Edition* version replaced it in 1963, the *General Introduction* had sold 45,672 copies for Boni and Liveright and 162,000 copies in cheap reprints licensed to Garden City Publishing, not to mention countless paperbacks (see below).[22]

On June 30, 1920, Bernays sent two copies to Freud in Vienna, explaining later "that the number of books in an edition varied, that it was customary to issue editions of 500 copies, that printing of sheets in quantity is done at one time, and bound copies are made up when a new edition is needed." Fifteen of these so-called editions (actually, new impressions from the original plates, with updated title pages) were issued before a true second edition appeared in 1935. Royalties did not follow as fast as new impressions, though, and Bernays had to twist Liveright's arm to get Freud what he was owed. "You did not seem to be puzzled or irritated at all by

First page of the Boni & Liveright internal ledger account for *General Introduction to Psychoanalysis*, 1920 (Boni and Liveright files, W.W. Norton & Company Records, Rare Book & Manuscript Library, Columbia University).

the attempt of the publishers to rob us of our royalties," Freud wrote to his nephew on April 24, 1921. "You seem to consider it a common business trick and I am sure you know your people. No doubt you were right in engaging an attorney to get the money out of them." Recounting the problem to Jones, Freud wrote that "Boni and Liveright, who printed the Bernays translation seem to be no better men [than pirates André Tridon and James McCann]. They confessed only to about 600 copies of the book and tried to cheat me for $2019. My nephew got the money from them by paying $100 to a lawyer."[23]

Jones considered the Boni and Liveright translation so hopelessly defective that for the 1922 London edition he had the text retranslated from scratch by Joan Riviere. This meant that two very different English-language versions were in circulation during the 1920s, one in New York and one in London. In 1933, Stanley Unwin offered to sell a duplicate set of the London plates to Liveright Inc. (the company's namesake had died), saying he did so because Freud requested it. Liveright Inc. agreed and began selling the Riviere translation in 1935, prefaced by this note by Freud:

> These lectures were brought out for the first time in English in 1920 by Horace Liveright, Inc., with an introductory preface by G. Stanley Hall. No translator was named. Two years later another translation made by Joan Riviere was published in London by G. Allen & Unwin. It is obviously undesirable to have the original German text presented to the English-reading public in more than one version. I therefore feel called upon to express my gratitude to the American publishers for their acceptance of the Riviere translation for their new edition.

Liveright printed 1,500 copies of the second edition in March 1935 and from that point on, Riviere's translation replaced the much-maligned 1919 translation by Hoch and Senner. By then 20,711 copies of the first, flawed, translation had been sold, compared to several hundred thousand copies which Riviere's went on to sell between 1935 and 1963.[24]

This 1935 second edition (412 pages) was bound in dark blue cloth printed in gold on its spine and front cover. In 1938 Liveright licensed it to Doubleday's reprint arm, Garden City Publishing Co., who brought out a "DeLuxe Edition" in February 1938 bound in gray cloth with a red spine panel and black, red, and white dust jacket, which went through seven impressions by 1952. Their less expensive "Star Edition" came out in 1943 with the same dust jacket and was printed 14 times by 1949, bound alternately in beige or blue cloth. These Garden City reprints sold a combined 162,000 copies by 1949. In addition, Liveright brought out its own "Black and Gold Library" issue of 5,000 copies in October 1946 with an ornately decorated spine; 3,500 of these had sold by the end of the following year.[25]

By then the paperback revolution was upending the book industry. In September 1948 Doubleday thought they could strike a middle path between the cheap new paperbacks and traditional hardcovers with a line of "Permabooks." These inexpensive volumes had "sewn pages, stained tops, colored end sheets, and three-color laminated covers, paper over boards" and were sold for 35 cents in custom wire racks supplied to retail outlets. The experiment quickly failed, however, and though the brand name was preserved, starting in 1951 Permabooks were manufactured as standard paperbacks. The third edition of *A General Introduction* (480 pages) appeared in both forms, published first in October 1949 as a "Permabook Giant" with plastic-coated covers that mimicked the dust jacket of the Garden City reprints and, starting in January 1953, as a

conventional paperback that
went through seven impressions over the next decade.
Both issues were printed on
highly acidic paper, which
helps account for their rela-
tive scarcity today. Between
1960 and 1968, the 480-page
paperback edition was also
issued six times by Simon
and Schuster's Washington
Square Press. Tens of thousands of additional copies
reached readers outside conventional publishing channels when the Encyclopædia
Britannica included it in
1952 in *The Major Works of
Sigmund Freud*, volume 54
of their *Great Books of the
Western World*. This sold
35,000–50,000 sets per year

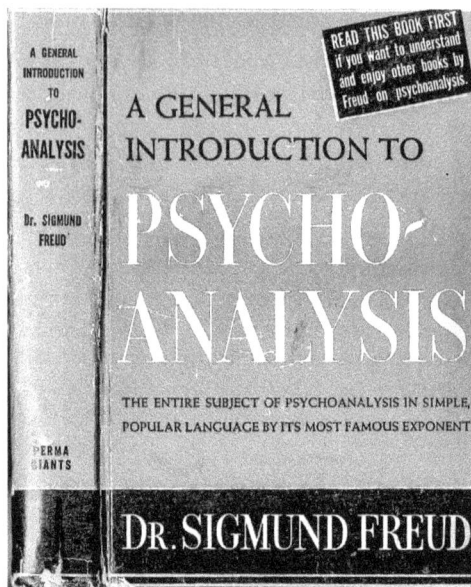

"Perma Giants" edition of Freud's *General
Introduction to Psychoanalysis,* October
1949 (author's collection).

during the 1950s and 1960s and totaled a million copies before the end of
the century.[26]

A *General Introduction to Psychoanalysis* was read by more Americans than any of Freud's other books. Total hardcover sales by Liveright
and Garden City topped 208,000 by 1963. The Permabook Giant and each
of the 14 paperback printings during the 1950s and 1960s numbered at least
10,000–20,000 copies, for a total of 150,000–300,000 more copies.[27] U.S.
sales of Freud's introductory lectures therefore approached half a million
before James Strachey's new translation appeared in 1963 in volumes 15–16
of the *Standard Edition*. In addition to conventional retail sales, the *Great
Books* edition peddled door-to-door sold roughly 400,000 copies between
1952 and 1962, though it's unclear how many of those typographically
impenetrable volumes were actually read.

Although it interrupts the chronological sequence, this is probably
the best place to discuss two other books by Freud that Horace Liveright
published in the early 1920s. Their history begins with Freud's own fortunes at the end of World War I.

In 1919 a grateful former patient, Anton von Freund (1880–1920),
established an endowment to support psychoanalysis. Freud decided
to use it to create a publishing house called the Verlag Internationaler

Psychoanalytischer as the movement's official publisher. "[Otto] Rank is in charge of this enterprise," he wrote on January 2, 1919, "which began work to-day. We shall publish, not only our journals, but also books, the first of which is to be the sixth edition of the *Everyday Life*." It was to have a subsidiary branch in London to handle English translations.[28]

In September 1919 Freud wrote to Bernays that Ernest Jones, "working in close cooperation with the international Psychoanalytic Press here in Vienna, is about to found a publishing house to publish translations and original works on psychoanalysis in England and in the United States." Jones's idea was to manufacture books on the continent where labor and materials were cheaper and then sell them in London and New York where prices were higher. He summarized its mission as "to distinguish between trustworthy psa [psychoanalytic] books and the rubbish otherwise published." In October 1919 Freud told Brill that "in the English Monograph Series there should be originals and translations, and of course it is also intended to place the outstanding translations of my books there. I want to be involved in this myself, maybe my daughter [Anna] can provide the raw material for the translation here, which can then be revised in London."[29]

In January 1920 Freud invited Bernays to be his America agent, asking him to consider "entering into business relations with our International Psychoanalytic Publishing company, which is creating just now an International Press in London for bringing out a new Anglo-American Journal of PSA? You could help us a great deal. I will advise my man, Dr. Otto Rank, to write you about it." Bernays negotiated the details with Rank and Jones, and in September 1920 distributed the following press release to his U.S. contacts:

> The International Psychoanalytic Press of London and Vienna announced the opening of its New York offices at 19 E. 48th St. [Bernays's office] A quarterly journal, the *International Journal of Psychoanalysis*, directed by Professor Sigmund Freud and edited by Ernest Jones, M.D., will be brought out by the organization.... The International Psychoanalytic Library, consisting of books by authorities on psychoanalysis, will be part of the new organization's activities. Three new books are announced: *Addresses on Psycho-Analysis* by Dr. J.J. Putnam, *Psycho-Analysis and War Neuroses, A Symposium* by doctors Karl Abraham (Berlin), S Ferenczi (Budapest), Ernest Jones (London), and Ernst Simmel (Berlin) with an introduction by Professor Sigmund Freud (Vienna), and *The Psycho-Analytic Study of the Family* by J.C. Fluegel.[30]

The arrangement lasted less than a year, however, because Jones and Rank were unable to provide enough funding to promote it adequately in New York. Jones could also be stubborn and pugnacious. "No one ever directed Ernest Jones," Anna Freud once said, "or gave him permissions, or even criticized him to his face. It was always the other way round." In

January 1921 Bernays resigned, and "so closed an undertaking I should not have entered into in the first place."[31]

By then Freud had temporarily lost faith in Brill—"he has become thoroughly Americanized"—and consequently found himself without effective representation in the U.S. just as his work was being aggressively promoted by Boni and Liveright. S.E. Jelliffe proposed to William White that they offer to step in and add Jones's books to the *Nervous and Mental Disease Monograph Series*, but nothing came of the idea. The first International Psycho-Analytic Press books appeared in Britain in the summer of 1921 with their title pages reading "London, Vienna and New York"—the editor was in London, the printer was in Vienna, and no one was in New York.[32]

Among the future books Jones promised that summer were Freud's *Group Psychology and the Analysis of the Ego* and *Beyond the Pleasure Principle*. These represented a shift in Freud's ideas and priorities, from the interior dynamics of personality to its outward relations with authority, and from the instincts of procreation and pleasure to the so-called death instinct. "Death is the mate of love," he told an interviewer, "together they rule the world. This is the message of my book, *Beyond the Pleasure Principle*." The books were badly received by reviewers, one commentator calling *Beyond the Pleasure Principle* "the most bizarre monster of all [Freud's] gallery of monsters." But in them Freud predicted the hero-worship of authoritarian leaders like Hitler and his early 21st-century descendants, explaining how their paranoid racism, xenophobia, and seductive conspiracy theories worked.[33]

The two books were translated by James Strachey (1887–1967) and Caroline Jane Mary Hubback (1871–1959?). Strachey and his wife Alix (1892–1973) had spent their honeymoon in Vienna in 1920 being analyzed by Freud and helping "in the desperate work of persuading the Viennese printers to master the peculiarities of English spelling." Hubback (1871–1959) worked for Jones on the *International Journal of Psycho-Analysis* but little more is known about her. Jones applauded her work to Freud, who protested that "even Miss Hubback, whom you praise so much, could not avoid errors and serious misconceptions, as Hiller and Anna pointed out to me." Jones had to revise her English translation of *Beyond the Pleasure Principle* several times before printing it.[34]

Strachey began his translation of *Group Psychology* while being analyzed by Freud in the spring of 1921. Freud recommended it to Jones that July: "I could only go through the first half of the translation shortly before I broke off, the latter is the more difficult one. I found it absolutely correct, free of all misunderstandings and I hope the rest will prove the same. I am no judge of the style, it seems to be plain and easy, your claims for elegance may be stronger than mine. In any case, don't be too hard on him, it is not easy for us to get efficient translators." In one of the most profound understatements of his career Freud added, "Strachey and his wife might become very useful to you. They are exceptionally nice and cultured people though are somewhat queer." *Beyond the Pleasure Principle* was published in London in October 1922 and *Group Psychology* followed in December. American editions did not appear for another two years since no one was representing Freud's interests on this side of the Atlantic.[35]

The challenges of editing and translating manuscripts in London, printing sheets in Austria, binding them in England, and distributing them across three continents were more than Jones's little cohort of amateur publishers could accomplish. So he contracted with Allen & Unwin to distribute the books in Britain until, in 1923, as Stanley Unwin recalled, "I ventured to publish a book critical of Freud. That was a heinous offense and the agency was forthwith transferred elsewhere." James Strachey approached his friend Leonard Woolf about taking over the International Psycho-Analytical Library at the Woolf's fledgling Hogarth Press. Woolf later wrote that "in 1924 the Institute had, I believe, made a considerable loss on their psycho-analytic publications. I know that at least one large publisher [Unwin] refused to risk money on Freud's *Collected Papers* and when he heard that we were going to do so he wrote to warn me 'in a friendly way' against it, saying that we should have to tie up over £1,000 in it (which was correct) and that in his opinion we should never see our money back."[36]

Woolf replied to Unwin, "I do not wonder at your being amused at our becoming your successor over the psycho-analysis undertaking. There has been plenty of amusement on my side already over the way that some of the people do business. I don't expect much profit, although the only thing which I have undertaken to publish (besides taking over the old stock) is the *Collected Papers*. The ideas of some people in the International Psycho-Analytical Press with regard to some of the other books contemplated seemed to me purely fantastic. My contract is with Dr Jones and Dr Rickman representing the Press. If I end up without loss, profit, or lawsuit, I shall congratulate myself. But I shall have had a good deal of amusement." Unwin replied, "My thankfulness that I am at the end of my troubles with this agency, and not in your shoes, is intense."[37]

Freud, Woolf, and Jones negotiated terms in the summer of 1924. Freud wanted to earn as much as possible to support the operation in Vienna and therefore insisted that American rights be omitted from the agreement so he could sell them separately. "I have made it clear to all people that I consider the American rights my own," he'd written to Bernays, "and that you should be the only person minding them." Woolf, on the other hand, needed to make sure that his very risky commitment of capital and energy would not undermine the Hogarth Press which, like Freud's Verlag, operated on a shoestring budget. Possessing the right to license Freud's books to America would considerably enlarge his earning potential. Jones was most interested in ensuring that all new English translations were accurate and, after seeing the fiascos that had unfolded in New York, believed that the London office should control Freud's texts and public image in America.[38]

In the end, Freud yielded to Woolf, which was acceptable to Jones, and from 1924 onward the Hogarth Press officially represented Freud in the English-speaking world in partnership with the International Psycho-Analytical Institute. American publishers had to license rights from Woolf and Jones before they could bring out a new edition, though the earlier translations by Brill and others continued to be reprinted and sold. In July 1924, the stock of the International Psycho-Analytical Press was shipped to Woolf's home office in Tavistock Square. "All the psycho-analyst books have been dumped in a fortress the size of Windsor castle in ruins on the floor," Virginia Woolf told a friend.[39]

This included nearly 5,000 copies each of *Beyond the Pleasure Principle* and *Group Psychology*. Woolf told an interviewer in 1956 that "we were amazed at the quantity that they had printed. No publisher at that time would have printed the amount they did. And we took over vast quantities and, of course, in the end we were very glad to have them. Actually, it took years to sell them. I know we were selling *Beyond the Pleasure Principle* in its original edition for years, and years, and years. I am not certain how many. I know we had an enormous quantity and *Group Psychology* in the same way."[40]

Nearly half of these, however, were exported from the Woolf's basement to Boni and Liveright in New York. Early in April 1924 Jones reported to Freud that "Boni and Liveright have practically agreed to buy two thousand sheets of 'Group Psychology' and 'Pleasure Principle' and to issue them there." Rank arrived in New York the next month "ready to take over," and it's possible that he helped broker the final arrangement. Bernays was also in contact with both Freud and Liveright at the time and may have played some role. The 2,000 sets of sheets for each book were imported in July 1924, American title pages were printed, and copies were bound in New York.[41]

There is no date on either of the books, which were published simultaneously at the end of August 1924. They were advertised together in the firm's fall 1924 catalog and reviewed together in the *New York Times* on September 7 and as part of a *Time* cover story on October 27. *Time* put Freud's name and face in front of not only 90,000 readers, but of countless

TIME

The Weekly News-Magazine

VOL. IV No. 17　　SIGMUND FREUD　　OCTOBER 27, 1924

Freud on the cover of *Time* magazine, October 27, 1924 (charcoal sketch by S.J. Woolf for Time, Inc., 1924).

more who saw the magazine on newsstands that week. The two books sold briskly at first, with about 1,200 copies of each selling in the first year. But sales quickly dropped off, and it took the rest of the decade for the entire editions to sell out. They remained out of print from 1929 until the spring of 1950, when Liveright published U.S. issues of both books, binding sheets from the second Hogarth Press editions in red cloth stamped in gold with a grey dust jacket; 2,500 sheets of *Group Psychology* were imported and 3,600 of *Beyond the Pleasure Principle*. Both titles appeared in volume 18 of the *Standard Edition* in 1955.[42]

During the 1920s Horace Liveright continued to raise and squander money, investing lavishly in unknown authors, Wall Street speculations, and Broadway plays. For a decade he flourished, his company often bringing in more than a million dollars a year (nearly $17 million today). In the summer of 1928, he had six of the country's top 10 best-sellers. Seven of his authors went on to win Nobel Prizes. But every time he ran out of cash he brought in a new partner, usually by selling his own stock, until by 1930 he had become a minority shareholder and was forced out by his accountant, who'd been buying up shares.

"As the years went on," Bernays recalled, "Liveright became more manic, more interested in pleasure and self-indulgence than in publishing. He branched out into the theater. But his major interests were parties, beautiful women, and drink."[43] In 1929 the stock market crashed, his Broadway hopes vanished like mist on a breeze, his old friends melted away, and his love life turned dysfunctional. In 1933 he was evicted from his midtown penthouse, where Manuel Komroff went to look for him. Instead of his old friend Komroff found

> the floor strewn with laundry, old shoes, socks, torn letters, newspaper clippings. And between empty gin bottles and other discarded fragments were all the favorite photographs from so many celebrities, autographed affectionately to Horace Liveright, but now with their frames and glasses broken. There was Sherwood Anderson and Bertrand Russell and John Reed. There was Eugene O'Neill and Rose Macauley and Gertrude Atherton. Robinson Jeffers and E.E. Cummings were split through the middle. Dorothy Parker and Elinor Wylie were also in ruins. Here were some original drawings by Van Loon and here a framed letter from George Moore. All smashed, all churned into wreckage.

Liveright survived only a few more months. "At the end," Komroff continued, "when he lost his business, his money, [he] had married a bitch who one night shot him, the bullet went through his arm and he was treated in the hospital for 'arthritis.'" He died on September 24, 1933, at the age of 49. "It was all rather crazy," Sherwood Anderson remembered later, "rather splendid. Horace was a gambler and if he believed in you would gamble on you. I have always thought, since the man's death, that too much emphasis has been put on the reckless splendor of the man rather than on his never-ending generosity and his real belief in men of talent."[44]

11

André Tridon, Boldest of the Pirates, 1921

"He is a thief," Freud told interviewer H.V. Kaltenborn in 1921. "My ideas belong to the world. He is welcome to those. But he stole the text of two of my books and combined them in a volume which he signed with his own name. I regret to say that under American law that kind of stealing seems to be permitted." With these heated words Freud denounced André Tridon (1877–1922), by far the boldest plunderer of his writings.[1]

Born outside Paris in 1877, Tridon claimed to have studied at the Sorbonne and the University of Heidelberg before coming to America in 1903. Although trained for the foreign service, he was anything but diplomatic. Van Wyck Brooks remembered him as "the Village eccentric," which must have been a remarkable feat in 1920. He wrote a play about sex for Moritz Jagendorf's Free Theatre, celebrated abstract painting and modern sculpture in art reviews, and wrote political essays for the *Masses* (where he briefly served as secretary) and the anarchist periodical *Revolt*. For some years Tridon earned his living by supplying the New York *Sun*, *Tribune*, *Times*, and other newspapers with articles on politics and culture. In 1914 *The Outlook* sent him to Mexico to cover Pancho Villa and the Mexican Revolution. When he returned in 1915 he declared bankruptcy, apparently to escape creditors. After the Russian Revolution broke out in 1917, he translated works by Lenin and Trotsky for communist publishers.[2]

After Freud captivated Greenwich Village, Tridon embraced psychoanalysis with the same enthusiasm he'd shown for Marx and modern art. He appointed himself an expert on the new psychology, printing stationery that billed himself as "Lecturer" and distributing postcards advertising his talks on psychoanalysis. He held salons in the homes of New York tastemakers. He lectured at the Literary Forum, the Labor Temple, the Fine Arts Guild, and other venues. When in 1919 he organized a "Psychoanalysis Study League," he claimed to have given 200 talks on psychoanalysis over the previous two years. With thick black hair, pince-nez, mustache, goatee, and a heavy French accent,

always dressed impecca-
bly, Tridon personified to
his American audiences
the sophisticated European
intellectual, the most *avant*
of the avant-garde.[3]

In 1919 publisher Ben-
jamin Huebsch asked Tri-
don to write a primer on
psychoanalysis for gen-
eral readers. "What I have
attempted to do in the present volume," he said in its
preface, "is to sum up in a
concise form the views of
the greatest American and
foreign analysts which at
present are scattered in hundreds of books, pamphlets
and magazine articles. I
have, whenever possible,
presented their thought in

André Tridon, popularizer and pirate, in February 1922 (*New York Sun*, February 19, 1922).

their own words, through either direct quotation or condensation." Like the
journalists writing about Freud for mass-market magazines, he simplified
nuanced ideas, avoided technical jargon, and condensed complex arguments.
He even included a glossary at the end "explaining in the simplest possible
way the meaning of every new word employed by the new science."[4]

Tridon was far from an orthodox Freudian. "While I profess the
deepest respect for Sigmund Freud," he wrote, "and believe that but for
his scientific insight and his untiring labors, psychoanalysis would probably be to-day an undeveloped, inaccurate set of hypotheses, I hold that
Jung's and Adler's theories are of inestimable value, and that no analysis would be complete which did not take into account the researches of
the 'Zurich School' and of the 'Individual Psychologists.'" This infuriated
Freud partisans like Jones, who in a review called Tridon's book "full of
mis-statements and inaccuracies, which are far too numerous for us to be
able to contemplate the task of pointing them out seriatim. We can only
say that the book gives a highly misleading account of psycho-analysis,
and is in no way to be recommended." Most of the reading public, however, didn't care about doctrinal schisms inside the "new psychology" and
the book went through six printings in less than four years, selling more
than 10,000 copies and far outpacing most of Freud's own books.[5]

Tridon's approach to psychoanalysis is revealed in an advertisement for his lecture series on "The New Science of the Unconscious Presented in a Simple, Clear and Popular Manner." His five weekly topics were to be "The Unconscious and Its Mysteries: or What Is Psychoanalysis?," "The Interpretation of Dreams: or Suppressed Desires and their Dream Gratification," "Problems of Childhood: or Heredity and Sexual Enlightenment," "Dual Personalities: or the Jekyll and Hyde Case in Actual Life," and "Love, Normal and Abnormal." He treated patients in his own private practice, and in 1922 the *New York Times* called him the "foremost psychoanalyst in America" despite the fact that he'd had no training and possessed no medical degree. Through it all Tridon kept a sharp eye on the profits. His mission could be summed up in the advice he gave Theodore Dreiser on dealing with publishers—"get the money *first*."[6]

As sales of his primer on psychoanalysis mushroomed, Tridon cranked out successors at an astonishing rate. *Psychoanalysis, Its History, Theory and Practice* was followed less than a year later by *Psychoanalysis and Behavior* in the fall of 1920, *Psychoanalysis, Sleep and Dreams* in the spring of 1921, *Easy Lessons in Psychoanalysis* in December 1921, and *Psychoanalysis and Love* and *Sex Happiness* in 1922. He produced books so fast that he had to scatter them among publishers, including Huebsch, Knopf, and Brentano's.[7]

At the end of 1919, Tridon crossed paths with a fledgling publisher looking for new manuscripts. James A. McCann (1887–1952) was born in Albany and came to New York City as a teenager, where he landed a job in the manufacturing department of Doubleday Page. Within a few years he was travelling books as a salesman for McBride Nast & Co. and in 1914 he was hired by the books division of the Hearst syndicate. He arrived shortly after Arthur Reeve's collection of Freudian detective stories, *The Dream Doctor*, appeared in Hearst's International Library and soon rose to be manager of the whole division. In 1919, when someone new was brought in over his head during a reorganization, he decided to break out on his own.[8]

The firm of James A. McCann Inc. opened its doors in the summer of 1919 with the sensational novels *The Bite of Benin: Where Many Go in but Few Come Out* and *The Trail of the Beast*, as if McCann was hoping to discover the next H. Rider Haggard or Edgar Rice Burroughs. Perusing his list today, one is struck not by how quickly his company folded but how it managed to stay in business as long as it did. During its brief life McCann published an eclectic mix of about 50 titles, not just adventure fiction but inspirational books like *Look Up: Sunshine Treatment for Shadowed Lives* and occult treatises such as *Birth Through Death: the Ethics of the Twentieth Plane*. He tried to stay current with books about radio, movies, and the women's movement (who could resist *Glint of Wings: the Story of a Modern Girl Who Wanted Her Liberty—and Got It*). His stable of authors was more like a carnival, relying heavily on emigré hacks like Alexander Romanoff who wrote imperialist thrillers under the pseudonym "Achmed Abdullah" and Scottish adventurer Robert Simpson, author of the memorably titled novel, *Swamp Breath*. McCann seems to have printed almost anything that might sell, including gardening, folklore, juveniles, and sentimental verse, all of it justly forgotten today. After five years he threw in the towel and went to work as sales manager for Bobbs-Merrill.[9]

It's unclear how McCann and Tridon met since they probably moved in very different circles. McCann was a young businessman living in Brooklyn while Tridon was the most bohemian of Bohemians in Greenwich Village. But they shared energy, ambition, and a willingness to bend the rules of publishing.

During 1920 one of them, probably Tridon, noticed that Freud's *Interpretation of Dreams* and *On Dreams* had not been copyrighted in the U.S. because their sheets were printed in England. Established American publishers had always tacitly acknowledged the rights of foreign authors and when they wanted to produce a U.S. edition usually entered into formal agreements that included compensation. Among themselves, they conformed to a gentlemen's agreement not to purloin each other's books by foreign writers.[10]

Tridon and McCann, on the other hand, decided that nothing legally prevented them from printing and selling a new edition of Freud's books on dreams and keeping the profits for themselves. They plunged ahead without contacting the author, translators, or original publishers. Given Tridon's better education, wider experience of the world, and domineering personality, it's hard to escape the conclusion that he suggested the plan to the younger, less-experienced McCann, who was only starting out as a publisher. Ernest Jones, inquiring discreetly among his American contacts, concluded that Tridon had instigated the theft.[11]

Tridon stole about 160 pages from Brill's translation of *The Interpretation of Dreams* and roughly 80 pages from M.D. Eder's translation of *On Dreams*, shuffling paragraphs and rearranging them into new chapters with new titles. In the preface he explained this was necessary because Freud's original books were too difficult for the common reader:

> The book in which he originally offered to the world his interpretation of dreams was as circumstantial as a legal record to be pondered over by scientists at their leisure, not to be assimilated in a few hours by the average alert reader. In those days, Freud could not leave out any detail likely to make his extremely novel thesis evidentially acceptable to those willing to sift data. Freud himself, however, realized the magnitude of the task which the reading

of his magnum opus imposed upon those who have not been prepared for it by long psychological and scientific training....

Tridon ended by praising his co-conspirator: "The publishers of the present book deserve credit for presenting to the reading public the gist of Freud's psychology in the master's own words, and in a form which shall neither discourage beginners, nor appear too elementary to those who are more advanced in psychoanalytic study.... There shall be no longer any excuse for ignorance of the most revolutionary psychological system of modern times."[12]

Freud misspoke when he told the interviewer that Tridon had published the book under his own name. *Dream Psychology* clearly stated on its title page that it was "by Prof. Dr. Sigmund Freud." When he applied for copyright on December 1, 1920, McCann listed it under Freud's name and claimed copyright only on Tridon's introduction. But Freud was correct that it was an outright theft. Tridon and McCann printed and sold his writing without permission and pocketed the profits.[13]

The book appeared in December 1920 with Tridon's preface dated the previous November and "1920" at the foot of the title page. But McCann must have realized that this would soon make the volume seem outdated, so he quickly put out a second issue with 1921 on its title page. Copies dated 1920 claim the entire book is an "Authorized English Translation by M.D. Eder," a statement dropped in the second issue. Both issues included a brief list of Tridon's other works on the title page but that from 1921 includes *Easy Lesson [sic] in Psychoanalysis*, which is doesn't appear on the 1920 list. *Dream Psychology* was priced comparatively high at $3.50. The number of copies printed is not known, but the edition was probably large since Tridon's first book on psychoanalysis was then selling thousands of copies, as was Freud's *General Introduction*. In fact, McCann bound *Dream Psychology* in dark blue cloth stamped in gilt like the *General Introduction* and laid it out to be virtually the same size and shape, as if the two books were intended to be companion volumes.

Dream Psychology was announced in the *New York Times* "Latest Books" column on February 20, 1921, which is perhaps where Brill came across it. Jones heard about it in London in late February and urged Stanley Unwin, Freud's British publisher, to find out more. "As far as we can see," Unwin wrote to Brill on March 13, 1921, "it is a clear case of piracy, but although, as your translation of 'The interpretation of Dreams' was never set up and copyrighted in America, there may be no legal remedy, we hardly think that even the American law entitles the McCann Company either (a) to attribute one man's work to another and treat your translation as being the work of M.D. Eder, or (b) to copyright a work that has been published for many years past that is still being imported from this country."[14]

Brill replied, "I beg to say that this James A. McCann Co. is no company at all; it is simply a case of an unscrupulous person collaborating with André Tridon, who is a quack, who would not hesitate at anything. No publisher here knows anything about McCann, and from personal investigation I find that he is a nobody. He took advantage of the fact that you have not copyrighted the book in this country. I agree with you that it is a piracy. From inquiries I find that I can do very little. I am, however, trying to bring pressure on him and will communicate with you further on the subject." Jones warned Freud that "your prestige is injured by having your work presented to the public through a long introduction written by a man, André Tridon, who has an unsavory reputation, and is an unscrupulous and ignorant exploiter of psychoanalysis, in short the very last man you would choose for such a purpose." Freud himself wrote to McCann requesting a copy for examination but received no reply.[15]

This set off more than a year of trans-Atlantic negotiation, persuasion, and threats that did nothing to stop the sale of the book. From the fragmentary records which survive, it appears that for several months McCann refused all demands, after which Unwin suggested in November 1921 that a campaign be launched to embarrass him among his peers. McCann parried by offering royalties to the original publishers, Macmillan and Rebman, though still not compensating Freud, Brill, or Eder. "As you know," Jones reported to Freud on January 26, 1922, "in America all virtues are measured by dollars, and McKann's [sic] offer to pay royalties has changed the position over there. The American agents of both the *Traumdeutung* and *Uber den Traum* are said to have expressed their entire satisfaction." Freud replied, "I will not accept anything but the withdrawal of the book and will not forgive publishing the scandal quite independently whether the two publishers go along with us or suffer themselves to be bribed by the promise of royalties."[16]

But legally there was nothing they could do beyond denouncing the book, which Jones did in a March 1922 review in the *International Journal of Psycho-analysis*:

> The present book is simply made up from a series of cuttings from the two authorized ones. These were re-arranged, given new chapter-headings, naturally without the knowledge of the author or either of the two previous translators or publishers, and offered to a publisher as a new book. We have reason to believe that the person guilty of this dishonourable act was Mr. Tridon. More surprising, however, is the circumstance that the publisher appears to have made no inquiry as to Mr. Tridon's bona fides, as to the authenticity of the book, or as to any arrangement for acquiring the publication rights from the author or original publisher. In logical accord with this behaviour the publisher, on being acquainted with the true state of affairs, refused to make the

only possible reparation—namely, of at once withdrawing the book from sale. It is not necessary for us to stigmatize conduct of this nature, about which no honest man can have two opinions. We have no doubt that it will meet with the opprobrium it deserves among publishing circles....

In the fall of 1922 Brill pressured Macmillan to manufacture its own edition of *The Interpretation of Dreams* so it could be copyrighted in the U.S. but Unwin was unwilling to agree, presumably because it would undercut his own American sales. Tridon died unexpectedly in November 1922, after which Brill, Jones, and Freud turned their attention to other matters. By then, sales of *Dream Psychology* probably totaled several thousand.[17]

Tridon and McCann joined forces again to bring out the former's *Easy Lessons in Psychoanalysis* in December 1921 and Tridon continued his frenzy of writing, lecturing, and publishing until he was diagnosed with inoperable cancer in the fall of 1922. After his death on November 22 his last publisher, Brentano's, continued to exploit his reputation by printing his manuscripts *Psychoanalysis and Gland Personalities* in 1923 and *Psycho-Analysis and Man's Unconscious Motives* in 1924. James McCann shut down his company early in 1924 and, after working for Bobbs-Merrill until 1928, joined forces with Thomas R. Coward to establish the Coward-McCann Publishing Company. This time he was successful, flourishing for two decades until his retirement in 1946. One can only imagine that he rationalized the Tridon piracy as a beginner's mistake and, having retroactively paid Macmillan and Rebman, cleared his conscience. He died in 1952.[18]

12

Freud in the Modern Library, 1924 and After

"America was on a spree," Manuel Komroff recalled, speaking of the early 1920s. "Even the older generation seemed weary of Puritanism and New England idealism. Youth was disillusioned with corruption in government (the scandals in President Harding's administration), with dissolution and useless wars, with a church that promised a spiritual way of life but delivered nothing, a society that seemed indifferent to education of any of the finer things in life.... Now the house itself, the house of society, had a rotten structure. Social termites had eaten away the inner beams. We were all living in a shell that seemed ready to collapse."[1]

Horace Liveright and Albert Boni started the Modern Library in 1917 for the disillusioned young people who surrounded them in Greenwich Village. "The main considerations governing the inclusion of works in the Modern Library were cultural," the leading historian of the company explained. "Young, Jewish, politically radical, in touch with new writing in Europe and culturally active at home, Boni embodied the European intellectual currents that were beginning to shake American culture. The Modern Library was a fully conscious attempt on his part to transmit these currents to the broader American audience." Liveright wanted to include new American authors in the mix, too, and their disagreement over the scope of the series was a reason he and Boni soon fell apart.[2]

By the time Boni left in July 1918, they'd already published 50 Modern Library titles. Attractively designed, bound in flexible imitation leather, priced low, and small enough to conveniently fit in a pocket, they became immensely popular. "For young people hungry for what was sophisticated, subversive, avant-garde in literature," Louis Kronenberger recalled, "the Modern Library signified to the early twenties, one can almost say, what the whole world of quality paperbacks does today [1965]. Inside its limp, oily, smelly leatherette covers were texts hard to come by at low prices, or at all: Schopenhauer and Nietzsche, Dostoevsky and Baudelaire, Whitman and Zola, Strindberg's plays and Chekhov's stories, Havelock Ellis, Stephen Crane, Sherwood Anderson, D.H. Lawrence."[3]

Liveright was extravagant with marketing funds and created compelling advertisements. Bennett Cerf recalled, "he was doing big ads with black, black type and eye-catching borders—something previously unknown in the industry, which at that time was mostly in the hands of middle-aged or older stuffed shirts who considered publishing a very respectable business, and they didn't approve of flamboyant advertising." With the help of Bernays, Liveright bombarded tastemakers and influencers with creative notices of new books and events related to their publication. They felt that if the opening of a Broadway play could be a media event, so too could the release of an important book from a trending author.[4]

Profits earned by the Modern Library subsidized Liveright's path-breaking books by modernist writers like Ezra Pound, T.S. Eliot, and Theodore Dreiser despite the fact that the reprint series was largely ignored by his staff. "It was done sort of at the last minute," Cerf recalled in an interview. "One editor would say, 'Hey, we've got to find a couple of new titles for the Modern Library.' And it would be done in a haphazard way. The Modern Library was a great success, but nobody cared much about it. It developed almost by itself. It was so successful; it was such a good idea. I very quickly became by default the editor of the Modern Library. If I wanted to put a book in the Modern Library, I could always talk Horace into it because he didn't give much of a damn. It wasn't exciting enough for him…. It was the kind of a place that any time you volunteered to do anything, you got it because most of them were busy drinking bootleg liquor." By the time Cerf began steering editorial choices in 1923–1924, more than 100 titles had been issued.[5]

This was precisely when Liveright's Modern Library decided to publish an anthology of essays on psychoanalysis. Seeing the success of Freud's *General Introduction*, which had sold 10,000 copies for the firm over the previous two years, Liveright's staff began work in the summer of 1923 on "a symposium of the latest expressions by the leaders of the various schools of the new psychology." Bernays claimed to have introduced the symposium format a decade earlier while working for Robinson and may have influenced the decision. The symposium's cornerstone was to be "The Origin and Development of Psychoanalysis," Freud's five Clark University lectures from 1909. At the end of 1921 Freud had brought out a new German edition of the lectures and asked Ernest Jones to "rescue" them from the obscure pamphlet printed by G. Stanley Hall back in 1910. Jones wrote to Hall but nothing came of the idea at the time.[6]

Two years later, in 1923–1924, the Modern Library editors built their

TheModernLibrary
of the world's best modern classics
Fall 1923 Titles

A BOOK BY JAS. BRANCH CABELL
Title and introduction to be announced later.

FREE AND OTHER STORIES
by Theodore Dreiser
Introduction to be announced later.

IN A WINTER CITY   *by Ouida*
With an introduction by CARL VAN VECHTEN.

PLAYS BY MOLIERE
With an introduction by WALDO FRANK.

ERIK DORN   *by Ben Hecht*
Introduction to be announced later.

THAIS   *by Anatole France*
Introduction to be announced later.

JOHN DAVIDSON'S POEMS
With introduction by R. M. WENLEY

AN OUTLINE OF PSYCHOANALYSIS
A symposium of the latest expressions by the leaders
of the various schools of the new psychology.
Edited by J. S. VAN TESLAAR

**THE LE GALLIENNE ANTHOLOGY OF
AMERICAN POETRY**
Introduction by RICHARD LE GALLIENNE

The publication dates will be announced later

"High brow, it will never sell," said the literary pundits in
1917. We think it a fair statement, that next to the popular
reprints The Modern Library is the *fastest selling* book store
series in America today. The M. L. idea and ideal have been
gloriously vindicated.

BONI & LIVERIGHT   **GOOD BOOKS**   **61 WEST 48TH STREET
NEW YORK, N.Y.**

Boni & Liveright advertisement for the Modern Library (*Publishers Weekly*,
July 7, 1923).

new anthology around the Clark lectures. Cerf likely played the key role in producing the book, but Bernays had a hand in it, too. *An Outline of Psychoanalysis* was advertised as a forthcoming Boni and Liveright title in July 1923 and as "In Prep" in August, though more than a year passed before it actually reached bookstores. "Mr. Edward Bernays had a note sent to me today," Otto Rank wrote to Freud in July 1924, "informing me that Boni and Liveright want to publish your American lectures in book form, and that you've referred them to me."[7]

In his letter to Rank, Bernays suggested a payment of $75 for the rights. Rank wanted $1,000, to which Freud replied, "I think you're intoxicated with money if you demand $1000; $300, even $250, would be appropriate, and still strike B&L as extravagant and impossible." Freud had no strong feelings about the matter: "I'm prepared to allow the Five Lectures to be published by the two swindlers, and accept 75 dollars for them." In the end they settled on $150, but Bernays had to threaten Liveright with a lawsuit before Freud was paid. Freud also wanted the five lectures to appear by themselves and was dismayed when "my nephew hinted that the publisher wants to take something else to add to the Five Lectures. This must be stopped." By then, however, the book was already being constructed as a compendium of different approaches with contributions not only by Freud but also Jung, Stekel, Adler, Jelliffe and others, and there was nothing he could do about it. "I'd have much preferred that the lectures appear alone as a special publication," Freud told Rank afterward. "Of course that doesn't seem to be the case, but we'll let it go."[8]

It's not clear how Liveright's team chose the editor of the little book. James Van Teslaar (1884–1926), a Boston analyst, had been born in a village in the Carpathian Mountains of northern Romania, moved with his family to Bucharest in 1894, and was at school in Germany when his family's fortunes collapsed and he was thrown on his own resources. "A boat was leaving on the Rhine for the north," he recalled. "I took that boat, making the trip all the way to the mouth of the river in Holland. From there I went to England and in a short time I was on a vessel bound for the new continent" where he landed in Quebec. "A passenger to whom I rendered useful service gave me as pay a ticket to Manitoba, as he had changed his destination and was going to New York.... I travelled slowly, as the ticket gave me the privilege to stop over in various places, and eventually reached the end of the journey. But I remained there only a short time. I wandered all the way back East, making my way over the Great Lakes and through the States. In the East I continued wandering about in various places from Massachusetts to Florida, trying my hand at a variety of odd jobs and occupations."[9]

But Van Teslaar had never abandoned his dream of a university education, so he again "crossed the Continent all the way to California.

I found that tuition was free at the State University which is located at Berkeley, across the bay from San Francisco. There I settled down to work and study. Instead of engineering I took up the medical course. I also graduated in the literary department in due time." According to records at the American Medical Association, he earned his medical degree at Berkeley in 1903, followed by a research fellowship in neurology at the University of Chicago and courses at Rush Medical School in 1903–1904. After living for some time in Connecticut, he moved about 1911 to Massachusetts, where he joined the early psychoanalysts who met on Friday afternoons at the home of Dr. James J. Putnam. He was an assistant in neurology at Massachusetts General Hospital in Boston in 1911–1912 and taught as an adjunct professor for G. Stanley Hall at Clark in 1915. Hall had written the preface for Liveright's 1920 book by Freud and could have suggested Van Teslaar as editor.[10]

Van Teslaar was not a strict Freudian. "In spite of the allegations of narrow partisanship to the contrary," he wrote in the introduction, "I have always held that the views of Freud and Jung are not mutually exclusive. Dr. James Jackson Putnam agreed wholeheartedly with me when I emphasized this point at the Friday afternoon meetings of the Boston group of psychoanalysts." Worse yet (from Freud and Brill's perspective), during a visit to Vienna he came under the influence of heretical Wilhelm Stekel, claiming that "the importance of Stekel is only beginning to dawn upon the English world. In the course of time he undoubtedly will be recognized as the spiritual heir of Freud—the man who more than any other has built upon the foundations laid by Freud, even though he has had the temerity of reconstructing those foundations here and there in accordance with his own observations and experience." Between 1922 and his sudden death from a heart attack in 1926 at the age of 40, Van Teslaar translated six of Stekel's books. This led one Freud loyalist to conclude that he had "hooked up with the wrong people," including "quacks in New York."[11]

For *An Outline of Psychoanalysis,* Van Teslaar selected 16 essays and articles, most of which had already been published elsewhere between 1909 and 1923. Their authors included not only Freud, Jung, and Stekel but also Brill, Jelliffe, Putnam, Jones, and half a dozen other psychologists. Only six of the 16 would have met Freud or Brill's definition of psychoanalysts; the majority represented other therapeutic and theoretical approaches. The quality of the essays ranged widely, from Beatrice Hinkle's excellent overview of Jung to pieces that suggest Van Teslaar was simply looking for filler. It also included a glossary.

The book appeared in the fall of 1924 bound in flexible imitation leather, without the usual catalog of other Modern Library titles at the end and with an off-white dust jacket printed in black and red. Later impressions bear the date 1925 on the verso of the title page rather than 1924. It received only lukewarm reviews, criticized for its haphazard selection, technical jargon, and often lugubrious prose and praised only for its physical format and low price. It nevertheless remained in print for 30 years, the text unchanged during that time but its bindings evolving with those of the Modern Library series.[12]

The number of copies first printed in 1924 is not known, but probably totaled several thousand. In the late 1920s, Modern Library titles sold an average of 3,000–4,000 copies per year. In 1928 Random House promised booksellers that they'd discontinue any book in the series selling fewer than 2,000 copies annually. Later the same year, when staff calculated the top-selling titles from January through June, *An Outline of Psychoanalysis* was number 56 out of 150 with 1,692 copies sold in six months. If it averaged 3,400 copies per year throughout the 1920s, it would have sold about 20,000 copies by the end of the decade, more than any of Freud's books except the *General Introduction* (see epilogue for comparative sales figures). If that annual average held for its 30-year lifespan—there is no hard evidence that it did or didn't—then *An Outline of Psychoanalysis* would have reached more than 100,000 readers between 1924 and 1955, when it was allowed to go out of print.[13]

In 1955, editors at the Modern Library replaced Van Teslaar's collection with a completely new anthology under the same title. Edited by Clara Thompson, Milton Mazer, and Earl Witenberg, this was more than 200 pages longer, contained none of the same essays, and focused on a wider range of theoretical and therapeutic issues. As if two different books with the same title from the same publisher were not sufficiently confusing, a third was already on the market. In 1939 Freud had drafted a short summary of his work to which he gave the same title, *An Outline of Psychoanalysis*; an English translation by James Strachey was published by W.W. Norton in 1949 and it was included in volume 23 of the *Standard Edition* in 1964. Besides the title, the three books—Van Teslaar's 1924 symposium, Freud's 1939 essay, and Thompson's 1955 anthology—have nothing in common.

In the spring of 1925, Liveright found himself strapped for cash again, so Cerf proposed over lunch on May 25 that Liveright sell him the Modern Library. They went back to the office and negotiated an agreement that called for Cerf to pay $200,000, including credit for a $50,000 investment he'd already made. Liveright's closest friend on the staff, Julian Messner, vigorously opposed the deal but had no chance to intervene because the spouse of one of Liveright's mistresses arrived at the door with a pistol, vowing to shoot his wife's lover. Messner had to rush downstairs and pacify the jealous husband while Cerf and Liveright, the latter fearing for his life, finalized the terms of the sale. Cerf's friend Donald Klopfer put up $100,000 and he borrowed the other $50,000. "I bought the Modern Library the night I sailed for Europe," Cerf later recalled. "It was May 25th, 1925—my [27th] birthday.... To tell you what an incredible purchase this was, in two years we had made back not only the $50,000 that we had borrowed, but we had made back the entire investment. The minute we put our full attention on it, this series simply boomed."[14]

The Modern Library began life in 1917 closely identified with the younger generation's revolt against their Victorian elders. The first pocket-sized, inexpensive volumes occupied a place rather like that of City Lights paperbacks for the Beat Generation, underground newspapers for the hippies, or zines for Generation X. But under Cerf and Klopfer's guidance, it evolved into a mainstream commodity valued by every public library and bookstore in America. Starting with a few dozen titles in 1925, they gradually built a line of several hundred of "the world's best books" aimed at what they called the "civilized minority." Like the Book-of-the-Month Club or the Harvard Classics, the Modern Library stood for self-edification, stability, and prosperity. As the rebellious youth of the 1910s grew into middle age, its advertisements depicted affluent buyers packing Modern Library books on golfing and yachting vacations. By the mid-thirties the series was selling a million books annually despite the hardships of the Great Depression.[15]

Throughout the 1920s and 1930s, Brill's translations of Freud also continued to be reprinted by their original publishers. Macmillan, Jelliffe and White, Dodd Mead (who bought Moffat Yard in 1924), Horace Liveright Inc., and their subsidiaries, successors, and licensees, all continued to issue their earlier Freud titles. Sales diminished in the mid–1920s as the Freud trend waned, though they picked up again in the early 1930s with the success of his book, *Civilization and Its Discontents*. Recognizing this shift in the market, Cerf proposed to Brill that Freud's most important books be gathered into a single omnibus volume.

"For some time," Cerf wrote to Brill on November 1, 1936, "we have been thinking over the idea of doing a one-volume edition of Freud's writings in the Modern Library Giant series. One thing is sure, and that is that if the book is to be done, there is only one logical editor for it, and that is yourself." Brill concurred. Cerf's team set to work getting permissions from the original publishers, downplaying the sales potential of the anthology. "The volume will be a costly one," he told Dodd Mead, perhaps disingenuously, "and obviously no one is going to make very much out of it." He claimed that his primary goal was to popularize Freud and argued that if he was successful, all Dodd Mead's Freud titles would benefit.[16]

Brill, meanwhile, began revising his 20-year-old translations and deleting passages in order to reduce the size of the final product. He explained the anthology this way to Freud: "it contains the works which I have translated except *Leonardo* and *Reflections on War and Death....* Some of these books like *Totem and Taboo*, and *Wit*, were out of print, as was also *The History of the P.A. Movement*. The others, which Jelliffe had, had been paying very little for years. The Random House who published the work bought all these rights from the various publishers and I practically retranslated all of the works ... the works are together and will be obtainable by students who could not spend $17.50 for the originals."[17]

Brill didn't mention that while preparing the manuscript he took great liberties with Freud's texts. The most dramatic of these was telescoping the 80-page opening chapter of *The Interpretation of Dreams* down to a mere two pages. "As the first chapter of this work is nothing but an introduction to the book proper," he explained in a note to readers, "it was deemed best for the purposes of this collection of Freud's basic writings to omit most of it and to give only those parts that are in any way pertinent to the themes under later consideration." He also requested permission from publisher Ernest Benn (who'd acquired T. Fisher Unwin's rights) to use only about two-thirds of *Psychopathology of Everyday Life*, and silently truncated or rewrote lengthy passages in four of its chapters. He told Cerf on October 20, 1937, that "the other three books I shall incorporate as they are with slight notations etc., etc."[18]

Random House announced *Basic Writings* as forthcoming in December 1937. Galleys reached Brill for correction in February 1938, when Modern Library advertised that it would "contain not only an interpretive biography by the editor, Dr. A.A. Brill, but include ALL of Freud's most significant writings, from his earliest down to the most recent. There is simply no comparative volume of Freud that competes with this one." Brill's warm 32-page introduction is part biography, part memoir, and part summary of Freud's central ideas.[19]

A first printing of 10,000 copies delivered to bookstores in mid–May 1938 sold out in less than two weeks. This first edition is explicitly identified on the title page verso; subsequent printings omit the "first edition" line. By mid–June total sales had doubled. Macy's department store reported 177 copies sold on a single Saturday. In mid–July *Publishers Weekly* reported it was the nation's top-selling reprint title, a position it maintained well into the autumn. The manager of the University of Chicago Bookstore highlighted the role that word-of-mouth played on college campuses: "By noon of the day that a shipment of this title has come into the store the news has filtered through the whole psychology department, and most of the students and faculty members are buying the book. And for one of them that may be the first book he has ever bought that he wasn't required to buy. No advertising campaign you could possibly have arranged would have improved upon that simple strategic setup."[20]

Brill sent the first royalties to Freud on November 25, 1938. "The enclosed check for $500 is for royalties on The Basic Writings etc. which I just received," he wrote. "The book has been selling very well for a few months but unfortunately it is sold for only $1.25. As it is, you will get more than you would have gotten on the individual works of which it consists." Freud replied, "The check enclosed in your letter contained a by no means unpleasant surprise in these times. I didn't know anything about the Basic Writings, and so far I've never made it clear to myself whether it's right that I accept these royalties that may be due to you. I've made myself comfortable by assuming that if you act like this, it will surely be all right." Brill reminded the octogenarian author, "I wrote to you about this long ago and have sent you a check for $500 to Vienna as soon as I completed the arrangements with the local publisher.... So far you have received $1000 which I am sure could not have come from the original translations. ... As to your right to the royalties, we discussed this many years ago and I repeat what I told you then: that whereas I have a legal right to them, I believe that under the circumstances you should receive them." Four months later he was able to send another $1,200 shortly before Freud died.[21]

Sales of Basic Writings averaged 10,000–20,000 copies per year for the next 25 years. Cerf admitted to an interviewer at the end of 1942, when over 100,000 copies had been sold, "we haven't the faintest idea why or who are the people that are reading this book so assiduously." By 1951 it had sold 203,000 copies. In the 25-year life of the Modern Library, only two titles had sold more (Tolstoy's War and Peace and Maugham's Of Human Bondage). By the time the Standard Edition was completed in 1967, Basic Writings had reached more than 345,664 readers.[22]

Epilogue

Freud's Books at Mid-Century

Between 1910 and 1920, Freud's ideas swept across America. In 1909 his name was known only to a handful of medical experts but four years later it was appearing on newsstands all around the nation. By 1925 the chorus of a popular showtune could end with the refrain, "Don't tell me what you dreamed last night, for I've been reading Freud."[1]

The table below shows annual sales of his books through 1929, so far as this can be determined. Data comes mostly from Brill's royalty reports, publishers' correspondence, internal account ledgers, and other archival sources.[2] Jelliffe and White's technical monographs and titles for which no information survives are omitted. For years in which sales data is missing, the number of copies printed or imported has been substituted if known; royalty years that span calendar years (such as March–February) have been shifted; in one case, a six-month royalty report has been doubled to estimate an annual total. Empty cells predate a book's publication; "?" indicates that data could not be found; "0" means that the publisher reported no copies sold; * signifies that the figure immediately below is the publisher's cumulative, "sold-to-date" total. Those edits and the numerous gaps mean that these figures should be used with caution; they merely suggest trends.

To put these statistics in context, during the year in which Freud sold the most books (1923) his total sales were 8,709. That same year Giovanni Papini's biography of Christ sold over 100,000 copies. In 1925, F. Scott Fitzgerald's *The Great Gatsby* sold 20,000 in its first month.[3]

The 1924 agreement drawn up by Freud, Jones, and Woolf centralized Freud's English-language copyrights for the first time. Woolf had insisted on retaining the American rights, but by then the initial wave of interest in Freud had passed and he "had to work very hard to try and get Freud taken in the United States, with no result at all." Brill's translations continued to appear with only modest results; some were allowed to go out of print.

Year	Interpretation of Dreams	Psychopathology of Everyday Life	Wit & Its Relation of the Unconscious	Leonardo da Vinci	Dream and Delusion	Totem & Taboo	General Introduction	Outline of Psychoanalysis	Group Psychology & Analysis of the Ego	Beyond the Pleasure Principle	TOTAL
1913	1,457										1,457
1914	590	?									590
1915	?	?									0
1916	700	412	*	*							1,112
1917	400	450	*	*	*						850
1918	300	91	*	*	*	*					391
1919	750	?	*	*	*	*					750
1920	816	?	*	*	*	*	4,366				5,182
1921	600	501	*	*	*	*	2,099				3,200
1922	250	500	*	*	*	*	2,763				3,513
1923	1,010	250	1,495	1,310	1,363	1,567	1,714				8,709
1924	250	?	26	?	?	19	1,400	?	1,200	1,253	4,148
1925	500	250	37	?	?	108	1,205	?	328	359	2,787
1926	?	264	?	?	?	?	1,610	?	154	160	2,188
1927	?	0	46	?	2,000	83	1,326	?	107	123	3,685
1928	?	250	41	?	?	2,008	1,009	3,384	48	10	6,750
1929	?	0	22	?	?	659	898	?	163	0	1,742
TOTAL	7,623	2,968	1,667	1,310	3,363	4,444	18,390	3,384	2,000	1,905	47,054

Annual sales of Freud's books through 1929.

Sales improved somewhat after 1930 with the success of *Civilization and Its Discontents*, but until the late 1930s Freud was not popular in the U.S.—with one notable exception.[4]

In 1919 Emmanuel Haldeman-Julius began publishing tiny pamphlet versions of classic works in 32 or 64 pages that sold for five or 10 cents. These shirt-pocket booklets were bought mostly by readers without college degrees who wanted to educate themselves; 95 percent were sold directly to customers through the mail. Popularly called the Little Blue Books, the series was an immediate success and sold 40 million copies in its first two years. In 1921, booklet no. 203, Havelock Ellis's essay *Love Rights of Women* was published; copies printed after 1925 also included Freud's essay "The Sexual Enlightenment of Children." In 1927 this sold

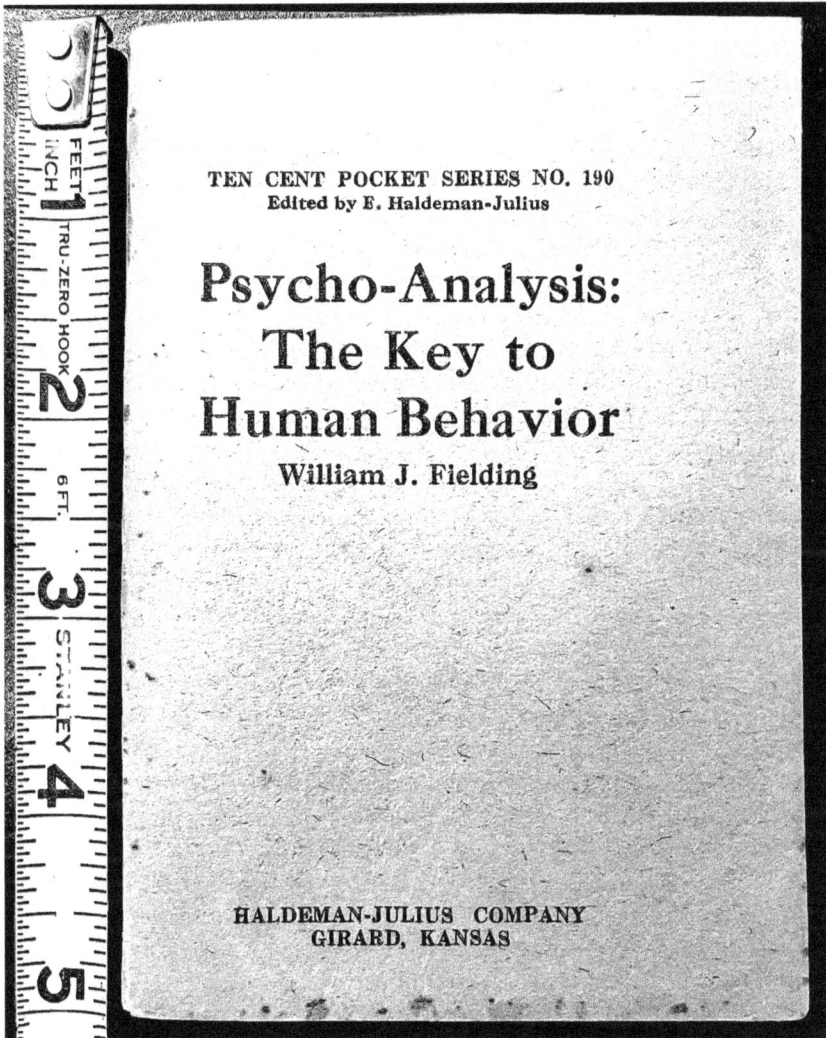

Haldeman-Julius Little Blue Books brought Freud's ideas to millions (author's collection).

39,000 copies. It remained in print until the early 1940s, so if the 1927 sales held as an annual average, nearly 600,000 copies of Freud's essay would have been sold by 1940. Other Little Blue Books summarizing or excerpting Freud's writings were equally popular. Anton S. Booker's *Freud on Sleep and Sexual Dreams* (1925) annually sold 61,000 copies, for a potential total of 900,000 by 1940, and William J. Fielding's *Psycho-Analysis: The Key to Human Behavior* sold 330,000 between 1921 and 1949. While

Freud's mainstream publishers were reaching thousands of middle-class customers in bookstores, Haldeman-Julius was reaching more than a million through the Little Blue Books.[5]

The rise of fascism and World War II were responsible for a Freudian renaissance in the U.S. Starting in the mid–1930s, Jewish psychoanalysts were denied the right to practice under the Third Reich; facing arrest and transportation to concentration camps, many fled Nazi-occupied countries. In 1935 American analysts formed a committee that eventually helped 149 psychoanalysts, doctors, social workers, teachers, and other professionals associated with Freud to relocate to the U.S. They soon went on to share his teachings not just in New York and Boston but as far west as the Menninger Institute in Kansas and fledgling psychoanalytic communities in California.[6]

In March 1938 Hitler's troops occupied Vienna. The gestapo raided Freud's home, seized his valuables, and arrested his daughter Anna, who concealed enough Veronal on her person to kill herself if tortured. Viennese Jews were abused, beaten, and killed by mobs in the streets. Soon more than 7,000 were shipped to concentration camps; many others committed suicide rather than wait to be arrested. On June 4, 1938, after intense international pressure, Freud and his immediate family were allowed to depart for England. His four elderly sisters were not allowed to leave and perished in Nazi death camps. Freud lived in London a little more than a year, choosing to end his own life on September 23, 1939, when his late-stage cancer became inoperable. His death prompted poet W.H. Auden to write, "he is no more a person now / but a whole climate of opinion / under whom we conduct our different lives."[7]

By then war had been declared in Europe. In America, psychoanalyst William Menninger was appointed to train 1,700 military counselors how to evaluate the mental health of new recruits and returning veterans. When the war ended, "brimming with confidence, armed with their radically simplified version of psychoanalysis," wrote historian Andrew Scull, "America's military psychiatrists persuaded the politicians, the public, and, just as important, themselves, that their techniques were immensely powerful, and, if implemented early enough, offered a revolutionary new approach to the cure of mental disorder." Financed by the G.I. Bill, the fledgling Freudians flooded university campuses where psychology departments flourished thanks to government funding. The pince-nez, homburg hats, and Havana cigars of first-generation analysts were replaced by skinny ties, horn-rimmed glasses, and filter cigarettes. The new generation eagerly snapped up Modern Library's *Basic Writings* and cheap paperback reprints of Freud's other books.[8]

Abraham Brill lived only long enough to see the start of this Freudian resurgence. His student May Romm recalled that "many of his friends (myself included) noticed a definite change in him after Freud died. A good deal of his buoyancy, his enthusiasm, and his lust for life seemed to have evaporated. There was a sadness in him that he could not conceal. He told me that, when he was informed of Freud's death, some part of him also died. On the last few times that I saw him during my biannual attendance at psychoanalytic meetings, he repeatedly referred to his acceptance of the idea that life was running out for him."[9] Brill told his friend Theodore Dreiser, "we must learn not to fear death, and therefore we will not be afraid of it, will accept it when the time comes…. As far as rewards are concerned, there is a new beatitude which says, 'Blessed are those who expect nothing, for they shall not be disappointed.'" He died from a heart attack on March 2, 1948, just before his 74th birthday.[10]

During the decade that followed, Andrew Scull writes, "the chairs of the great majority of university departments were analysts by training and persuasion, and the discipline's major textbooks heavily emphasized psychoanalytic perspectives." Freud's ideas dominated not just universities but mental health clinics as well after they were woven into the *Diagnostic and Statistical Manual of Mental Disorders* (DSM) in 1952. Outsiders joked that psychoanalysis had become a religion with Freud its infallible pope, his writings scripture, and his theories dogma; heretics were excommunicated. Aldous Huxley, a guest at the 1953 American Psychological Association conference in Los Angeles, playfully crossed himself whenever Freud's name was mentioned. But the narrow orthodoxy of the profession's leadership also prompted rebellion in the ranks, and for decades feuding raged inside American psychoanalysis over doctrinal differences and therapeutic variations.[11]

Psychoanalytic in-fighting didn't prevent Freud's central ideas from thoroughly penetrating education, advertising, religion, social work, economics, literature, criminology, filmmaking, law, sociology, and child-rearing during the 1950s. Their widest circulation came through Dr. Benjamin Spock's *Commonsense Book of Baby and Child Care*, which sold nearly a million copies per year and more than 50 million copies over its lifetime. Trained at the New York Psychoanalytic Society and Institute, Spock was a loyal Freudian, and without ever mentioning the master's name he helped "indoctrinate a whole generation of young parents into the psychoanalytic perspective on life."[12] So, too, did Hollywood, as directors like Alfred Hitchcock, Joseph L. Mankiewicz, and Nicholas Ray put explicitly Freudian themes in front of millions of movie-goers. Freud's ideas became so popular that the Basic Book Club, formed in 1945 to provide one psychoanalytic book each month to its members, had enrolled 45,000 subscribers by 1952.[13]

That's the year that a second massive collection of Freud's writings appeared when the Encyclopædia Britannica completed its *Great Books of the Western World* series with volume 54, *The Major Works of Sigmund Freud,* in nearly 900 pages. It contained 18 works, including the 1909 Clark Lectures, *The Interpretation of Dreams, Reflections on War and Death, A General Introduction to Psychoanalysis, Group Psychology and the Analysis of the Ego,* and *Beyond the Pleasure Principle* as well as several essays and later books. The *Great Books* were peddled door-to-door like an encyclopedia and sold 35,000–50,000 sets per year, totaling a million copies by the end of the century.

Volume 54 of the *Great Books* undoubtedly put Freud's ideas into more hands than any other publication, but they didn't necessarily move from buyers' hands into their heads. Historian Alex Beam concluded that very few copies of the *Great Books* were actually read, since the books "were in fact icons of unreadability—32,000 pages of tiny, double-column, eye-straining type. There were no concessions to contemporary taste, or even pleasure." For most customers they were merely a status symbol decorating a suburban mid-century-modern living room. Virtually unread sets can still be found today, and the Freud volume can be bought by itself in pristine condition for less than $10 from antiquarian book dealers.[14]

During the 1950s the paperback revolution carried Freud's writings out of libraries and bookshops into newsstands, railway stations, drugstores, and supermarkets; 10 of his books were available in softcover by 1955. With profit margins of only pennies on each copy sold, paperback publishers needed to turn over hundreds of thousands of copies to make a profit. Anchor, Avon, Beacon, Pocket Books, and Vintage, all of whom published Freud in paperback, typically printed 10,000 to 20,000 copies per impression. Anchor set a break-even point at 27,000 copies and often printed more; Avon announced initial print runs of 50,000. Between 1946 and 1966, a dozen paperback firms issued at least 89 impressions of Freud's books. With a minimum of 10,000–20,000 copies per impression, at least one to two million copies of his works must have been distributed in paperback during the post-war years; the actual total could have been much higher. Like the Little Blue Books, they put Freud's ideas into the hands of less affluent readers, especially the hundreds of thousands of students flooding college campuses with help from the G.I. Bill.[15]

During those decades two firms emerged as the leading publishers of Freud's work in the U.S. Basic Books, founded in 1945 as a psychoanalytic book club, was acquired three years later by Arthur Rosenthal (whose mother had been analyzed by Otto Rank). In 1952 Rosenthal reorganized it as Basic Books Publishing Co. and began printing hardcover editions that

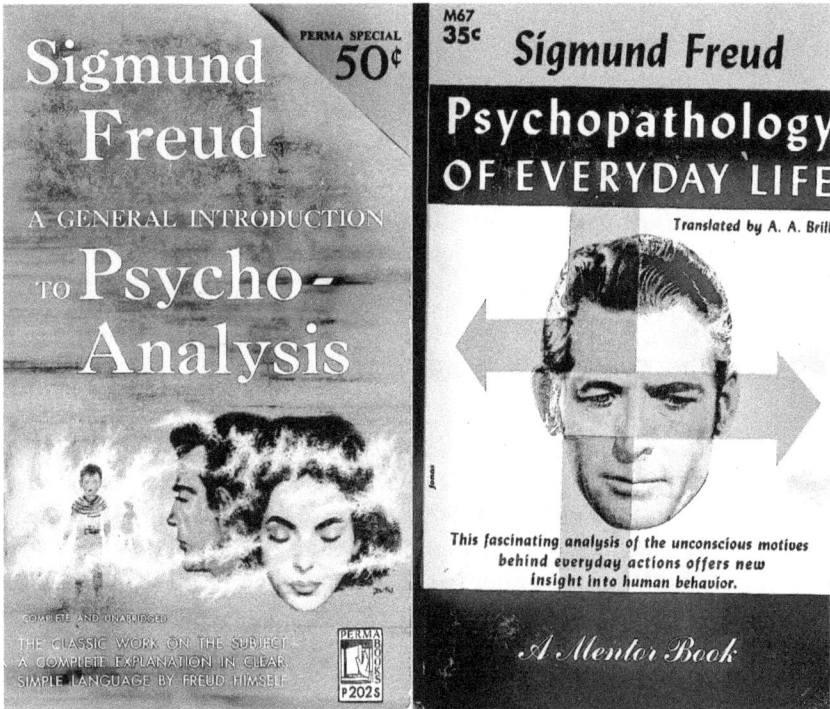

Freud encounters the 1950s paperback revolution (author's collection).

included Freud's correspondence with Wilhelm Fliess (much sanitized) in 1954, Ernest Jones's three-volume biography 1954–1957, the first U.S. edition of Freud's *Collected Papers* in five volumes in 1959, and six other titles, including three more volumes of Freud's letters between 1954 and 1964.[16] The second company, W.W. Norton, had been founded in 1923 to publish psychology and serious non-fiction; proprietor Warder W. Norton was also instrumental in distributing millions of Armed Services paperbacks to troops during World War II. Starting in 1933 Norton licensed rights from the Hogarth Press and went on to issue American editions of Freud's works as they were produced in London for the *Standard Edition*, eventually bringing out 20 titles in all.[17]

During the 1920s both Brill and Jones had contemplated a collected edition of Freud's works, and prior to the war Leonard Woolf had taken initial steps toward producing one. The war delayed it, but work resumed as soon as hostilities ceased. The project was headed by James Strachey, whom Woolf praised for his "psychoanalytical knowledge, brilliance, and accuracy as a writer and translator, and indomitable severity both to himself and to his publisher." Woolf recalled in his autobiography that

Freud's American copyrights were in such a tangled and chaotic condition that the moment we began definitely to face the problem there seemed to be no way of acquiring all the rights or even of being quite sure of who controlled them. What made the task of our approach to Dr Brill, and after his death to his heirs and executors, doubly delicate was that we had to obtain their consent first to our publishing in America translations of the works in which they held the American rights, and second to our using not Dr Brill's translations but James's. For a long time every attempt to find a way through the maze of copyrights and overcome the other difficulties failed, but eventually, largely owing to Ernst Freud's tact and perseverance, an agreement with the Brill executors made publication in America possible.[18]

The initial volume of the *Standard Edition of the Complete Psychological Works of Sigmund Freud* appeared in 1953, the last in 1967; in 1974 a volume of indexes and bibliographies completed the project. Over the last 60 years its texts have been read in countless paperback versions from Norton and Penguin, completely overshadowing the work of Brill and his contemporaries who first made Freud a household name.[19]

By the time the last volume of the *Standard Edition* came out in 1974, Freud's reputation had begun to suffer a complete reversal. Historians declared that his conclusions were based on a small sample, that he played fast and loose with data, that he saw in his patients only what he wanted to see, that they told him only what he wanted to hear, and that many of his claims were factually wrong. One critic went so far as to call psychoanalysis "the most stupendous intellectual confidence trick of the 20th century." The most compelling critiques came from second wave feminists. Freud had famously confessed in 1927 that "the sexual life of adult women is a 'dark continent' for psychology" and after 1970 his ignorant stumblings in the dark were carefully dissected and justly denounced by a generation of feminist critics. The heroic warrior-genius of Jones's 1950s biography crumbled. In 2014, in an unintentionally symbolic act, vandals broke into the cemetery where Freud's remains are kept and toppled the urn containing his ashes off its pedestal.[20]

By then the harshest anti–Freudian critiques had been internalized by the general public, even though they haven't held up well under careful analysis. For example, Seymour Fisher and Roger Greenberg devoted 30 years to examining more than 2,500 psychoanalytic studies according to modern standards of scientific research. They concluded that Freud's most important claims were strongly supported by the available data. These included his overall topography of the mind (id, ego, and superego), his model of psychosexual developmental (oral, anal, phallic, latent, and genital stages, as well as the Oedipal conflict), and the psychodynamics of repression and ego defense.[21]

Freud's ideas were rejected not because they were wrong but because a more simplistic, easily digested paradigm replaced them. The discovery of chemical neurotransmitters in the 1950s, development of psychiatric drugs during the 1960s, and the invention of brain imaging in the 1970s convinced many people that mental life consists of nothing more than electrical impulses and chemical reactions inside a slab of meat. Millions of prescriptions for Thorazine, Miltown, and Prozac—promoted by Big Pharma through Bernaysian marketing campaigns aimed at doctors—reinforced the notion that "mental troubles are brain diseases for which drugs are the logical form of treatment." At the end of his life, Freud himself had entertained this possibility: "The future may teach us to exercise a direct influence, by means of particular chemical substances, on the amounts of energy and their distribution in the mental apparatus." Today the vast majority of psychiatrists provide no therapy at all but only medication. One in eight American adults currently takes anti-depressants, totaling nearly 100 million prescriptions per year. They relieve vast amounts of suffering despite their success rate of only about 60 percent. And while they shed much light on how the brain functions, they do little to explain how our minds work.[22]

Today, psychotherapists who offer counseling usually employ a form of cognitive behavioral therapy, which rejects depth psychology in favor of teaching clients to notice and interrupt repeated harmful thoughts. Rather than spend years unearthing the root causes of inner conflict, they try to eliminate the conscious sources of current misery. Freud would say that they treat the symptoms but ignore the disease. CBT's origins can be traced back to the pragmatic methods of his early disciple Alfred Adler, resurrected in new forms in the 1950s by Aaron Beck and Albert Ellis. It's now the most popular therapeutic approach because it works for many people faced with depression and anxiety, at least temporarily, and because insurance companies will often pay for it.[23]

Despite half a century of criticism, Freud's ideas settled into a sort of common sense. His name may evoke scorn, but like Copernicus and Darwin (to whom he was often compared) his central concepts were embraced by millions of Americans unaware that their silent assumptions about life came from his revolutionary insights. Freud, in the words of historian Mark Edmundson, was "the man who had probably done more than any other to change the way people in the West thought about who and what they were." This happened because between 1900 and 1924 a handful of translators, editors, and publishers—chief among them Ely Jelliffe, Abraham Brill, George Brett, Joseph Coit, Edward Bernays, Horace Liveright, and Bennett Cerf—turned his ideas into tangible objects and put them into the hands of readers.[24]

Appendix

First American Editions of Freud, 1900–1924

The descriptions below, arranged chronologically, attempt to show how Freud's books looked and felt when they first reached American readers. Intact first editions are scarce, so I'm grateful to the curators of rare books around the country who generously examined their copies for me and provided dozens of photographs. Books I've handled in person are identified with an asterisk; a pair of asterisks indicates that someone else examined a physical copy for me. Digital facsimiles and photographs of copies offered for sale by rare book dealers provided more data. The rarest items are accompanied by photographs.

*1. *What Are Dreams?* New York: Tucker Publishing Co., April 5, 1900. Three cents.

Title Page: WHAT ARE DREAMS? | [leaf decoration] | From the German | [publisher's logo] | Office of Publication: | Rooms 2128-29-30-31, Park Row Building

Pagination: [cover] ; [verso of cover] blank ; [1] title page ; [2] blank ; [3, text begins. At foot:] Originally printed in "Die Grenzboten," Leipzig, March 15, 1900 ; 3–15 text ; [16] blank.

Binding: Paper wrappers. Front wrapper printed in reddish-brown within an art nouveau floral design inside a ruled border: *The* | *Balzac* | *Library* | WHAT ARE DREAMS ? | FROM THE GERMAN | PRICE, 3 CENTS | New York | The Tucker Pub. Co | [beneath the floral design is the artist's name:] Edward Dewson 1900 | [outside the ruled border at foot of page:] Six times a week. | No. 29–April 5, 1900 | Subscription, $10 a year. Front wrapper verso, back wrapper verso, and back wrapper are all blank.

Notes: This piracy reprints a German review composed largely of quotations from and condensations of Freud's *Die Traumdeutung* (*The Interpretation of Dreams*), published three months earlier in Vienna. The number of copies printed is not known. OCLC WorldCat records only two surviving copies, at Harvard and at the University of Michigan; a third is in private hands. The cover artist, Edward Dewson, was a furniture designer and interior decorator who worked in Boston and New York; in 1897 he edited the monthly *Home Decorator and Furnisher*. See Chapter 1 for details.

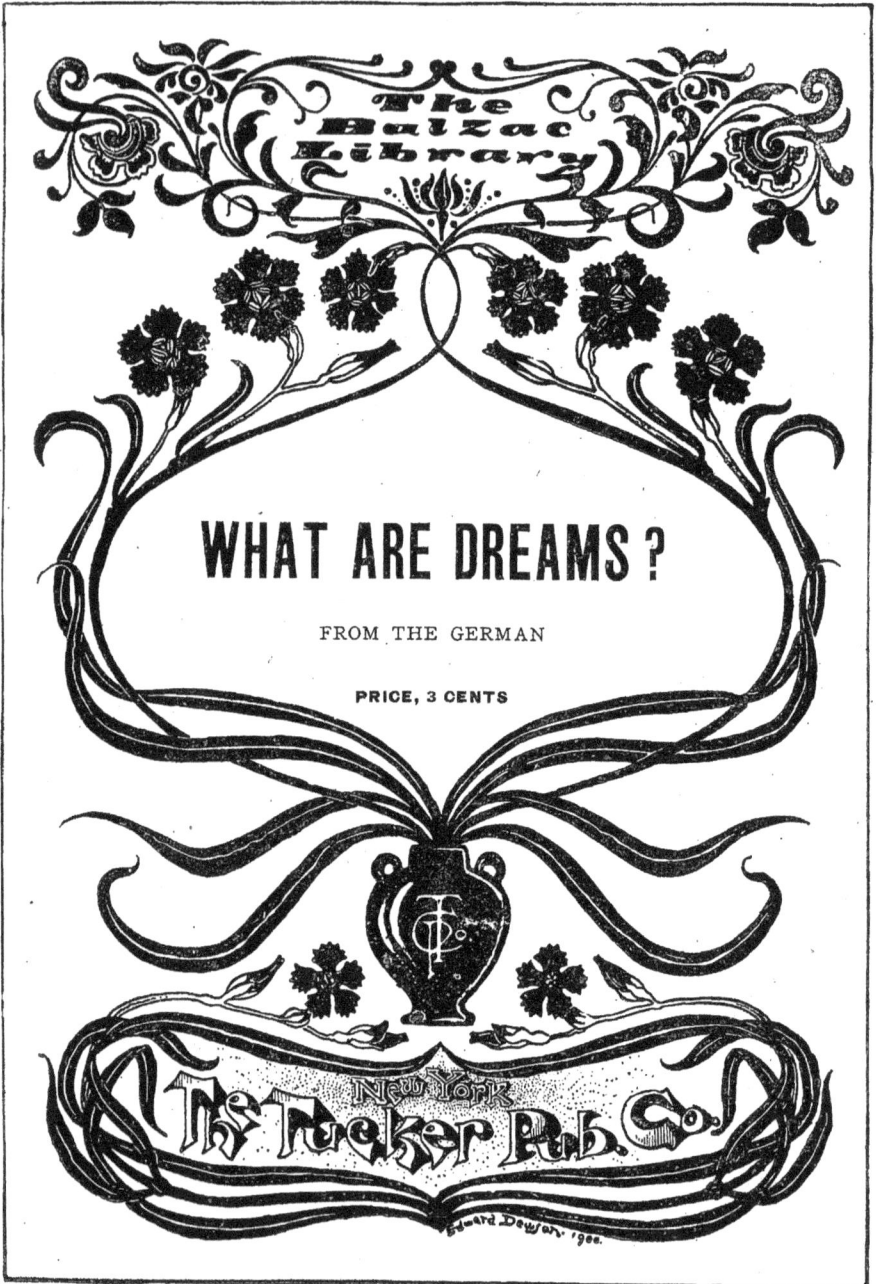

THE BALZAC LIBRARY

WHAT ARE DREAMS ?

FROM THE GERMAN

PRICE, 3 CENTS

New York
The Tucker Pub. Co.

What Are Dreams?, pirated by Benjamin Tucker in 1900 (author's collection).

Nervous and Mental Disease Monograph Series No. 4

Selected Papers on Hysteria

and

Other Psychoneuroses

PROF. SIGMUND FREUD
VIENNA

NEW YORK
1909

Front wrapper of *Selected Papers on Hysteria*, 1909 (author's collection).

*2. *Selected Papers on Hysteria and Other Psychoneuroses* New York: The Nervous & Mental Disease Publishing Co., September 30, 1909. [2]+vi+200 pages. $2.00

    Title Page: SELECTED PAPERS ON HYSTERIA | AND | OTHER PSY-CHONEUROSES | BY | PROF. SIGMUND FREUD | VIENNA | AUTHORIZED TRANSLATION | BY | A. A. BRILL, PH.D., M.D. | CHIEF OF NERVOUS DISPENSARY, BETH ISRAEL HOSPITAL, CLINICAL ASSISTANT, DEPARTMENT OF | PSYCHIATRY AND NEUROLOGY, COLUMBIA UNIVERSITY; ASSISTANT IN MENTAL AND | NERVOUS DISEASES, O. P. D., BELLEVUE HOSPITAL; ASSISTANT VISITING | PHYSICIAN, HOSPITAL FOR NERVOUS DISEASES. | NEW YORK | THE JOURNAL OF NERVOUS AND MENTAL DISEASE | PUBLISHING COMPANY | 1909

    Pagination: the title page and its verso precede inferred Roman page numbers: [title page as above] ; [title page verso:] Copyright 1909, by | THE JOURNAL OF NERVOUS AND MENTAL DISEASE | PUBLISHING COMPANY. ; [i] contents ; [ii] blank ; [iii]–vi translator's preface ; 1–200 text.

    Binding: Dark brown paper wrappers printed in black. On front wrapper: Nervous and Mental Disease Monograph Series No. 4 | Selected Papers on Hysteria | and | Other Psychoneuroses | PROF. SIGMUND FREUD | VIENNA | NEW YORK | 1909 Inside of back wrapper contains advertisements for the series; back wrapper is printed with an advertisement for the *Journal of Nervous and Mental Disease*.

    Notes: The number of copies printed is not known. The first four chapters had appeared in 1895 in Freud and Josef Breuer's *Studien über Hysterie*, which contained two articles by Breuer, five by Freud, and one written jointly. *Selected Papers…* omits three case histories printed there (Fraulein Anna O., Frau Emmy von N., and Katharina) as well as Breuer's opening theoretical chapter. For its subsequent publishing history, see chapter 2.

    3. *Three Contributions to the Sexual Theory*. New York: Nervous and Mental Disease Publishing Co., 1910 [January 1911]. x+92 pages. $2.00.

    Title Page: THREE CONTRIBUTIONS TO THE | SEXUAL THEORY | BY | PROF. SIGMUND FREUD, LL.D., | VIENNA. | AUTHORIZED TRANSLATION | BY | A. A. BRILL, PH.B., M.D., | CLINICAL ASSISTANT DEPARTMENT OF PSYCHIATRY AND NEUROLOGY, COLUMBIA UNIVERSITY ; | ASSISTANT IN MENTAL DISEASES, BELLEVUE HOSPITAL; ASSISTANT VISITING PHYSICIAN, | HOSPITAL FOR NERVOUS DISEASES | WITH INTRODUCTION | BY | JAMES J. PUTNAM, M.D. | NEW YORK | THE JOURNAL OF NERVOUS AND MENTAL DISEASE | PUBLISHING COMPANY | 1910

    Pagination: [i] title page ; [ii] [list of numbers 1–7 in series. At foot:] Copyright, 1910, by | THE JOURNAL OF NERVOUS AND MENTAL DISEASE | PUBLISHING COMPANY | NEW YORK | PRESS OF | THE NEW ERA PRINTING COMPANY | LANCASTER, PA. ; iii contents ; [iv] blank ; [v] author's preface to the second German edition, dated December 1909 ; [vi] blank ; vii–x introduction by James J. Putnam ; 1–86 text ; 87–91 index ; [92] blank.

    Binding: Brown paper wrappers printed in black. On front wrapper: Nervous and Mental Disease Monograph Series No. 7 | Three Contributions to the Sexual Theory | By | Prof. Sigmund Freud, LL.D. | Vienna. | New York | 1910. Inside of

LECTURES AND ADDRESSES

DELIVERED BEFORE THE
DEPARTMENTS OF

PSYCHOLOGY AND PEDAGOGY

IN CELEBRATION OF THE

TWENTIETH ANNIVERSARY

OF THE OPENING OF

CLARK UNIVERSITY

SEPTEMBER, 1909

Part I
LECTURES BEFORE THE DEPARTMENT OF PSYCHOLOGY

Part II
LECTURES BEFORE THE DEPARTMENT OF PEDAGOGY

WORCESTER, MASS.
1910

Front wrapper of Clark University twentieth anniversary lectures, privately issued in 1910 (University of Wisconsin copy).

---

back wrapper contains advertisements for the series; back wrapper is printed with an advertisement for the *Journal of Nervous and Mental Disease*.

Copyright entered: December 1, 1910

Notes: The title was changed to *Three Contributions to the Theory of Sex* with the second edition. For its subsequent publishing history, see chapter 2.

*4. Lectures and Addresses Delivered Before the Departments of Psychology and Pedagogy in Celebration of the Twentieth Anniversary of the Opening of Clark University. September, 1909... Worcester, Mass., October 1910. Part 1: xiv+1–176; Part 2: viii+80 pages.

Title Page: LECTURES AND ADDRESSES | DELIVERED BEFORE THE | DEPARTMENTS OF PSYCHOLOGY AND PEDAGOGY | IN CELEBRATION OF THE | TWENTIETH ANNIVERSARY /OF THE OPENING OF | CLARK UNIVERSITY | [rule] SEPTEMBER, 1909 | [rule] | Part I | LECTURES BEFORE THE DEPARTMENT OF PSYCHOLOGY | Part II | LECTURES BEFORE THE DEPARTMENT OF PEDAGOGY | [rule] | WORCESTER, MASS. | 1910

Pagination (on heavy laid paper with visible chain lines): blank leaf ; frontispiece photograph, with tissue overlay identifying people in the photo ; [i] title page ; [ii] blank ; [iii] list of lecturers ; [iv] blank ; [v]–viii Introduction ; [ix] section title ; [x] blank ; [xi] section title ; [xii] blank ; [xiii] Contents of Part I ; [xiv] blank ; [1]–38 Freud's five lectures under the title "Origin and Development of Psychoanalysis" ; [39]–175 essays by other conference presenters ; [176] blank. Part Two, *Lectures on Pedagogy*, then follows with a separate pagination, viii+80.

Binding: Light blue paper wrappers printed like the title page. Inside of front wrapper and both sides of back wrapper are blank.

Copyright entered: No copyright registration found.

Notes: The number of copies printed is not known, but only 150–200 people attended the conference so the edition size was probably small. Printed by Worcester printer Oliver B. Wood from the same setting of type as in the *American Journal of Psychology* 21 (April 1910): 181–218; opening words on each page are identical in both, and Freud's name is mis-spelled "Frued" in the running head on the final two pages of both. Freud received his copy on November 5, 1910, so it must have been mailed in late October. Clark's own copies were accessioned in November. For its subsequent publishing history, see chapter 3.

*5. *The Interpretation of Dreams*. New York: MacMillan Co. April 1913. xiv+1–510 pages. $4.00

Title Page: THE INTERPRETATION | OF DREAMS | BY | PROF. DR. SIGMUND FREUD, LL.D. | AUTHORISED TRANSLATION OF THIRD EDITION | WITH INTRODUCTION BY A. A. BRILL, PH.B., M.D. | CHIEF OF THE NEUROLOGICAL DEPARTMENT OF THE BRONX HOSPITAL AND DISPENSARY | CLINICAL ASSISTANT IN NEUROLOGY AND PSYCHIATRY, COLUMBIA UNIVERSITY | FORMER ASSISTANT PHYSICIAN IN THE CENTRAL ISLIP STATE HOSPITAL | AND IN THE CLINIC OF PSYCHIATRY, ZÜRICH/ " *Flectere si nequeo superos, Acheronta movebo* " | NEW YORK | THE MACMILLAN COMPANY | 1913

Pagination: [i] blank ; [ii] blank ; [iii] title page ; [iv] Printed by BALLANTYNE, HANSON & CO. | At the Ballantyne Press, Edinburgh. ; v–vi Introductory

Remarks ; vii–[viii] Preface to the Second [1908 German] Edition ; ix– × Preface to the Third [1911 German] Edition ; xi–xii Translator's Preface ; xiii Contents ; [xiv] blank ; [1]–493 text ; 494–499 Literary Index [bibliography] ; [500] blank ; 501–510 Index [at foot of 510:] Printed by Ballantyne, Hanson & Co., Edinburgh & London. ; [two blank leaves].

Binding: Blue cloth printed in gold on cover: THE INTERPRETATION | OF DREAMS | PROF. SIGMUND FREUD, LL.D. and on spine: THE | INTERPRE-TATION | OF DREAMS | SIGMUND FREUD, LL.D. | A. A. BRILL, M.D. | THE MACMILLAN | COMPANY

Copyright entered: No copyright registration located.

Notes: Bound from sheets printed in England. Found in two states. *First state*: A typographical error omits the word "confronted" on page 87. Some copies had a small erratum slip pasted in opposite page 1 noting, "Page 87, line 3 from bottom, *for* 'I shall certainly be with doubts,' *read* 'I shall certainly be confronted with doubts." The verso of the title page identifies the printer. *Second state*: The error on page 87 has been corrected but otherwise the book appears identical to the first state. In later printings, the versos of the title pages list the earliest impression as having been issued in London in February, March, or April 1913. The correct month is April 1913: *The Interpretation of Dreams* was listed in *The Bookseller* (London) on April 11, 1913, and William Allen wrote Brill on April 17th, "by now you will have received your copies..." The impressions of April and May 1913 probably numbered 250 or 500 copies each, most of which were exported to Macmillan in New York: a year earlier Macmillan had agreed to import 500 copies but reduced that to only 250 in June 1912.[1] A balance sheet dated December 31, 1913, in box 15 of the Brill Papers at LOC reports a total of 1,763 copies printed and bound during the book's first year, 1,457 of which were sold to Macmillan in New York, 246 sold in London, and 60 distributed free to the press and others. For its subsequent publishing history, see chapter 5.

**6. On Dreams. New York: Rebman Company, July 1914. xxxii+110 pages. $1.00

Title Page: ON DREAMS | BY | PROF. DR. SIGM. FREUD | ONLY AUTHO-RISED ENGLISH TRANSLATION | BY | M. D. EDER | FROM THE SECOND GERMAN EDITION | WITH AN INTRODUCTION BY | W. LESLIE MACKEN-ZIE, M.A., M.D., LL.D. | MEDICAL MEMBER OF THE LOCAL GOVERNMENT BOARD FOR SCOTLAND; | LATE FERGUSON SCHOLAR IN PHILOSOPHY; LATE EXAMINER IN | MENTAL PHILOSOPHY, UNIVERSITY OF ABER-DEEN | [publisher's logo] | NEW YORK | REBMAN COMPANY | HERALD SQUARE BUILDING | 141–145 West 36TH STREET

Pagination: blank leaf ; half-title ; advertisement for Jung's *Studies in Word Association* ; [i] title page ; [ii] *All rights reserved | Printed in Great Britain* ; iii Contents ; [iv] blank ; v–xxxii Introduction ; 1–110 text [foot of 110, below a ruled line:] WOODS & SONS, LTD., PRINTERS, LONDON, N. ; blank leaf.

Binding: Light gray/off-white cloth printed on spine in black, reading head to foot: FREUD [rule] ON DREAMS

Copyright entered: No copyright registration located.

Notes: Bound from sheets printed in England. The number of copies issued is not known. Found in two states, neither of which is dated. *First state*: The title page includes a line at the foot giving the publisher's location above the street address as "Herald Square Building" and its verso has *"All rights reserved"* at center and *"Printed in Great Britain"* at lower left. The printer is identified at the foot of page 110 as Woods and Sons, London, below a ruled line. *Second state:* The title page does not include the line "Herald Square Building" and its verso contains only the single line, "All Rights Reserved." The printer's acknowledgment at the foot of page 110 does not include a ruled line above the text but is otherwise identical to the first state. A 1915 issue was bound in yellow cloth and identified the printer on page 110 as, "BILLING AND SONS, LTD., PRINTERS, GUILDFORD." For its subsequent publishing history, see chapter 5.

**7. *Psychopathology of Everyday Life*. New York: Macmillan Co., August 1914. viii+342. $3.50

Title Page: PSYCHOPATHOLOGY | OF EVERYDAY LIFE | BY | PROFESSOR DR. SIGMUND FREUD, LL.D. | AUTHORIZED ENGLISH EDITION, WITH | INTRODUCTION BY | A. A. BRILL, Ph.B., M.D. | *Chief of Clinic of Psychiatry Columbia University ; Chief of the | Neurological Department, Bronx Hospital and Dispensary ; | former Assistant Physician in the Central Islip State | Hospital, and in the Clinic of Psychiatry, Zurich* | NEW YORK | THE MACMILLAN COMPANY | 1914

Pagination: [i] half-title ; [ii] blank ; [iii] title page ; [iv, at foot:] (All rights reserved) ; v–vi Introduction by Brill ; vii Contents ; [viii] blank ; [1] section title ; [2] blank ; 3–338 text ; 339–[342] Index [at foot of 342:] UNWIN BROTHERS, LIMITED, THE GRESHAM PRESS, WOKING AND LONDON

Binding: Bluish-gray cloth printed in gold on spine: PSYCHOPATHOLOGY | OF | EVERYDAY LIFE | [rule] | FREUD | [rule] | BRILL | [at foot:] MACMILLAN [four dots]

Copyright entered: No copyright registration found.

Notes: Bound from sheets printed in England. The number of copies printed is not known. For its subsequent publishing history, see chapter 5.

**8. *Modern Sexual Morality and Modern Nervousness*. New York: Critic and Guide Co., October 1915. 16 pages. 25 cents

Title Page: Self-wrappers; see binding description below.

Pagination: [cover] ; [inside cover with advertisements] ; 1–15 text ; [16] blank ; [inside rear cover, with advertisement] ; [back cover]. This is essentially the same setting of type as in Robinson's *American Journal of Urology*, October 1915, pages 391–405, with the layout slightly adjusted and new page numbers inserted to accommodate the pamphlet format.

Binding: Paper wrappers, printed as follows on front wrapper: Modern Sexual Morality | and | Modern Nervousness | By Sigmund Freud, M.D., LL.D. | VIENNA | CRITIC AND GUIDE CO. | 12 MT. MORRIS PARK W. | NEW YORK | Copyright 1915, by Dr. Wm. J. Robinson.

Copyright entered: No copyright registration found, despite Robinson's claim on the cover.

Notes: Only one copy is known to survive (at the Library of Congress). For its subsequent publishing history, see chapter 7.

**9. *Wit and Its Relation to the Unconscious*. New York: Moffat, Yard and Company, September 30, 1916. x+388 pages. $1.25

Modern Sexual Morality
and
Modern Nervousness

By Sigmund Freud, M. D., LL.D.

VIENNA

CRITIC AND GUIDE CO.
12 MT. MORRIS PARK W.
NEW YORK

The only known copy of Freud's *Modern Sexual Morality and Modern Nervousness*, pirated by William Robinson in 1915 (Library of Congress, Sigmund Freud Collection, call no. RC530.F73513, 1915).

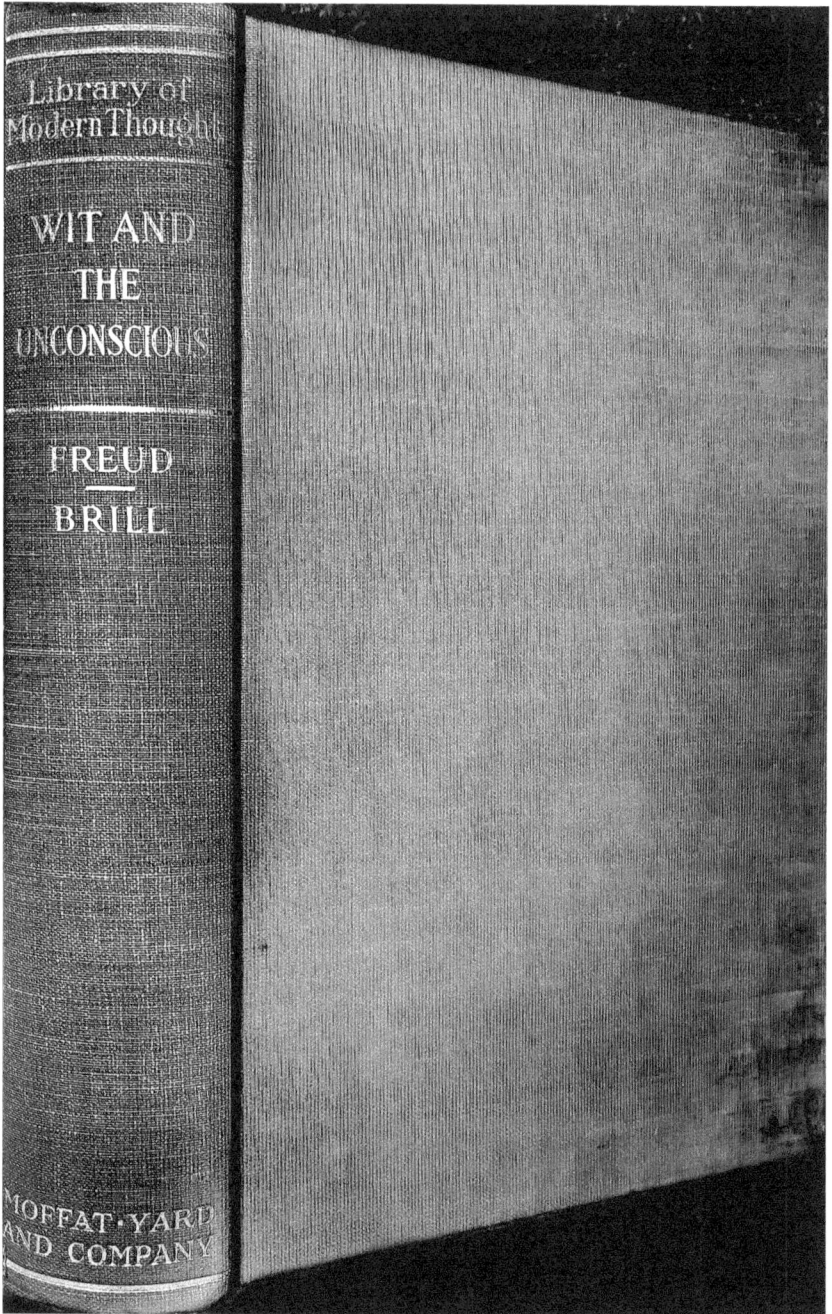

First edition, third issue of *Wit and Its Relation to the Unconscious* for the
Library of Modern Thought, 1917 (author's collection).

Title Page: WIT AND ITS RELATION | TO THE UNCONSCIOUS | BY | PROFESSOR DR. SIGMUND FREUD, LL.D. | Authorized English Edition, with Introduction by | A. A. BRILL, PH.B., M.D. | Lecturer in Psychoanalysis and Abnormal Psychology, | New York University; former Chief of Clinic | of Psychiatry, Columbia University | [publisher's logo] | NEW YORK | MOFFAT, YARD AND COMPANY | 1916

Pagination: [i] half-title ; [ii] blank; [iii] title page ; [iv] Copyright, 1916, BY | MOFFAT, YARD AND COMPANY | NEW YORK | [rule] *All Rights Reserved* ; v–[vii] Translator's Preface ; [viii] blank ; [ix] Contents ; [x] blank ; [1] section title ; [2] blank ; 3–384 text ; 385–388 Index.

Binding: Blue-gray cloth stamped in gold on the spine: [double rule] | WIT AND | THE | UNCONSCIOUS | [rule] | FREUD | [rule] | BRILL | [at foot:] MOFFAT YARD | AND COMPANY | [double rule]

Copyright entered: September 30, 1916.

Notes: A second issue was published by Kegan Paul in London in December 1916 made up from the American sheets. A third issue, also bound from the original 1916 sheets, was published in Moffat, Yard & Co.'s "Library of Modern Thought" in September 1917 bound in red cloth stamped in gold, with a frontispiece photo of Freud not found in the trade issue. A fourth issue was printed in November 1917 bound in blue cloth stamped in black on its spine. The number of copies published in each issue is not known, but on January 31, 1924, Moffat, Yard & Co. reported that a total of only 1,465 copies had been sold to date and they still had 300 in stock.[2] For its subsequent publishing history, see chapter 8.

**10. *Leonardo da Vinci, A Psychosexual Study of an Infantile Reminiscence.* New York: Moffat, Yard & Co., September 30, 1916. vi+130 pages. $1.25

Title Page: Leonardo da Vinci | A PSYCHOSEXUAL STUDY OF AN | INFANTILE REMINISCENCE | BY | PROFESSOR DR. SIGMUND FREUD, LL.D. | (UNIVERSITY OF VIENNA) | TRANSLATED BY | A. A. BRILL, PH.B., M.D. | Lecturer in Psychoanalysis and Abnormal | Psychology, New York University | [publisher's logo] | NEW YORK | MOFFAT, YARD & COMPANY | 1916

Pagination: [i] blank ; [ii] portrait of Leonardo; [iii] title page ; [iv] COPYRIGHT, 1916, BY | MOFFAT, YARD & COMPANY ; [v] list of illustrations ; [vi] blank ; 1–130 text [foot of 130: THE END]

Binding: Dark green cloth printed in gold: LEONARDO | DA VINCI | [rule] | FREUD | [rule] | BRILL | [at foot:] MOFFAT | YARD & CO

Copyright entered: September 30, 1916.

Notes: In March 1919 the book was challenged as obscene by the New York Society for the Suppression of Vice and taken to court (see Chapter 9). The number of copies printed is not known, but on January 31, 1924, Moffat, Yard & Co. reported that a total of just 1,310 copies had been sold to date, only 94 them in 1923.[3] For its subsequent publishing history, see chapters 8 and 9.

11. *Delusion and Dream, An Interpretation in the Light of Psychoanalysis of Gradiva, a Novel.* New York: Moffat, Yard, September 22, 1917. viii+244 pages. $2.00.

Title Page: DELUSION AND DREAM | An Interpretation in the Light of Psychoanalysis | of *Gradiva*, a Novel, by Wilhelm Jensen, | Which is Here Translated |

BY | DR. SIGMUND FREUD | Author of "WIt and its Relation to the Unconscious," | "Leonardo da Vinci," etc. | TRANSLATED BY | HELEN M. DOWNEY, M.A. | INTRODUCTION BY | DR. G. STANLEY HALL | President of Clark University | [publisher's logo] | NEW YORK | MOFFAT, YARD AND COMPANY | 1917

Pagination: [blank leaf] ; [i] title page ; [ii] Copyright, 1917, by | MOFFAT, YARD AND COMPANY | [rule] ; *Published September, 1917* ; [iii–iv] Preface by Helen Downey ; [v–vi] Introduction by G. Stanley Hall ; [vii] contents ; [viii] blank ; [1] half-title ; [2] blank ; [3]-118 Jensen's *Gradiva* ; [119] section title ; [120] blank ; 121–243 Freud's commentary ; [blank leaf]

Binding: Blue cloth with spine printed in gold: [double rule] | DELUSION | AND | DREAM | [rule] FREUD [at foot] MOFFAT YARD | AND COMPANY | [double rule]

Copyright entered: September 22, 1917.

Notes: The number of copies printed is not known, but on January 31, 1924, Moffat, Yard & Co. reported that it had sold a total of 1,363 copies to date. In 1939, the Overbrook Press, a private press specializing in fine illustrated books, requested and received permission from Dodd Mead to bring out a limited edition of 175 copies illustrated by Salvador Dali, who had proposed the idea but no evidence has been found that this edition was ever printed.[4] For its subsequent publishing history, see chapter 8.

12. *The History of the Psychoanalytic Movement.* New York: Nervous & Mental Disease Pub. Co., February 1917. iv+58 pages. 60 cents.

Title Page: NERVOUS AND MENTAL DISEASE MONOGRAPH SERIES No. 25 | THE HISTORY OF THE | PSYCHOANALYTIC MOVEMENT | BY | PROF. DR. SIGMUND FREUD, LL.D. | OF VIENNA | AUTHORIZED ENGLISH TRANSLATION BY | A. A. BRILL, PH.B., M.D. | LECTURER IN PSYCHOANAL-YSIS AND ABNORMAL PSYCHOLOGY, NEW YORK UNIVERSITY | FORMER CHIEF OF CLINIC OF PSYCHIATRY, COLUMBIA UNIVERSITY | NEW YORK | THE NERVOUS AND MENTAL DISEASE | PUBLISHING COMPANY | 1917

Pagination: [i] title page ; [ii] verso of title page, including advertisement for series numbers 1–25 and: Copyright, 1917 by | NERVOUS AND MENTAL DISEASE PUBLISHING COMPANY | PRESS OF | THE NEW ERA PRINTING COMPANY | LANCASTER, PA ; iii *Fluctuat nec mergitur* ["It is tossed by the waves, but does not sink"] | From the Coat of Arms of the City of Paris ; [iv] blank ; 1–58 text ; [six pages of advertisements for the series, the *Journal of Nervous and Mental Disease*, and the *Psychoanalytic Review*, dated October 1916]

Binding: The earliest copies were issued in brown paper over boards and the title page dated at foot 1916; later copies were issued in paper wrappers but dated 1917 on the title page. Inside front cover and both sides of the back cover contain advertisements for the monograph series; six pages of advertisements are also present at the end.

Copyright entered: February 15, 1917.

Notes: The number of copies printed is not known. For its subsequent publishing history, see chapter 2.

*13. *Reflections on War and Death.* New York: Moffat, Yard, April 13, 1918. viii+72. 75 cents.

Title Page: REFLECTIONS | ON WAR AND DEATH | *By* | PROFESSOR DR. SIGMUND FREUD, LL.D. | *Authorized English Translation By* | DR. A. A. BRILL and | ALFRED B. KUTTNER | [pendant leaf decoration] | MOFFAT, YARD AND COMPANY | NEW YORK | 1918

Pagination: [i] half title ; [ii] blank ; [iii] title page ; [iv] Copyright, 1918, by | MOFFAT, YARD , AND COMPANY ; [v] translators' note ; [vi] blank ; [vii] [section title] ; [viii] blank ; 1–72 text.

Binding: Red cloth printed in white, on cover: REFLECTIONS ON | WAR AND DEATH | [at foot:] SIGMUND FREUD [and on spine, reading head to foot:] REFLECTIONS ON WAR AND DEATH–FREUD

Copyright entered: April 13, 1918.

Notes: The number of copies printed is not known. In 1922, a second edition of 500 copies was printed, bound in red stamped in gold with the single-word title, "Reflections." In January 1924 Moffat, Yard & Co. reported that a total of 423 copies had been sold to date.[5] For its subsequent publishing history, see chapter 8.

*14. *Totem and Taboo, Resemblances between the Psychic Lives of Savages and Neurotics.* New York: Moffat, Yard and company, May 31, 1918. xii+266 pages. $2.00.

Title Page: TOTEM AND TABOO | RESEMBLANCES BETWEEN THE PSYCHIC | LIVES OF SAVAGES AND NEUROTICS | BY | PROFESSOR DR. SIGMUND FREUD, LL. D. | Authorized English Translation | with Introduction by | A. A. BRILL, Ph. B., M.D. | Asst. Prof. of Psychiatry, N.Y. Post Graduate Medical | School; Lecturer in Psychoanalysis and Ab- | normal Psychology, New York University; | former Chief of Clinic of Psychiatry, | Columbia University | [publisher's logo] | NEW YORK | MOFFAT, YARD AND COMPANY | 1918

Pagination: [blank leaf] ; [i] title page ; [ii] Copyright, 1918, by | MOFFAT, YARD AND COMPANY ; iii–v author's preface ; [vi] blank ; vii–x translator's preface ; [xi] contents ; [xii] blank ; 1–265 text ; [266] blank ; [blank leaf]

Binding: Blue cloth stamped in gold on spine: [double rule across head] | TOTEM | AND | TABOO | FREUD [rule] | BRILL | [at foot:] MOFFAT YARD / AND COMPANY | [double rule}

Copyright entered: May 24, 1918. Library of Congress deposit copy accessioned May 31, 1918.

Notes: The number of copies printed is unknown. In January 1924 Moffat, Yard & Co. reported that a total of 1,567 had been sold to date.[6] For its subsequent publishing history, see chapter 8.

**15. *A General Introduction to Psychoanalysis.* New York: Boni and Liveright, June 30, 1920. xii+406 pages. $4.50

Title Page: A General Introduction | to | Psychoanalysis | BY | PROF. SIGMUND FREUD, LL.D. | AUTHORIZED TRANSLATION | WITH A PREFACE | BY | G. STANLEY HALL | PRESIDENT, CLARK UNIVERSITY | BONI AND LIVERIGHT | PUBLISHERS NEW YORK

Pagination: [i] half-title ; [ii] blank ; [frontispiece] ; [iii] title page ; [iv] Published, 1920, by | BONI & LIVERIGHT, INC. | *Printed in the United States of America* | COPYRIGHT, 1920, BY EDWARD L. BERNAYS ; v–vii Preface by G. Stanley Hall ; [viii] blank ; ix–x contents ; [xi] section title ; [xii] blank ; 1–402 text; [403]–406 index ; blank leaf.

Binding: Dark blue cloth printed in gold on spine: A GENERAL | INTRO-DUCTION TO | PSYCHOANALYSIS | SIGMUND | FREUD, L.L.D. | [at foot:] BONI AND | LIVERIGHT Front cover printed in gold: A GENERAL INTRO-DUCTION TO | PSYCHOANALYSIS | PROF. SIGMUND FREUD, LL.D. Light blue paper dust jacket printed in black.

Copyright entered: June 22, 1920, in Bernays's name rather than Freud's.

Notes: Boni and Liveright's account ledgers show that two printings were ordered in June 1920 before the book was published, totaling 2,200 copies. 1,250 copies of these were bound and delivered on June 30, 1920. Another 1,353 were bound and delivered in July, after another impression (the third) of 2,000 had been printed. Subsequent impressions are listed on the verso of title pages through 1935.[7] For its subsequent publishing history, see chapter 10.

16. Dream Psychology: Psychoanalysis for Beginners. New York: The James A. McCann Co., late 1920. xii+237 pages. $3.50

Title Page: DREAM PSYCHOLOGY | PSYCHOANALYSIS FOR BEGIN-NERS | BY | PROF. DR. SIGMUND FREUD | AUTHORIZED ENGLISH TRANS-LATION | BY /M. D. EDER | WITH AN INTRODUCTION BY ANDRÉ TRIDON | Author of "Psychoanalysis, its History, Theory and | Practice." "Psychoanaly-sis and Behavior"' and | "Psychoanalysis, Sleep and Dreams" | NEW YORK | THE JAMES A. McCANN COMPANY | 1920

Pagination: [blank leaf] [i] title page ; [ii, title page verso:] Copyright, 1920, by | THE JAMES A. McCANN COMPANY | All Rights Reserved | PRINTED IN THE U.S. A | [rule] ; [iii]–xi Introduction dated November 1920 ; [xii blank] ; [xiii] contents ; [xiv] blank ; 1–237 text ; [238 blank] ; [blank leaf]

Binding: Dark blue cloth printed in gold or white on spine: DREAM | PSY-CHOLOGY | [three dots in triangle] | SIGMUND | FREUD

Copyright entered: December 1, 1920, with protection claimed only for the introduction.

Notes: The first issue is dated 1920 on the title page. A second issue appeared in February 1921 with a new title page on which the lines crediting the translation to Eder are omitted, the list of Tridon's works is expanded to include *Easy Lesson [sic] in Psychoanalysis*, and the company logo appears. The number of copies printed is not known. For further details, see chapter 11.

17. Group Psychology and the Analysis of the Ego. New York: Boni and Liv-eright, September 1924. viii+136 pages. $2.00

Title Page: GROUP PSYCHOLOGY | AND | THE ANALYSIS OF THE EGO | BY | SIGMUND FREUD, M.D., LL.D. | AUTHORIZED TRANSLATION | BY | JAMES STRACHEY | [oval logo with silhouette of scribe at desk] | BONI AND LIVERIGHT | PUBLISHERS :: :: NEW YORK

Pagination: blank leaf ; [i] half-title ; [ii] blank ; [iii] title page ; [iv] blank ; [v] translator's note ; [vi] blank ; [vii] contents ; [viii] blank ; 1–127 text ; [128] blank ; [129]–134 index ; [135] advertisement for six titles in International Psycho-ana-lytical Library and International Journal of Psycho-Analysis ; [136] Printed by K. Liebel in Vienna, II. | Grosse Mohrengasse 23

Binding: Gray cloth printed in gold on spine: [rule] GROUP | PSYCHOLOGY | AND THE | ANALYSIS | OF THE | EGO | FREUD | [rule at foot]. Dust jacket off-white paper heavily printed with text, including a series title "Researches [*sic*] in Human Herd Instincts" and price of $2.00 on cover.

Copyright entered: copyright not registered.

Notes: In the spring of 1924 2,000 sets of sheets were imported from the Hogarth Press in London and given a new title page.[8] No date is printed anywhere on the book, but it was reviewed in the *Boston Evening Transcript* on September 6, 1924, and the *New York Times Book Review*, September 7, 1924. For its subsequent publishing history, see chapter 10.

**18. *Beyond the Pleasure Principle.* New York: Boni & Liveright, September 1924. viii+92 pages. $1.50

Title Page: BEYOND THE | PLEASURE | PRINCIPLE | BY | SIGMUND FREUD, M.D., LL.D. | AUTHORIZED TRANSLATION | FROM THE SECOND GERMAN EDITION | BY C. J. M. HUBBACK | [oval logo with silhouette of scribe at desk] | BONI AND LIVERIGHT | PUBLISHERS :: :: NEW YORK

Pagination: [i] half-title ; [ii] blank ; [iii] title page ; [iv] blank ; [v] editorial preface ; [vi] blank ; [vii] half-title ; [viii] blank ; 1–83 text ; [84] blank ; 85–90 index ; [91] advertisement listing six books and journal ; [92] PRINTED IN VIENNA BY THE | SOCIETY FOR GRAPHIC INDUSTRY

Binding: Gray cloth printed in gold on spine: [rule] | BEYOND | THE /PLEASURE | PRINCIPLE | FREUD | [rule] | [at foot:] BONI & | LIVERIGHT

Copyright entered: no copyright registered.

Notes: In the spring of 1924 2,000 sets of sheets were imported from the Hogarth Press in London and given a new title page.[9] No date is printed anywhere on the book, but it was reviewed in the *Boston Evening Transcript* on September 6, 1924, and the *New York Times Book Review*, September 7, 1924. The printer, Society for Graphic Industry or Gesellschaft für Graphische Industrie, had printed the original German edition in 1921. For its subsequent publishing history, see chapter 10.

*19. Van Teslaar, James, ed. ***An Outline of Psychoanalysis.*** New York: Boni and Liveright, September 1924. xx+384 pages. 60 cents.

Title Page: [within double-ruled page border] AN OUTLINE OF | PSYCHO-ANALYSIS | [rule] EDITED BY J.S. VAN TESLAAR | [rule] | [torch bearer logo by Lucian Bernhart] | THE MODERN LIBRARY | [rule] | PUBLISHERS :: :: NEW YORK

Pagination: [i] half-title ; [ii] paragraph describing Modern Library series ; [iii] title page as above ; [iv] AN OUTLINE OF PSYCHOANALYSIS | [rule] | COPYRIGHT, 1924, BY | BONI & LIVERIGHT, INC | [at foot:] MANUFACTURED IN THE UNITED STATES OF AMERICA | FOR THE MODERN LIBRARY, INC., BY H. WOLFF ; [v]–xvi Editor's Introduction ; xvii–xviii Contents ; [xix] section title ; [xx blank] ; 21–383 text ; [384 blank]

Binding: Imitation leather ("leatherette") in brown, blue, or green. Spine stamped in gold as follows: [double rule] | AN | OUTLINE | OF | PSYCHO | ANALYSIS | [triangle of three dots] | VAN TESLAAR | [at foot:] MODERN | LIBRARY | [double rule]. Front cover is stamped in gold with Bernhart torch bearer logo. No catalog of other Modern Library titles appears at the end. Dust jacket off-white paper printed in black and red. Endpapers printed in diamond pane design by Lucian Bernhart.

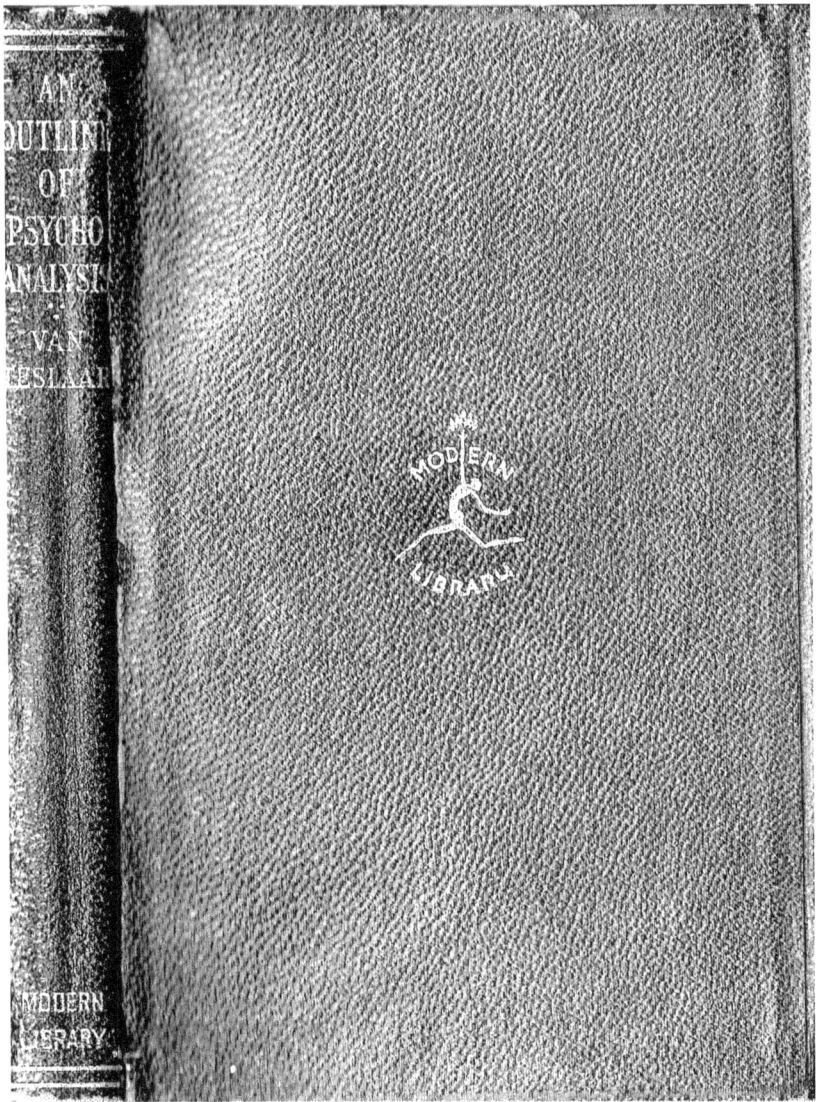

Modern Library's anthology *An Outline of Psychoanalysis*, 1924 (author's collection).

Copyright entered: No copyright registered.
Notes: Modern Library title no. 66. The first issue, rarely met with, is dated 1924 on the verso of the title page; later impressions include on the verso of the title page, *"Copyright, 1925, by* | THE MODERN LIBRARY." Announced in *Publishers Weekly*'s "Weekly Record" of new books on September 20, 1924; advertised as "Just Published in the Modern Library" in the *New York Times Book Review*

on November 2, 1924. Three completely different books bear the title *An Outline of Psychoanalysis*: in 1955 Modern Library let Van Teslaar's collection go out of print and issued a new one compiled by Clara Thompson and others with entirely different contents. Neither of these Modern Library volumes should be confused with Freud's own *An Outline of Psychoanalysis* published in 1949 in London by the Hogarth Press and in New York by W.W. Norton. For subsequent publishing history, see chapter 12.

20. Contributions to Works by Other Authors.

Freud was generous in providing introductions and prefaces to colleagues: volume 24 of the *Standard Edition* lists 23 such contributions to the works of other authors and editors. Listed below are those that appeared in American books through the year 1924.

20a. Pfister, Oskar. *The Psychoanalytic Method.* New York: Moffatt & Yard, 1917. xx+588 pages. Published in late January 1917. Blue cloth with spine printed in gold. Freud's introduction is on pages v–viii, dated February 1913. The book also includes a one-page introductory note by G. Stanley Hall and a translator's note by Charles Rockwell Payne stating that "the author entirely revised the book in 1915 and sent me these revisions and changes to be incorporated in my translation." Printed in *Standard Edition*, vol. 12.

20b. Putnam, James Jackson. *Addresses on Psychoanalysis, with a Preface by Sigmund Freud.* London and New York: International Psycho-analytical Press, 1921. x+470 pages. Green cloth printed in gold on spine and front cover. International Psycho–analytical Library, no. 1. Freud's preface on pages iii–v is dated January 1921. Printed in *Standard Edition*, vol. 18.

20c. Varendonck, Julien. *The Psychology of Day-Dreams.* London: G. Allen & Unwin, Ltd.; New York: The Macmillan Company, 1921. 368 pages. Black cloth printed in gold on spine, with gold ruled border on front cover. Written in English by the author. Freud's introduction is on pages 9–10. Printed in *Standard Edition*, vol. 18.

20d. *A Young Girl's Diary, with a Preface by Sigmund Freud.* New York: Thomas Seltzer, 1921. Translated by Eden and Cedar Paul. 285 pages. Boards covered in green cloth, spine in off-white cloth with printed paper label. Preface contains Freud's two-page letter dated April 27, 1915. For Seltzer's career and the prosecution of this book under U.S. obscenity laws, see Chapter 9. Printed in *Standard Edition*, vol. 14.

20e. Ferenczi, Sandor, et al. *Psycho-Analysis and the War Neuroses* by Drs. S. Ferenczi (Budapest), Karl Abraham (Berlin), Ernst Simmel (Berlin) and Ernest Jones (London). Introduction By Prof. Sigm. Freud. (Vienna). London, Vienna, and New York: The International Psycho-Analytical Press, 1921. vi+59 pages. Green cloth printed in gold on spine and front cover. International Psycho-analytical Library, no. 2. Freud's introduction is on pages 1–4. Papers given at the Fifth International Psycho-Analytical Congress at Budapest, September 1918, supplemented with a paper by Jones. Printed in *Standard Edition*, vol. 17.

20f. *These Eventful Years: The Twentieth Century in the Making.* London and New York: Encyclopedia Britannica Company Limited, 1924. Two volumes. Black cloth printed in gold with pictorial dust jackets. 1,500 copies were specially bound in dark olive leather with top edges gilt and ornate floral design in gold on front covers. Vol. II (xii+695 pages) contains Freud's essay, "Psycho-Analysis: Exploring the Hidden Recesses of the Mind" on 511–523. Freud was unhappy with the first translation of his essay, writing to Brill on March 24, 1924, "Thank you very much for taking on the unsuccessful translation for the History of our own times. She [unnamed translator] really was scandalously bad, unscrupulous, in the most vulgar manner, and I have to give Mr. Hooper credit for making no attempt to apologize. I'm glad you've acted as my translator again, and the whole affair may give you an indication that the severing of this one relationship hasn't changed anything else between us."[10] Printed in *Standard Edition*, vol. 19.

Chapter Notes

Introduction

1. Sigmund Freud, "Origin and Development of Psychoanalysis," *American Journal of Psychology* 21 (April 1910): 206. Freud, *An Autobiographical Study* (New York: W.W. Norton, 1935), 87.

2. Theodore Dreiser, *Twelve Men* (New York: Modern Library, 1928), 212.

3. Edward Bok, *The Americanization of Edward Bok* (New York: Scribner's, 1920), 345–350. Ernest Jones, *The Life and Work of Sigmund Freud. Volume 2: Years of Maturity 1901–1919* (New York: Basic Books, 1955), 88. Mabel Dodge, *European Experiences* (New York: Harcourt, Brace, 1935), 36.

4. Freud, "Preface to the Third (Revised) English Edition," *The Interpretation of Dreams* (London: Hogarth Press, 1953), *Standard Edition* vol. 4, xxxii. Fritz Wittels, "Brill: The Pioneer," *The Psychoanalytic Review* 35 (1948): 394.

5. "mistake": Ernest Jones, *The Life and Work of Sigmund Freud. Volume 2: Years of Maturity, 1901–1919* (New York: Basic Books, 1955), 60; this comment is recalled slightly differently in Jones's memoir, *Free Associations* (New York: Basic Books, 1959), 191: "Yes, America is gigantic, but a gigantic mistake." Freud to Brill, January 27, 1923, in the Freud Papers at the Library of Congress: General Correspondence, Freud to Brill, Transcripts, viewed online August 12, 2022, at https://www.loc.gov/resource/mss39990.01905/?sp=12. Freud to Downey, March 1, 1922, in the Freud Papers at the Library of Congress: General Correspondence, 1871–1996; Downey, Helen, 1922, viewed online September 28, 2022, at https://hdl.loc.gov/loc.mss/ms004017.mss39990.00535.

6. G.C. Meynell, "Freud Translated: An Historical and Bibliographical Note," *Journal of the Royal Society of Medicine* 74 (April 1981): 306.

7. Louis Menand, "Why Freud Survives," *New Yorker*, August 28, 2017. Andrew Scull, *Desperate Remedies: Psychiatry's Turbulent Quest to Cure Mental Illness* (Cambridge: Harvard University Press, 2022), xv, 252, 377–378. See Epilogue for more on the history of Freud's reputation.

8. Matt Ffytche, *Sigmund Freud* (London: Reaktion Books, 2022), 13–14.

Chapter 1

1. G. Stanley Hall, *Life and Confessions of a Psychologist* (New York: Appleton, 1924), 333. Junius F. Brown, "Freud's Influence on American Psychology," *Psychoanalytic Quarterly* 9 (1940): 283. Barbara Sicherman, "The New Psychiatry: Medical and Behavioral Science, 1895–1921" in Jacques M. Quen and Eric T. Carlson, *American Psychoanalysis: Origins and Development* (New York: Brunner/Mazel, 1978), 20.

2. Alexander Grinstein, "Freud's First Publications in America," *Journal of the American Psychoanalytic Association* 19, no. 2 (1971): 241–264. See Part B of the bibliography below for references to Freud's work, 1882–1909.

3. "Spina's Studies on the Bacillus of Tuberculosis," *Medical News* (April 7, 1883): 401–402 (unsigned). A two-column, 13-paragraph review of *Studien über Tuberculose* by Arnold Spina (Vienna: W. Braumüller, 1883).

4. "Prospectus," *Medical News and Library* 1, no. 1 (January 1843): 1.

5. Freud's letter is quoted in Grin-
stein, "Freud's First Publications in Amer-
ica," 241. Peter Gay, *Freud: A Life for Our
Time* (New York: W.W. Norton, 2006), 32.
William James, "Über den Psychischen
Mechanismus Hysterischer Phänomene,"
Psychological Review 1 (March 1894): 199;
a one-paragraph abstract of Freud and
Breuer's article, signed only with initials.
James Strachey, "Editor's Introduction" in
Freud and Breuer, *Studies on Hysteria*, vol.
2 of *The Standard Edition of the Complete
Psychological Works of Sigmund Freud*
(London: Hogarth Press, 1955), x–xii.

6. *Alienist and Neurologist* 17 (October 1896): 519–520, and 20 (January 1899):
113–114.

7. Mark Sullivan, *Our Times; the United
States, 1900–1925* (New York: Scribner's,
1936), vol. 1, 61–64. Centers for Disease
Control, "Achievements in Public Health,
1900–1999: Healthier Mothers and
Babies," *Morbidity and Mortality Weekly
Report* 48, no. 38 (October 1, 1999): 849.

8. William James, *The Principles of Psychology* (New York: Henry Holt, 1891),
vol. 1, 164–170. Hugo Münsterberg, *Über
Aufgaben und Methoden der Psychologie*
(Leipzig: Ambr. Abel, 1891), 110.

9. James Strachey, "Editor's Intro-
duction" in Freud, *The Interpretation of
Dreams*, vol. 4 of the *Standard Edition*
(London: Hogarth Press, 1958), xviii–xx.
Freud, "Foreword to the Third English Edi-
tion," *The Interpretation of Dreams* (New
York: Macmillan, 1932), [9].

10. Ernest Jones, *The Life and Work of
Sigmund Freud. Edited and Abridged in
One Volume by Lionel Trilling and Steven Marcus* (New York: Basic Books,
1961), 234. Alexander Grinstein, *Sigmund
Freud's Writings: A Comprehensive Bibliography* (New York: International Universities Press, 1977). The book's reception is
described in Frank Sulloway, *Freud: Biologist of the Mind* (New York: Basic Books,
1979), 449–451, and Milton Kramer,
"Sigmund Freud's The Interpretation
of Dreams: The initial Response (1899–
1908)," *Dreaming* 4, no. 1 (March 1994):
47–52.

11. Carl Metzentin, "Wissenschaftliche
Traumdetung," *Der Deutsche Correspondent*, January 21, 1900, 6.

12. Library of Congress, "About Der
Deutsche Correspondent," *Chronicling

America* Web page accessed March 4,
2022, at https://chroniclingamerica.
loc.gov/lccn/sn83045081/. "Die Gegenwart," *Wikipedia* (German edition), accessed March 4, 2022, at https://
de.wikipedia.org/wiki/Die_Gegenwart_
(1872%E2%80%931931). Sigmund Freud,
*The Complete Letters of Sigmund Freud
to Wilhelm Fliess 1887–1904* (Cambridge:
Harvard University Press, 1985), 392.

13. "Mystery of Dreams Revealed," *San
Francisco Call*, March 18, 1900, 8.

14. Library of Congress, "About *The
San Francisco Call*," *Chronicling America* Web page accessed March 4, 2022, at
https://chroniclingamerica.loc.gov/lccn/
sn85066387/.

15. Charles A. Madison, *Critics and
Crusaders* (New York: Henry Holt,
1947), 194–214. Joseph Ishill, "Benjamin
R. Tucker: In Appreciation," *Free Vistas II* (Berkeley Heights, NJ: Oriole Press,
1937[?]), 399.

16. "The Life of Benjamin R. Tucker
Disclosed by Himself in the Principality of Monaco at the Age of 74," 43–44 and
79–80, *Benjamin R. Tucker Papers*, Box 8,
New York Public Library.

17. George Schumm, "Benj. R. Tucker—A Brief Sketch of His Life and Work,"
Freethinkers Magazine XI (July 1893):
439–440.

18. Quoted in Madison, *Critics and
Crusaders*, 216. Benjamin Tucker, *Liberty*,
July 17, 1886. James J. Martin, *Men Against
the State: The Expositors of Individualist
Anarchism in America, 1827–1908* (New
York: Libertarian Book Club, 1957), citing
circulation figures published by Tucker,
July 17, 1886, and November 2, 1895.

19. Ishill, "Benjamin R. Tucker," 299.
Horace Traubel, *With Walt Whitman in
Camden*, vol. 1 (Boston: Small, Maynard,
1906), 58 and 350.

20. Benjamin Tucker, "Are Anarchists
Thugs?" *New York Tribune*, December 4,
1898.

21. Tucker, "Are Anarchists Thugs?"

22. Levitas, *The Unterrified Jeffersonian*, 293–296.

23. "Was Ist der Traum?" *Die Grenzboten* 59 (March 15, 1900): 540–548.

24. William J. Lloyd, "Memories of
Benjamin R. Tucker" in Ishill, *Free Vistas
II*, 282.

25. Charles A. Madison, "Benjamin R.

Tucker: Individualist and Anarchist," *New England Quarterly* 16, no. 3 (September 1943): 448.

26. At Harvard and the University of Michigan. A third is in private hands.

27. Levitas, *The Unterrified Jeffersonian*, 186–187. Renate Perkons, *Benjamin R. Tucker—A Fighter Against His Age* (PhD dissertation, California State University, Fullerton, 1989), 182–188. Madison, "Benjamin R. Tucker," 451–452.

28. In the years between Tucker's 1900 pamphlet and Freud's 1909 visit to the U.S., only one article about his work appeared in a popular periodical, Frederick Peterson's "The New Divination of Dreams" in *Harper's Monthly Magazine* for August 1907.

Chapter 2

1. Smith E. Jelliffe, "The Editor Himself and His Adopted Child," *Journal of Nervous and Mental Disease* 89 (April 1939): 555–556. Jelliffe's name first appears as editor in the issue of September 1, 1900.

2. U.S. Bureau of the Census, *Occupations at the Twelfth Census* (Washington, D.C.: GPO, 1904), liv.

3. *Jelliffe: American Psychoanalyst and Physician [with] His Correspondence with Sigmund Freud and C.G. Jung*, ed. John C. Burnham and William McGuire (Chicago: University of Chicago, 1983), 59.

4. Smith E. Jelliffe, "The Editor Himself," 570–572. *Ayer & Son's American Newspaper Annual and Directory* (Philadelphia: N.W. Ayer, 1910). *Jelliffe*, 53–56.

5. Nolan D.C. Lewis, "Smith Ely Jelliffe 1866–1945: Psychosomatic Medicine in America" in *Psychoanalytic Pioneers*, ed. Franz Alexander, Samuel Eisenstein and Martin Grotjahn (New York: Basic Books, 1966), 233. John Burnham, *Psychoanalysis and American Medicine, 1894–1918* (New York: International Universities Press, 1967), 60 and 85–86. *Jelliffe*, 96 and 149–151.

6. John C. Burnham, *Jelliffe: American Psychoanalyst and Physician [with] His Correspondence with Sigmund Freud and C.G. Jung*, ed. John C. Burnham and William McGuire (Chicago: University of Chicago Press, 1983), 57 and 291.

7. Barbara Sicherman, "The New Psychiatry: Medical and Behavioral Science, 1895–1921" in Jacques M. Quen and Eric T. Carlson, *American Psychoanalysis: Origins and Development* (New York: Brunner/Mazel, 1978), 20–24.

8. A.A. Brill, "Jelliffe, the Psychiatrist and Psychoanalyst," *Journal of Nervous and Mental Disease* 89 (1939): 536.

9. *Jelliffe*, 14–16, 48–51.

10. Item 44 in Appendix 1.

11. Nathan G. Hale, ed., *James Jackson Putnam and Psychoanalysis: Letters Between Putnam and Sigmund Freud, Ernest Jones, William James, Sandor Ferenczi, and Morton Prince, 1877–1917* (Cambridge: Harvard University Press, 1971), 16–18 and 37. Clarence Oberndorf, *A History of Psychoanalysis in America* (New York: Grune and Stratton, 1953), 56 and 81–83. Burnham, *Psychoanalysis*, 7, 29, and 157–158. On Meyer, see Scull, *Desperate Remedies*, 43–55.

12. Belinda Jelliffe, interview recorded June 12, 1954, by Kurt Eissler, in the *Sigmund Freud Papers at the Library of Congress: Interviews and Recollections, 1914–1998*, image 49, viewed online August 4, 2022, at https://www.loc.gov/item/mss3999001494. Quoted in *Jelliffe*, 32.

13. Karl Menninger, "Contributions of A.A. Brill to Psychiatry," *Bulletin of the Menninger Clinic* 13, no. 5 (1949): 185. Freud, "Foreword to the Third English Edition," [9].

14. C.P. Oberndorf, "Obituary: Abraham Arden Brill," *Psychoanalytic Review* 35 (1948): 392. Jones, *Free Associations*, 230–231. Mabel Dodge Luhan, *Movers and Shakers* (Albuquerque: University of New Mexico Press, 1985), 506.

15. C.P. Oberndorf, "Obituary: Abraham Arden Brill," *Psychoanalytic Review* 35 (1948): 389.

16. A.A. Brill, "The Introduction and Development of Freud's Works in the United States," *American Journal of Sociology* 45 (November 1939): 318–319 and "Introduction" in *The Basic Writings of Sigmund Freud* (New York: Modern Library, 1938), 24.

17. William A. White, *The Autobiography of a Purpose* (New York: Doubleday, 1938), 79. White to Jelliffe May 23, 1916, Records of St. Elizabeths Hospital, National Archives, Washington, D.C.,

Record Group 418.3.3, Records of Superintendent William Alanson White, personal correspondence 1906–37, box 13.

18. Review of White's *Outlines of Psychiatry* in the *American Journal of the Medical Sciences* 136, no. 5 (May 1908): 750.

19. Burnham, *Jelliffe*, p. 60. G.C. Meynell, "Freud Translated: An Historical and Bibliographical Note," *Journal of the Royal Society of Medicine* 74 (April 1981): 306.

20. *Freud/Jung Letters*, ed. William McGuire (Princeton: Princeton University Press, 1974), 118. Ernest Jones, *Free Associations: Memories of a Psycho-Analyst* (New York: Basic Books, 1959), 168–169. Brill, "Introduction," *Basic Writings*, 27.

21. Brill, "Psychotherapies I Encountered," *Psychiatric Quarterly* 21 (1947): 581–582, and "The Introduction and Development," 324. White, *Autobiography*, 79.

22. A.A. Brill, "Reflections, Reminiscences of Sigmund Freud" in Hendrik Marinus Ruitenbeek, *Freud as We Knew Him* (Detroit: Wayne State University Press, 1973), 155. Brill to Freud on August 17, 1908, in Sigmund Freud Papers at Library of Congress: General Correspondence, 1871–1996, Brill to Freud, transcripts viewed online August 12, 2022, at https://www.loc.gov/resource/mss39990.01908/?sp=6.

23. A.A. Brill, "A Psychoanalyst Scans His Past," *Journal of Nervous & Mental Disease* 95, no. 5 (1942): 540. Jones, *Free Associations*, 231. B.D. Lewin, "Reminiscences and Retrospect" in M. Waugh, *Fruition of an Idea* (New York: International Universities Press, 1962), as quoted in Riccardo Steiner, "A World Wide International Trade Mark of Genuineness?" 82.

24. Brill to Freud, October 23, 1908, in Sigmund Freud Papers: General Correspondence, Brill to Freud, Transcripts, viewed online August 12, 2022, at www.loc.gov/resource/mss39990.01908/?sp=10.

25. *William Alanson White: The Washington Years, 1903–1937* (Washington, 1976), 69. Library of Congress, *Sigmund Freud Papers* and *www.freud-edition.net*.

26. White to Brill, July 20 and August 4, 1909, in "Nervous and Mental Disease Publishing Co.," Brill Papers at the Library of Congress, Box 5, folder 9. Brill later translated Breuer and Freud's 1895 book as

Studies in Hysteria and Jelliffe and White published it as Nervous & Mental Disease Monograph 61 in 1937.

27. Saul Rosenzweig, *Freud, Jung and Hall the King-Maker: The Expedition to America (1909)* (St. Louis: Rana House, 1992), 58. Library of Congress. Copyright Office, *Catalog of Copyright Entries, 1909* (November 11, 1909), 5992, entry 5988. The book was copyrighted on September 30 and deposit copies received October 2.

28. A.A. Brill Papers (MSS51748) at the Library of Congress, Box 5, folder 9. Interview with Mrs. S.E. Jelliffe June 12, 1954, in Interviews and Recollections recorded by Kurt Eissler in the *Sigmund Freud Papers at the Library of Congress: Interviews and Recollections, 1914–1998*, viewed online August 3, 2022, at https://www.loc.gov/item/mss3999001494.

29. The reviews appeared in *Medical Record* 77, no. 4 (January 22, 1910): 16. *American Journal of the Medical Sciences* 139, no. 3 (March 1910): 430, review signed T.H.W. *Old Dominion Journal of Medicine and Surgery* 10 (March 1910): 236. *New England Medical Gazette* 45 (July 1910): 321–322. *Interstate Medical Journal* 17 (November 1910): 892.

30. In 1909, 62.5 Kronen was equivalent to about $360 in 2022.

31. Alex Beam, *A Great Idea at the Time: The Rise, Fall, and Curious Afterlife of the Great Books* (New York: Public Affairs, 2008), 106 and 135.

32. White to Brill June 10, 1935, and W.A. Barbour to Brill, October 15, 1935, Brill Papers at the Library of Congress, Box 5, folder 9.

33. Havelock Ellis, "The Symbolism of Dreams," *Popular Science Monthly*, July 1910, 50.

34. Ely Smith Jelliffe, "Glimpses of a Freudian Odyssey," *Psychoanalytic Quarterly* 2, no. 2 (1933): 325.

35. Henry May, *The End of American Innocence* (New York: Knopf, 1959), 235.

36. Brill, "Introduction," *Basic Writings of Sigmund Freud* (New York: Modern Library, 1938), 14. William A. White, *Forty Years of Psychiatry* (New York: Nervous and Mental Disease Publishing Co., 1933), 56.

37. Brill to Freud, November 18, 1908, in Sigmund Freud Papers: General Correspondence, Brill to Freud, Transcripts,

viewed online August 12, 2022, at www. loc.gov/resource/mss39990.01908/?sp=13. Oberndorf, "Obituary," 392–393. Putnam to Jones, September 14, 1910, in Nathan G. Hale, ed., *James Jackson Putnam and Psychoanalysis: Letters* (Cambridge: Harvard University Press, 1971), 229.

38. Burnham, *Jelliffe*, 71.

39. White to Brill, June 10, 1933, Brill Papers at the Library of Congress, Box 5, folder 9.

40. Burnham, *Jellliffe*, 187–188. Brill to Freud, December 12, 1913, in Sigmund Freud Papers: General Correspondence, Brill to Freud, Transcripts, viewed online August 12, 2022, at www.loc.gov/resource/ mss39990.01908/?sp=17. *The Complete Correspondence of Sigmund Freud and Karl Abraham, 1907– 1925: Completed Edition*, ed. Ernst Falzeder (London: Karnac, 2002), 162. Mrs. Smith Ely (Belinda) Jelliffe, interview with Kurt Eissler, June 12, 1954, in the Sigmund Freud Papers at the Library of Congress: Interviews and Recollections, 1914–1998, viewed online August 3, 2022, at https://www.loc.gov/item/mss3999001494.

41. Jones to Freud, October 22 and December 15, 1914, and Freud to Jones, December 25, 1914, in *Complete Correspondence* (letters 205, 208 and 209). *The Psycho-Analytic Review* 3 (October 1916): 406–454.

42. William White to Brill, May 9, 1916, in the Brill Papers at the Library of Congress, Box 5, folder 9.

43. White to Brill, March 15, May 13, October 10, and December 28, 1916, and Brill to White, May 12, 1916, Records of St. Elizabeth's Hospital, National Archives, Washington, D.C., Record Group 418.3.3, Records of Superintendent William Alanson White, Personal correspondence 1906–37, box 12.

44. *Jelliffe*, 24–28 and 153. Robert W. Rieber, *Freud on Interpretation* (New York: Springer, 2012), 122–125. Mrs. Smith Ely (Belinda) Jelliffe, interview with Kurt Eissler, June 12, 1954, in the Sigmund Freud Papers at the Library of Congress.

45. *Jelliffe*, 117–120.

Chapter 3

1. Excellent brief accounts are in chapter five of Peter Gay's *Freud: A Life for Our Time* (New York: W.W. Norton, 1988), chapter four of Andrew Scull's *Desperate Remedies* (Cambridge: Harvard University Press, 2022), and Richard Skues, "Clark Revisited: Reappraising Freud in America," in John Burnham, *After Freud Left* (Chicago: University of Chicago Press, 2012), 49–84. The standard book-length treatment, with lengthy quotations from unpublished primary sources, is Saul Rosenzweig, *Freud, Jung and Hall the King-Maker: The Expedition to America (1909)* (St. Louis: Rana House, 1992).

2. Quoted in Christopher D. Green, "Where Did Freud's Iceberg Metaphor of Mind Come from?" *History of Psychology, Psychology and Psychiatry in the Global World Part II* 22, no. 4 (November 2019): 370–371.

3. Clark University, *Lectures and Addresses Delivered Before the Departments of Psychology and Pedagogy in Celebration of the Twentieth Anniversary of the Opening of Clark University September 1909* (Worcester, MA: [publisher not identified], 1910), v–vi. Skues, "Clark Revisited," 66.

4. R.B. Evans and W.A. Koelsch, "Psychoanalysis Arrives in America: The 1909 Psychology Conference at Clark University," *American Psychologist* 40, no. 8 (1985): 942–948. Emma Goldman, *Living My Life* (Salt Lake City: G.M. Smith, 1982), 173 and 454–56.

5. Rosenzweig, *Freud, Jung and Hall the King-Maker*, passim. Burnham, *Jelliffe*, 189. William A. Koelsch, *Incredible Day-Dream: Freud and Jung at Clark, 1909* (Worcester, MA: Clark University, Friends of the Goddard Library, 1984), unpaginated.

6. Freud to Hall, October 21, November 21, and December 14, 1909, and January 11, 1910, Hall to Freud, October 7, November 4, December 3, and December 8, 1909, quoted in Rosenzweig, *Freud, Jung and Hall the King-Maker*.

7. Freud's five lectures were published as "The Origin and Development of Psychoanalysis" in *American Journal of Psychology* 21, no. 2 (April 1910): 181–218.

8. Koelsch, *Incredible Day-Dream*, unpaginated. Freud to Brill, November 6, 1910, in Sigmund Freud Papers: General Correspondence, 1871–1996; A.A. Brill, from Freud; Transcripts and translations;

1908–1911; translation at https://www. freud-edition.net/briefe/freud-sigmund/ brill-abraham-arden/1910/11/06, viewed August 12, 2022. Clark University Goddard Library accession books, November 1910 (personal communication from Cynthia A. Shenette, Head of Archives and Special Collections, Clark University, March 22, 2022). G. Stanley Hall Papers, Clark University, series B1–10–1: Publishers Accounts book for the *American Journal of Psychology* (personal communication from Cynthia Shenette, Head of Archives and Special Collections, Clark University). The Harvard copy is online at Hathitrust.org.
    9. Beam, *A Great Idea at the Time*, 106 and 135. *New York Times*, June 23, 1996.
    10. Ernest Jones, *The Life and Work of Sigmund Freud* (New York: Basic Books, 1953), vol. 2, 115.

Chapter 4

1. Evans and Koelsch convincingly document Hall's authorship. Circulation statistics were reported by publishers each year to *N.W. Ayer & Son's Directory of Newspapers and Periodicals* but are notoriously unreliable; I cite them here as found in the 1910 or 1911 editions of *Ayers*, but they should be taken cautiously.
    2. G. Stanley Hall, "Twentieth Anniversary of Clark University" *Nation* 89 (September 23, 1909): 284–285.
    3. Based on searches in the full-text databases *Newspapers.com*, Readex *American Newspapers*, Library of Congress *Chronicling America*, and *Reader's Guide Retrospective*. The interview was Albert Albrecht, "Prof. Sigmund Freud. The Eminent Vienna Psycho-Therapeutist Now in America," *Boston Evening Transcript*, September 11, 1909, 31.
    4. Based on searches for "Freud" or "psychoanalysis" and "psycho-analysis" in 10 full-text newspaper and periodicals databases 1900–1924, excluding brief references such as letters to the editor or footnotes.
    5. Ernest Jones, *Free Associations*, 193. A.A. Brill, "The Introduction and Development of Freud's Works in the United States," *American Journal of Sociology* 45 (November 1939): 322–323. Skues, "Clark

Revisited," 77. *Index Medicus*, January–December 1910. Freud, "On the History of the Psycho-Analytic Movement," *Standard Edition* vol. 14, 32.
    6. A.A. Brill, "Thoughts on Life and Death," *Psychiatric Quarterly* 21 (1947): 200. C.P. Oberndorf, "Obituary: Abraham Arden Brill," *The Psychoanalytic Review* 35 (January 1, 1948): 391. Samuel Atkin, "The New York Psychoanalytic Society and Institute: Its Founding and Development" in Jacques M. Quen and Eric T. Carlson, *American Psychoanalysis: Origins and Development* (New York: Brunner/Mazel, 1978), 74.
    7. H. Addington Bruce, "Masters of The Mind," *American Magazine* (November 1, 1910): 81. Jung to Freud, November 11, 1912, in *Freud/Jung Letters*, 515.
    8. The best discussion of the role and impact of mass-market magazines in the spread of Freud's ideas is in Jessamyn Hatcher's 2004 Duke University PhD dissertation, *Psychoanalysis and Everyday Life*. Although Hatcher largely ignores the first wave of articles discussed here, she devotes considerable space to analyzing those discussed in chapter 6 and examines the social, political, and personal significance of magazine articles about Freud, 1912–1918.
    9. "Science Discovers Reality of Dreams," *New York Times, Sunday Magazine*, May 8, 1910: 14. A.A. Brill, "Dreams and Their Relations to the Neurosis," *New York Medical Journal* 91 (April 23, 1910): 842–846.
    10. "Alden March Dies," *New York Times*, September 15, 1942, 23.
    11. Bruce, "Masters of The Mind," 71.
    12. Frank Luther Mott, *A History of American Magazines, 1865–1885* (Cambridge: Harvard University Press, 1938), vol. III, 512–513.
    13. H. Addington Bruce, "Some Books on Mental Healing," *Forum* 43 (March 1, 1910): 316.
    14. P.M. Dennis, "Psychology's First Publicist," *Psychological Reports* 68, no. 3 (1991): 755–765. F.H. Matthews, "The Americanization of Sigmund Freud," *Journal of American Studies* 1, no. 1 (April 1967): 39–62.
    15. Bruce, "Masters of The Mind," 81.
    16. Personal communication from Matthew Mason, image archivist at Yale's

Beinecke Library, March 15, 2022. No earlier copy of the image could be found in the full-text databases ProQuest American Periodicals, Newspapers.com, Chronicling America, or Readex American Newspapers.

17. Frank Luther Mott, *A History of American Magazines, Vol. 4: 1885–1905.* (Cambridge Harvard University Press, 1958), 506–510.

18. E.W. Scripture, "Neurology in Zurich," *Medical Record* 78, no. 26 (December 24, 1910): 1129–1135. "Medical Report from a New Psychological World," *Current Literature* 50 (February 1, 1911): 167–169. "Psychanalysis [sic]," *Scientific American Supplement* 71 (April 15, 1911): 256.

19. Niel M. Johnson, *George Sylvester Viereck: Pro-German Publicist in America, 1910–1945* (PhD dissertation, University of Iowa, 1971), 12–13, 40. The friend was Alfred Rau, quoted in Phyllis Keller, "George Sylvester Viereck: The Psychology of a German-American Militant," *Journal of Interdisciplinary History* 2, no. 1 (1971): 76.

20. Keller is the source for Viereck's study of Freud "in the first decade of the century." Viereck, *Confessions of a Barbarian* (New York: Jackson, 1910), 115–116. Viereck, "Surveying Life at Seventy" [interview with Freud], *American Monthly* (October 1927): 10. Freud, *Letters* (New York: Basic Books, 1960), 417.

21. Harry W. Chase, "Freud's Theories of the Unconscious," *Popular Science Monthly* 78 (April 1, 1911): 355–363.

22. Hall, *Life and Confessions*, 232, 335. J. McKeen Cattell, "Some Psychological Experiments: Address of the retiring President of the American Association for the Advancement of Science, given at Kansas City on December 28, 1925," *Science* (January 1, 1926): 5.

23. "Freud's Discovery of the Lowest Chamber of the Soul," *Current Opinion* 50 (May 1, 1911): 512–514.

24. Freud to Brill May 11, 1911, in Sigmund Freud Papers: General Correspondence, 1871–1996; A.A. Brill, from Freud; Transcripts and translations; 1908–1911; translation viewed at www.freud-edition.net/briefe/freud-sigmund/brill-abraham-arden/1911/05/11, August 12, 2022.

25. Rosenzweig, *Freud, Jung and Hall the King-Maker*, 365.

26. Edwin T. Brewster, "Dreams and Forgetting," *McClure's Magazine* 39 (October 1, 1912): 714–16. Brewster's article is discussed in Hatcher, *Psychoanalysis and Everyday Life*, 96–97.

27. *Who's Who Among North American Authors*, 1921. OCLC WorldCat.

28. Brewster, "Dreams and Forgetting," 716–719.

29. Reeve, "The Dream Doctor," *Cosmopolitan*, August 1913, 325–334.

30. Freud, "The Origin and Development of Psychoanalysis," *American Journal of Psychology* 21 (April 1910): 209.

31. Jones, *Free Associations*, 234. Burnham, *Psychoanalysis and American Medicine*, 32–33.

Chapter 5

1. George Brett to Sir Frederick Macmillan, April 1, 1913, in *Archives of George Allen & Co., 1893–1915* in the series "British Publisher's Archives on Microfilm" (Thetford: Chadwyck-Healey, 1974), reel 8. John A. Tebbel, *A History of Book Publishing in the United States: Vol. 2—The Expansion of an Industry, 1865–1919* (New York: Bowker, 1972), 18, 354–355. Charles Morgan, *The House of Macmillan* (London: Macmillan, 1943), 164.

2. The four articles that may have sparked Brett's interest were "Medical Report from a New Psychological World," *Current Opinion*, February 1911; Harry Chase, "Freud's Theories of the Unconscious," *Popular Science*, April 1911; "Psychanalysis: Getting at the Facts of Mental Life," *Scientific American Supplement*, April 22, 1911; and "Freud's Discovery of the Lowest Chamber of the Soul," *Current Literature*, May 1911. Freud to Brill, June 11, 1911, in Sigmund Freud Papers: General Correspondence, 1871–1996; A.A. Brill, from Freud; Transcripts and translations; 1908–1911; translation viewed at https://www.freud-edition.net/briefe/freud-sigmund/brill-abraham-arden/1911/06/11, August 12, 2022. 35 Stat. 1075, March 4, 1909, "An Act to Amend and Consolidate the Acts Respecting Copyright," section 15, viewed June 20, 2022, at https://www.copyright.gov/history/1909act.pdf.

3. *Medical Critic and Guide* 24 (March

1921): 87–88. F.A. Mumby and F.H.S. Stallybrass, *From Swan Sonnenschein to George Allen & Unwin, Ltd.* (London: George Allen & Unwin, 1955), 7–8. Freud to Brill, June 11, 1911, in Sigmund Freud Papers: General Correspondence, 1871–1996; A.A. Brill, from Freud; Transcripts and translations; 1908–1911; translation viewed at https://www.freud-edition.net/briefe/freud-sigmund/brill-abraham-arden/1911/06/11, viewed August 12, 2022. Macmillan-Allen correspondence April–June 1912 in *Records of George Allen & Unwin Ltd, 1884-1983*, folder AU FSC 20/127/2, University of Reading.

4. Freud, "Foreword to the Third English Edition," *The Interpretation of Dreams* (New York: Macmillan, 1932), [ix]. *Freud/Jung Letters*, 120; Freud's sentence was in English in the original. Freud, *The Interpretation of Dreams* (London: Hogarth Press, 1953), *Standard Edition* vol. 4, 99.

5. Ronald Steel, *Walter Lippmann and the American Century* (London: Bodley Head, 1980), 45.

6. Mumby and Stallybrass, 7–8. Brill to Allen, March 6, 1913, in Brill Papers at Library of Congress, Box 4.

7. Allen to Brill, December 31, 1913, and annual balance sheets in Brill Papers at Library of Congress, Box 15. *Records of George Allen & Unwin Ltd, 1884-1983*, folder AU FSC 20/127/2, University of Reading. Allen to Brill, April 17, 1913, Brill Papers at Library of Congress, Box 4, folder 15.

8. Allen to Brill, December 31, 1913, and annual balance sheets in Brill Papers at Library of Congress, Box 15. Allen to Brill, May 21, 1913, in the Brill Papers at the Library of Congress, Box 4, folder 15. Copy offered for sale by the seller Bookbid (Beverly Hills, CA) on June 20, 2022, at Abebooks.com, with photograph of publisher's note.

9. Stanley Unwin to Brill, November 14, 1922, in the Brill Papers at the Library of Congress, Box 4, folder 15. Freud to Werner Achelis, January 30, 1927, in Freud, *Letters*, 375.

10. Freud to Brill, July 29, 1913, in Sigmund Freud Papers: General Correspondence, 1871–1996; A.A. Brill, from Freud; Transcripts and translations; 1908–1911; translation at https://www.freud-edition.

net/briefe/freud-sigmund/brill-abraham-arden/1913/07/29, viewed August 12, 2022. *Dial* 55 (August 1, 1913): 80.

11. James Strachey, "Editor's Introduction," *The Interpretation of Dreams* (New York: Basic Books, 2010), xxi.

12. Eight serious reviews appeared before the end of the year: *Nation*, May 15, 1913; *New York Times*, June 1, 1913; *Scientific American*, June 14, 1913; *Dial*, August 1, 1913; *Life*, August 14, 1913; *American Theosophist*, September 1, 1913; *Science*, September 5, 1913; and *Delinquent* [for prison reform advocates], October 1, 1913.

13. Allen to Brill, December 31, 1913, and annual balance sheets in Brill Papers at Library of Congress, Box 15.

14. Brill Papers at Library of Congress, Box 4.

15. Brill Papers at Library of Congress, Boxes 4 and 15.

16. Freud, *Über Den Traum* (Wiesbaden: J.F. Bergmann, 1901).

17. Freud to Brill, June 7, 1911, in Sigmund Freud Papers: General Correspondence, 1871–1996; A.A. Brill, from Freud; Transcripts and translations; 1908–1911; translation at https://www.freud-edition.net/briefe/freud-sigmund/brill-abraham-arden/1911/06/11, viewed August 12, 2022. Jones to Freud, August 31, 1911, in *Complete Correspondence*. Freud to Brill, December 14, 1911, in Sigmund Freud Papers: General Correspondence, 1871–1996; A.A. Brill, from Freud; Transcripts and translations; 1908–1911; translation viewed at https://www.freud-edition.net/briefe/freud-sigmund/brill-abraham-arden/1911/12/14, August 12, 2022.

18. *Oxford Dictionary of National Biography*. Jones, *Life and Work*, vol. 2, 88.

19. Jones to Freud, July 30, 1912, in *Complete Correspondence*. J.B. Hobman, ed., *David Eder: Memoirs of a Modern Pioneer* (London: Gollancz, 1945), 18–21.

20. John St. John, *William Heinemann: A Century of Publishing, 1890–1990* (London: Heinemann, 1990), 152.

21. P. Kuhn, "The Sexual Life of Our Time: Medical Censorship in Early-20th-Century England," *History of Psychology* 23 (2020): 46–48. OCLC WorldCat.

22. *Southern Medical Journal* 7, issue 9 (September 1914): 764. *Maryland*

Medical Journal (November 1914). *Johns Hopkins Medical Bulletin* (November 1914). *Monthly Cyclopedia and Medical Bulletin* (December 1914). *Publishers Weekly* 88 (October 9, 1915): 30

23. *American Journal of Clinical Medicine* 21 (1914): 1038.

24. Brill to Freud, January 11, 1914, Sigmund Freud Papers at Library of Congress: General Correspondence, Brill to Freud, transcripts viewed online August 12, 2022, at https://www.loc.gov/resource/mss39990.01908/?sp=19.

25. Philip Unwin, *The Publishing Unwins* (London: Heinemann, 1972), 46.

26. Brill to Unwin, December 19, 1913, in Brill Papers, Library of Congress, Box 5, folder 18.

27. Brill to Freud, undated but before April 1914, Sigmund Freud Papers at Library of Congress: General Correspondence, Brill to Freud, transcripts viewed online, August 12, 2022, at www.loc.gov/resource/mss39990.01908/?sp=21&st=image.

28. Brill, "Introduction," *Psychopathology of Everyday Life* (New York: Macmillan, 1914), v. James Strachey, "Editor's Introduction" in Freud, *Psychopathology of Everyday Life* (London: Hogarth Press, 1960), *Standard Edition* vol. 6, xi.

29. Brill to Fisher Unwin, December 19, 1913, in Brill Papers at Library of Congress, Box 5, folder 18. Freud to Edward Bernays, July 20, 1920, quoted in Edward Bernays, *Biography of Idea* (New York: Simon & Schuster, 1965), 259. Burnham, *Psychoanalysis and American Medicine*, 143–147.

30. Brill to Fisher Unwin, November 8 and December 19, 1913, and Unwin to Brill, May 19, 1914, in Brill Papers at Library of Congress, Box 5, folder 18. Brill to William Allen, January 11, 1914, in Brill Papers at Library of Congress, Box 4, folder 15. Brill to Freud, June 7, 1914, Sigmund Freud Papers at Library of Congress: General Correspondence, Brill to Freud, transcripts viewed August 12, 2022, at www.loc.gov/resource/mss39990.01908/?sp=23.

31. Reviews appeared in the *Nation*, September 24, 1914; *New York Times Sunday Magazine*, October 18 ("What Causes Slips of the Tongue?"); *Pittsburgh Press*, October 18 ("Tricks by Which Your Mind Betrays You"); *Independent*, October 19

("The Cause of Forgetfulness"); *St. Louis Post-Dispatch*, November 7 ("Glimpse into the Soul"); *Dallas Morning News* and *Galveston Daily News*, both on November 8 under the same headline ("Do You Forget Easily?"); and *Boston Evening Transcript*, November 27, 1914.

32. Brill to Fisher Unwin, January 30, 1914, in the Brill Papers at the Library of Congress, Box 5, folder 18. Annual royalty statements from Unwin and Benn to Brill in the Brill Papers, Box 15. Precise figures are impossible because statements for some years are missing, including 1914–1915 and 1915–1916. Brill to Ernest Benn, November 23, 1937, in Brill Papers, Box 5, folder 18.

33. Steve Hare, *Penguin Portrait: Allen Lane and the Penguin Editors, 1935-1970* (London: Penguin, 1995), 148. *New York Times*, February 1, 1948, BR8.

Chapter 6

1. Searches were conducted in *Index Medicus*, which tried to cite every article in every major medical journal; *Readers Guide to Periodical Literature*, which indexed the 100 most popular American magazines; the Library of Congress's *Chronicling America*, which contains 55,000 newspaper issues dated 1909–1918; Readex's *America's Historical Newspapers*, which contains more than 30 million pages printed during that decade; and *Publishers Weekly*, the industry trade journal that announced new books as they were published.

2. Celia Burns Stendler, "New Ideas for Old: How Freudianism Was Received in the United States," *Journal of Educational Psychology* 38, no. 4 (1947): 206.

3. For general background on Greenwich Village, see Steven Watson's *Strange Bedfellows: The First American Avant-Garde* (New York: Abbeville Press, 1991). For psychoanalysis in Greenwich Village see chapter 2 of Frederick Hoffman's *Freudianism and the Literary Mind* (Baton Rouge: Louisiana State University Press, 1957), F.H. Matthews, "The Americanization of Sigmund Freud," *Journal of American Studies* 1 (April 1967): 39–62 and Leslie Fishbein's "Freud and the Radicals: The Sexual Revolution Comes to

Greenwich Village," *Canadian Review of American Studies* 12, Issue 2 (1981): 173–189.

4. Keith N. Richwine, *The Liberal Club: Bohemia and the Resurgence in Greenwich Village, 1912–1918* (PhD dissertation, University of Pennsylvania, 1968), 8–15.

5. Nathan G. Hale, *The Rise and Crisis of Psychoanalysis in the United States, 1917–1986* (New York: Oxford University Press, 1995), 59. Ruitenbeek, *Freud in America*, 62.

6. Lois P. Rudnick, *Mabel Dodge Luhan: New Woman, New Worlds* (Albuquerque: University of New Mexico Press, 1984), 360.

7. "East Village Tenement Housed 'the Most Dangerous Woman in America,'" *Off the Grid* (Greenwich Village Society for Historic Preservation), November 29, 2011. Emma Goldman, *Anarchism and Other Essays* (New York: Mother Earth, 1910), 178. Hoffman, *Freudianism and the Literary Mind*, 48. Brill's article was "Science Discovers Reality of Dreams," *New York Times*, May 8, 1910. *Harvard Alumni Directory* (volumes for 1908, 1910, and 1914). Ronald Steel, *Walter Lippmann and the American Century* (New York: Vintage, 1981), 18.

8. Steel, *Walter Lippmann*, 18, 39. Lippmann to Graham Wallas, October 30, 1912, quoted in Steel, *Walter Lippmann*, 46.

9. Brenda Wineapple, *Sister Brother: Gertrude and Leo Stein* (New York: Putnam's, 1996), 326. Patricia Everett, *Corresponding Lives: Mabel Dodge Luhan, A.A. Brill, and the Psychoanalytic Adventure in America* (New York: Routledge, 2016), 43–48.

10. Max Eastman, *Enjoyment of Living* (New York: Harper, 1948), 490–491. Sherwood Anderson, *Memoirs* (New York: Harcourt Brace, 1942), 243. Floyd Dell, letter, September 17, 1942, to Hoffman, quoted in *Freudianism and the Literary Mind*, 58.

11. Richwine, *The Liberal Club,* 145. Peter Hulme, "The Liberal Club and Its Jamaican Secretary," Acdemia.edu, last updated March 2017; viewed April 10, 2022, at academia.edu/33324262/The_Liberal_Club_and_its_Jamaican_Secretary, 11–15.

12. Bobby Jones, "The Story of Greenwich Village. Part VI," *Greenwich Village Quill* 13, no. 1 (July 1923): 10–11 and no. 6

(December 1923): 16–17 and 21. Frenanda Perrone, "Inventory to the Modern School Collection," Rutgers University Libraries, 1996, viewed April 26, 2022, at http://www2.scc.rutgers.edu/ead/manuscripts/Modernf.html.

13. Paul Avrich, *Anarchist Voices: An Oral History of Anarchism in America* (Princeton: Princeton University Press, 1995), 219–222. Sarah Bean Apmann, "Anarchy in the East Village! The Ferrer Modern School," *Off the Grid* (Greenwich Village Society for Historic Preservation), September 24, 2015. Lincoln Steffens, *The Autobiography of Lincoln Steffens* (New York: Harcourt Brace, 1958), 655–666.

14. A.A. Brill, "The Introduction and Development of Freud's Works in the United States," *American Journal of Sociology* 45 (November 1939): 322. Luhan, *Movers and Shakers*, 142.

15. Based on searches in 10 full-text newspaper and periodicals databases. Circulation statistics, always subject to exaggeration by publishers, are from *Ayer's Newspaper and Periodical Directory*, 1916–1918.

16. Alfred Booth Kuttner, "What Causes Slips of the Tongue?" *New York Times*, October 18, 1914, and "Note on Forgetting," *New Republic*, November 28, 1914. Alfred Booth Kuttner, "Freudian Theory," *New Republic*, March 20, 1915. Walter Lippmann, "Freud and the Layman," *New Republic,* April 17, 1915.

17. Max Eastman, "Exploring the Soul and Healing the Body," *Everybody's Magazine*, June 1, 1915, and "Mr.-er-er- oh! What's His Name?" *Everybody's Magazine*, July 1, 1915. The $1,000 payment is noted by E. Fuller Torrey, *Freudian Fraud* (New York: Harper Perennial, 1993), 24, without a citation to his source. Eastman's articles are discussed at greater length in Hatcher, *Psychoanalysis and Everyday Life*, 51–58, 67–75, and 79–80.

18. Henry Addington Bruce, "Stammering and Its Cure," *McClure's Magazine*, February 1, 1913, and "Fears of Childhood," *Good Housekeeping*, October 1, 1915.

19. "Peter Clark Macfarlane Tells How He Writes," *Writer's Monthly* 22, no. 3 (August 1923): 105–107. "Macfarlane Dies by His Own Hand," *New York Times*, June 10, 1924.

20. Peter Clark Macfarlane, "Diagnosis by Dreams," *Good Housekeeping* 60 (February and March 1915): 215–133 and 278–286. Macfarlane is discussed at greater length in Hatcher, *Psychoanalysis and Everyday Life*, 58–64.

21. *Who's Who in New York City and State*, vol. 8 (New York: L.R. Hamersly Co., 1924). "William Bigelow, a Former Editor: Good Housekeeping's Head from 1913 to 1942 Is Dead," *New York Times*, March 7, 1966. Frank Luther Mott, *A History of American Magazines, Vol. 5: 1905–1930* (Cambridge: Harvard University Press, 1968), 133–136.

22. "John Peter Toohey," IMDb.com. Dale Kramer, *Ross and the New Yorker* (New York: Doubleday, 1952), 39–40 and 60–61.

23. John P. Toohey, "How We All Reveal Our Soul Secrets," *Ladies' Home Journal*, November 1, 1917, 97. Toohey's article is discussed in Hatcher, *Psychoanalysis and Everyday Life*, 85–87.

24. Edward Bok, *The Americanization of Edward Bok* (New York: Scribner's, 1920), *passim*. Rob Wagner, *Hollywood Bohemia* (Santa Maria, CA: Janeway Books, 2019), 30. Mike Ashley, "Blue Book—The Slick in Pulp Clothing," *Pulp Vault* 14 (Barrington Hills, IL: Tattered Pages Press, 2011), 210–53. Claire Bruyère, "From Boston, MA, to Kingsport, TN: Joseph Hamblen Sears (1865–1946), a Forgotten Figure in American Publishing," *Papers of the Bibliographical Society of Canada* 52, no. 1 (2014): 311.

25. See introductions and notes in Patricia Everett, *Corresponding Lives* and Lois P. Rudnick, *The Suppressed Memoirs of Mabel Dodge Luhan: Sex, Syphilis, and Psychoanalysis in the Making of Modern American Culture* (Albuquerque: University of New Mexico Press, 2012).

26. Mabel Dodge Luhan, *Movers and Shakers* (Albuquerque: University of New Mexico Press, 1985 [1933]), 161, 507–510.

27. Dodge, *Movers and Shakers*, 510.

28. Editorial page, *Washington Times*, November 24, 1917.

29. "Mabel Dodge Talks on Mothers of Men," *Washington Times*, September 13, 1917. "Mabel Dodge Talks of Women Who Seek Masters," *Washington Times*, August 28, 1917. "Mabel Dodge's Article on Looking Ahead," *Washington Times*, September 4, 1917.

30. Arthur B. Reeve, "The Dream Doctor," *Cosmopolitan*, August 1913, 325.

31. Arthur B. Reeve, "The Dream Doctor," *Cosmopolitan*, August 1913, 332–335.

32. Reeve made explicit use of Freudian concepts in three stories, "The Dream Doctor," *Cosmopolitan*, August 1913, 325–334; "The Soul-Analysis," *Cosmopolitan*, May 1916, 869–81; "The Psychic Scar," *Cosmopolitan*, April 1918, 85–88, 128–34. The first two were collected in 1913 in his book *The Dream Doctor* (New York: Hearst International Library, 1914) and "The Psychic Scar" was collected in *The Panama Plot* (New York: Harper, 1918). Hatcher discusses Reeve's work and its effects at length in the second chapter of her dissertation, *Psychoanalysis and Everyday Life*. Ffytche, *Sigmund Freud*, 86.

33. Hutchins Hapgood, *A Victorian in the Modern World* (Seattle: University of Washington Press, 1972 [1939]), 382–383. Glaspell and Kenton quoted in J. Ellen Gainor, *Susan Glaspell in Context* (Ann Arbor: University of Michigan, 2004), 20 and 25. Alfred Booth Kuttner, "Nerves" in *Civilization in the United States, an Inquiry by Thirty Americans*, ed. Harold E. Stearns (New York: Harcourt, Brace, 1922), 464–465. Freud, "Wild Psycho-Analysis," *Standard Edition* vol. 11, 221–230.

34. *New York Times*, September 16, 1922, 7. Bernays, *Biography of an Idea*, 253. Brief review of Ralph in *Psychoanalytic Quarterly* 9, no. 4 (October 1922): 469.

35. Ruitenbeek, *Freud in America*, 77. MacFarlane, "Diagnosis by Dreams," *Good Housekeeping*, February 1, 1915.

Chapter 7

1. For more information, see Andrew Scull, *Desperate Remedies* (Cambridge: Harvard University Press, 2022), chapter three, and Erika Janik's engaging history, *Marketplace of the Marvelous: The Strange Origins of Modern Medicine* (Boston: Beacon Press, 2015).

2. Nathan G. Hale's *Freud and the Americans: The Beginnings of Psychoanalysis in the United States, 1876–1917* (New York: Oxford University Press, 1971) treats this background in detail; C.P. Oberndorf's "History of the Psychoanalytic

Movement in America," *Psychoanalytic Review* 14 (1927): 281–297, is a good short account. Freud's prosecuted publishers were William Robinson, Moffat Yard & Co., Thomas Seltzer, and Horace Liveright.

3. Ben Reitman, "William J. Robinson: Estimate," *Medical Review of Reviews* 42 (February 1936): 61.

4. William J. Robinson, *A Few Minutes in the Confessional: A Page from My Inner Life* (New York: Altrurians, [1910?]), 12. "Biographical Introduction" by Eden and Cedar Paul in William J. Robinson, *A Doctor's Views on Life* (London: Allen & Unwin, 1927), 18–22. 1910 U.S. Census, Population Schedule.

5. Henry P. DeForest, "William J. Robinson: Eulogy," *Medical Review of Reviews* (February 1936): 54. Robinson, *A Doctor's Views on Life*, 27–28. *Victor Robinson Memorial Volume* (New York: Froben Press, 1948), 431. 1910 U.S. Census, Population Schedule. Advertisement in December 1910 issue of *Practical Druggist*.

6. William Robinson, *Fewer and Better Babies, or, the Limitation of Offspring* (New York: Race Betterment League, 1916), 7, 175. Robinson, *A Doctor's Views on Life*, 30. Ben Reitman, "William J. Robinson: Estimate," 61.

7. Robinson, *A Doctor's Views on Life*, 37–38.

8. [Fred Robinson,] "A Review of the 'Medical Review of Reviews,'" *Medical Review of Reviews* 22 (January 1916): 1–4.

9. Not to be confused with the American Medical Association's index of the same name.

10. Bernays, *Biography of an Idea*, 50–51.

11. Robinson, *A Doctor's Views on Life*, 36.

12. Robinson, *A Doctor's Views on Life*, 500–501. "A Review of the 'Medical Review of Reviews,'" 2.

13. *Critic and Guide* (September 1915): 320. Freud, "'Civilized' Sexual Morality and Modern Nervous Illness," *Standard Edition* vol. 9, 204.

14. *American Journal of Urology* (October 1915): 391–405. *Publishers Weekly* (December 2, 1922): 2006. James Strachey, "Bibliographical note," *Standard Edition* vol. 9, 179.

15. The unique copy is in the Sigmund Freud Collection at the Library of Congress (OCLC WorldCat Number 2284222). I'm grateful to my friend Katie Mullen for examining and photographing it for me. This Freud pamphlet should not be confused with Clement Wood's *Modern Sexual Morality* (Girard, KS: Haldeman-Julius, 1924), number 717 in the well-known Little Blue Books series, which was in print at the same time and sold exponentially more copies.

16. Freud to Brill, October 25 and December 15, 1915, in Sigmund Freud Papers at Library of Congress: General Correspondence, Freud to Brill, Transcripts; translations viewed at https://www.freud-edition.net/briefe/freud-sigmund/brill-abraham-arden. A copy of the letter to the A.M.A. is also in the Freud Papers at the Library of Congress.

17. Advertising supplement at the back of the December 1917 issue of *Critic and Guide*, 8.

18. *Critic and Guide* 23, no. 6 (June 1920): 175.

19. The sole copy is at Drew University, Madison, New Jersey, according to OCLC WorldCat (record number 43274912).

20. *Sexual Problems of Today*. Robinson's own 1916 edition had escaped the censors because he was a medical publisher, but Lewis's popular edition did not. Jay Gertzman, *Bookleggers and Smuthounds: The Trade in Erotica, 1920–1940* (Philadelphia: University of Pennsylvania Press, 2001), 25–26. William Robinson, *If I Were God* (New York: Freethought Press, 1930), [5].

21. Freud, *Modern Sexual Morality and Modern Nervousness* (New York: Eugenics Publishing Co., 1931), v–vi.

22. Robinson, *A Doctor's Views on Life*, 297.

23. Jones to Freud, May 2, 1919, and Brill to Jones March 7, 1920, in *Complete Correspondence*, 344.

24. Robinson, *A Doctor's Views on Life*, 19, 37. Charles Leinenberger, "Introduction" to *Dr. Robinson's Voice in the Wilderness, 1917–1920* (Westport, CT: Greenwood, 1970), 3–4. "Drop Case Against Soviet Defender: Judge Knox Quashes Indictments against John Reed and Three Other Radicals," *New York Times*, April 5, 1919.

25. William Fielding to Robinson, October 26, 1920, in the Fielding Papers

at New York University, Box 3, folder 16. "Book Many Endorsed Held to Be Obscene," *New York Times*, April 23, 1921. Robinson, letter to the editor, "Suppressing Sex Information," *Appeal to Reason* (Girard, KS), May 14, 1921, 4. *Penal Law and the Code of Criminal Procedure of the State of New York* (Albany: M. Bender, 1919), Article 106: Indecency, Section 1141. There is no biography of Robinson beyond the introduction to *A Doctor's Views on Life* and the "Memorial Number to William Josephus Robinson: December 8, 1867–January 6, 1936" in the *Medical Review of Reviews* for February 1936.

Chapter 8

1. Bernays, *Biography of an Idea*, 277. Jay Corey Satterfield, *"The World's Best Books": Taste, Culture, and the Modern Library* (Amherst: University of Massachusetts Press, 2002), 11–12.

2. John Tebbel, *A History of Book Publishing in the United States*, vol. 2 (New York: Bowker, 1972), 378, and vol. 3 (New York: Bowker, 1978), 92. *The Trow Copartnership and Corporation Directory of Boroughs of Manhattan and the Bronx*, March 1906. *Who's Who in New York City and State* (New York: W.F. Brainerd, 1911), 676 and 1016. *Publishers Weekly*, January–May 1913. Yard, *The Publisher* (Boston: Houghton Mifflin, 1913).

3. *Trow Copartnership and Corporation Directory*, 1908–1916. *New York Times*, June 7, 1912. August Hecksher, *St. Paul's: The Life of a New England School* (New York: Scribner's, 1980), 109. August Hecksher, *A Brief History of St. Paul's School, 1856–1996* (Concord, NH: St. Paul's School, 1996), 34. Obituary of Coit in *Alumni Horae* 10, no. 2 (Concord, NH: St. Paul's School, December 1930), 59–60.

4. *Publishers Weekly*, December 7, 1907, 35; January 11, 1908, 31; April 25, 1908, 8. *The Dial*, December 1, 1908, 386.

5. *Publishers Weekly*, 1908–1919; quote is from February 10, 1917, issue. Frankwood E. Williams, *A Selected List of Books on Mental Hygiene and Allied Subjects* (New York: National Committee for Mental Hygiene, 1924), 333–335. *New Republic*, July 20, 1918, 347.

6. Brill to Freud, January 11, undated,

and October 27, 1914, in Sigmund Freud Papers at Library of Congress: General Correspondence, Brill to Freud, Transcripts, https://www.loc.gov/item/mss3999000471/.

7. James Strachey, "Editor's Preface" in Freud, *Jokes and Their Relation to the Unconscious* (New York: Norton, 1963), 6–7. Brill to Freud, October 27, 1914, in Sigmund Freud Papers at Library of Congress: General Correspondence, Brill to Freud, Transcripts, https://www.loc.gov/item/mss3999000471/. *Wit and Its Relation to the Unconscious* (New York: Moffat, Yard & Co., 1916), vii. Freud, *Der Witz und seine Beziehung zum Unbewussten* (Vienna: Deuticke, 1905) and (Vienna: Dueticke, 1921), 13.

8. Grant Overton, *Portrait of a Publisher* (New York: Appleton, 1925), 10–11.

9. Brill-Appleton correspondence February and March 1916 in the Brill Papers at the Library of Congress, Box 4, folder 7.

10. Brill to Appleton, April 28 and May 6, 1916, in the Brill Papers at the Library of Congress, Box 4, folder 7.

11. Brill-Moffat Yard correspondence for May–October 1916 is in the Brill Papers at the Library of Congress, Box 4, folder 7.

12. Dodd, Mead Mss., Lilly Library, Indiana University, boxes 8 and 15.

13. *Publishers Weekly*, October 7, 1916, 19.

14. *The Normal Instructor and Primary Plans* (June 1917): 10. *Reedy's Mirror* (November 23, 1917): 754.

15. Moffat to Brill May 9, 1916, in the Brill Papers at the Library of Congress, Box 4, folder 7. Library of Congress, "Shadows of War" online presentation at https://www.loc.gov/classroom-materials/immigration/german/shadows-of-war/, viewed May 16, 2022.

16. *Pearson's Magazine* (May 1918): 60. *The Expositor* (September 1918): 954.

17. Brill Papers at the Library of Congress, Box 4, folder 7. Dodd, Mead Mss., 1855–1992; LMC 2415, Lilly Library, Indiana University, Series: Authors, Publishers, and Other Correspondents: Freud, Sigmund, Box 8.

18. Hale, *James Jackson Putnam*, 295. Jones to Freud, December 15, 1921, in *Complete Correspondence*, letter 331.

19. Freud, *Leonardo* (London: Kegan Paul, 1922), vii.

20. Brill to Dodd, August 24 and November 11, 1931, in Brill Papers at Library of Congress, Box 23, folder 7.

21. Gordon B. Neavill, "Modern Library Paperbacks: Checklist and Dating Key, 1955–1960, Revised Version 2005," viewed online September 14, 2022, at http://www.modernlib.com/General/paperbackDatingKey.htm. Gordon B. Neavill, *The Modern Library Series: A Dissertation* (Chicago: University of Chicago, 1984), 388–389, 468.

22. Brill to Robert Appleton, October 19, 1917, in the Brill Papers at the Library of Congress, Box 4, folder 7.

23. Moffat to Brill, October 22, and Brill to Moffat, October 25, 1917, in the Brill Papers at the Library of Congress, Box 4, folder 7.

24. Downey to Appleton, November 5, 1917, in S.E. Jelliffe Papers at the Library of Congress, Box 3, Folder 1. Ernest Jones to Freud, January 26, 1922, in *Complete Correspondence*. Brill to Appleton, November 17, 1917, in the Brill Papers at the Library of Congress, Box 4, folder 7. Freud to Downey, March 1, 1922, in the Freud Papers at the Library of Congress: General Correspondence, 1871–1996, Downey, Helen, 1922, viewed online September 28, 2022, at https://hdl.loc.gov/loc.mss/ms004017.mss39990.00535.

25. Dodd, Mead Mss., 1855–1992, LMC 2415. Lilly Library, Indiana University, Box 15. John Tebbel, *A History of Book Publishing in the United States: Vol. 2: The Golden Age Between the Two Wars, 1920–1940* (New York: Bowker, 1978), 501–502. Freud, *Jensen's Gradiva and Other Works, Standard Edition*, vol. 9 (London: Hogarth Press, 1959), 4 and 94.

26. Brill Papers at the Library of Congress, Box 4, folder 7. Alfred Booth Kuttner to Mabel Dodge, May 15, 1916, Mabel Dodge Luhan Papers, Yale Collection of American Literature, Beinecke Rare Book and Manuscript Library, viewed online July 9, 2022, https://collections.library.yale.edu/catalog/17085356.

27. Dodd, Mead Mss., 1855–1992, LMC 2415. Lilly Library, Indiana University, Box 15.

28. Brill Papers at the Library of Congress, Box 4, folder 7, contains the November–December 1917 correspondence.

29. *Publishers Weekly*, February 16 and March 9, 1918. Dodd, Mead Mss., 1855–1992, LMC 2415, Lilly Library, Indiana University, boxes 8 and 15. Appleton to Brill April 19, 1918, in Brill Papers at the Library of Congress, Box 4, folder 7.

30. Dodd, *Movers and Shakers*, 151.

31. *New York Times* obituaries, October 26, 1930, January 20 and May 19, 1945, and October 1, 1946. Hecksher, *St. Paul's*, 109.

Chapter 9

1. Anthony Comstock, "The Work of the New York Society for the Prevention of Vice and Its Bearing on the Morals of the Young," *Proceedings of the Child Conference for Research and Welfare 1909* (New York: G.E. Stechert, 1910), 91 and 95.

2. May, *The End of American Innocence*, 340–341.

3. Helen Lefkowitz Horowitz, "Victoria Woodhull, Anthony Comstock, and Conflict over Sex in the United States in the 1870s," *Journal of American History* 87, no. 2 (September 2000): 408–409.

4. *U.S. Statutes at Large 42nd Congress, 3rd Session*, ch. 258, 17 Stat. 598 (1873). William Lee Curry, *Comstockery: A Study in the Rise and Decline of a Watchdog Censorship* (Ph.D. dissertation, Columbia University, 1957), 122.

5. John S. Sumner, "The New York Society for the Suppression of Vice," *Publishers Weekly*, May 17, 1930. "Censoring the Censors," *Current Opinion* 73 (October 1922): 451.

6. Curry, *Comstockery*, 238–241.

7. Curry, *Comstockery*, 130–131 and 148–149. Dardis, *Firebrand, The Life of Horace Liveright* (New York: Random House, 1995), 164. Cerf is quoted in Satterfield, "The World's Best Books," 11–12. Manuel Komroff, unpublished memoir "The Liveright Story" in the Manuel Komroff Papers 1897–1979 (MS#0723), Rare Book & Manuscript Library, Columbia University, box 15.

8. Freud, "The Sexual Life of Human Beings," in *Introductory Lectures on Psycho-Analysis*, Standard Edition, vol. 16 (London: Hogarth Press, 1963), 303. Everett, *Corresponding Lives*, 40, quoting Luhan's memoir, *European Experiences* (New York: Harcourt, Brace, 1935), 36. Horace Liveright, "Unpublished

Autobiography" in Horace Liveright Papers, Ms. Coll. 896, Univ. of Pennsylvania, box 3, 128. Edward Bok, *The Americanization of Edward Bok* (New York: Scribner's, 1920), 345–350.

9. May, *The End of American Innocence*, 346.

10. Brill Papers at the Library of Congress, Box 4, folder 15.

11. Freud, *The Interpretation of Dreams* (New York: Macmillan, 1913), 240.

12. Freud to Brill, January 31, 1913, in Sigmund Freud Papers at Library of Congress: General Correspondence, Freud to Brill, Transcripts at Library of Congress; translation viewed at https://www.freud-edition.net/briefe/freud-sigmund/brill-abraham-arden/1913/01/31. Brill Papers at the Library of Congress, Box 4, folder 15.

13. Copy offered by the bookseller Bookbid (Beverly Hills, CA) on June 20, 2022, at Abebooks.com, with photograph of the publisher's note.

14. Brill Papers at the Library of Congress, Box 4, folder 7.

15. Brill Papers at the Library of Congress, Box 4, folder 15.

16. Moffat to Brill May 9, 1918, Brill Papers at the Library of Congress, Box 4, folder 7.

17. Brill to Joseph Coit, May 24, 1916, in the Brill Papers at the Library of Congress, Box 4, folder 7. Freud, *Leonardo da Vinci*, 92. A detailed analysis of Freud's argument in light of modern research is in Élisabeth Roudinesco, *Freud: In His Time and Ours* (Cambridge: Harvard University Press, 2017), 159–164.

18. Freud, *Leonardo da Vinci*, 37–40.

19. Freud, *Leonardo da Vinci*, 37–38. Coit to Brill, November 14, 1916, and Brill's November 17 reply, in the Brill Papers at the Library of Congress, Box 4, folder 7.

20. John S. Sumner Papers at the Wisconsin Historical Society, Box 2, folder 7. Dodd, Mead Mss., 1855–1992, LMC 2415. Lilly Library, Indiana University. Series: Moffat, Yard and Company. Agreements, correspondence, bills, catalogs, royalty reports, etc., 1923–1924, Box 15.

21. Brill to Dodd Mead, August 24, 1931, in Brill Papers at Library of Congress, Box 23, folder 7. Freud to Brill, September 15, 1919, in Sigmund Freud Papers: General Correspondence, 1871–1996; A.A.

Brill, from Freud; Transcripts and translations; 1912–1919 in Library of Congress; translation viewed at https://www.freud-edition.net/briefe/freud-sigmund/brill-abraham-arden/1919/09/15. Much of Brill's hours-long defense found its way into his 30-page introduction to the 1947 Vintage paperback edition (see Part II).

22. Dodd, Mead Mss., 1855–1992, LMC 2415, Lilly Library, Indiana University, Series: Authors, Publishers, and Other Correspondents. Freud, Sigmund. Box 8.

23. Alexandra Lee Levin, "Thomas Seltzer: Publisher, Fighter for Freedom of the Press, and the Man Who 'Made' D. H. Lawrence," *American Jewish Archives* 41, no. 2 (1989): 217. Dzwonkoski, *American Literary Publishing Houses, 1900-1980*, 333.

24. *A Young Girl's Diary* (New York: Thomas Seltzer, 1921), 7.

25. Roudinesco, *Sigmund Freud*, 293.

26. Martin J. Drell, "Hermine Hug-Hellmuth, A Pioneer in Child Analysis," *Bulletin of the Menninger Clinic* 46, no. 2 (March 1, 1982): 143–145. Elaine Showalter, "A Freudian Fraud?" *Times Literary Supplement*, July 6, 1990, 12.

27. Quoted in Tanselle, "The Thomas Seltzer Imprint," 396–404, where the legal proceedings are traced in detail.

28. Showalter, "Freudian Fraud?" 12.

Chapter 10

1. Liveright, "Unpublished Autobiography," University of Pennsylvania, Ms. Coll. 896, box 3, 128.

2. Jones, *Life and Work*, vol. 2, 218–219. Satterfield, *"The World's Best Books,"* 37–38. Walker Gilmer, *Horace Liveright* (New York: David Lewis, 1970), 4–5.

3. Scott Cutlip, *The Unseen Power: Public Relations, A History* (Hillsdale, NJ: Lawrence Erlbaum Associates, 1994), 163–164, 172. Edward L. Bernays, "Uncle Sigi," *Journal of the History of Medicine* 35, no. 2 (April 1980): 217–218.

4. Bernays, *Biography of an Idea*, 277–278.

5. Tom Tye, *Firebrand: The Life of Horace Liveright* (New York: Random House, 1995), 117. Gordon B. Neavill, *The Modern Library Series* (Ph.D. dissertation, University of Chicago, 1984), 86 and 119. Bernays and Doris Fleischman did

not marry until 1922, but their two families had been close since childhood. Fleischman left Boni and Liveright in 1920 to live in Paris, where he directed expatriate American authors to the firm.

6. Bernays, *Biography of an Idea*, 217–221. Cutlip, *Unseen Power*, 169–170. Their work for Boni and Liveright is examined in detail in Susan Henry, *Anonymous in Their Own Names: Doris E. Fleischman, Ruth Hale, and Jane Grant* (Nashville: Vanderbilt University Press, 2012), 14–16. For Fleischman's role in the firm, see Margot Opdycke Lamme, "Outside the Prickly Nest: Revisiting Doris Fleischman," *American Journalism* 24, no. 3 (2007): 85–107. "'There Is Nothing in This Profession . . . That a Woman Cannot Do': Doris E. Fleischman and the Beginnings of Public Relations," *American Journalism* 16, no. 2 (April 1, 1999): 85–111.

7. Cutlip, *Unseen Power*, 170. Bernays, *Biography of an Idea*, 386–387, 395.

8. Bernays, *Biography of an Idea*, 77, 122–123, 277, and 442. Also, as quoted in Henry, *Anonymous in Their Own Names*, 34.

9. Komroff's unpublished memoir, "The Liveright Story," is in the Manuel Komroff Papers 1897–1979 (MS#0723), Rare Book & Manuscript Library, Columbia University, box 15. He and Liveright remained good friends until the latter's death in 1933.

10. Roazen, *Freud and His Followers*, 178. Edith M. Stern quoted in Satterfield, "The World's Best Books," 33. Bennett Cerf, "Horace Liveright. An Obituary—Unedited," *Publishers Weekly*, October 7, 1933, 1230. Manuel Komroff, "The Liveright Story" in the Manuel Komroff papers, 1897–1979, Rare Book & Manuscript Library, Columbia University, Box 15.

11. Bernays devotes a long chapter to publishing Freud's lectures in 1919–1920, with many quotes from Freud's and his own letters, in his memoir *Biography of an Idea*. Cerf, "Horace Liveright. An Obituary," 1230. Bernays, *Biography of an Idea*, 265.

12. Bernays, *Biography of an Idea*, 253–254.

13. Brill to Ernst Freud, May 22, 1947, in Brill Papers at Library of Congress, box 23, folder 7. Freud to Brill September 15, 1919, in Sigmund Freud Papers: General Correspondence, 1871–1996; A.A. Brill, from Freud; Transcripts and translations; 1912–1919 in Library of Congress; translation viewed at https://www.freud-edition. net/briefe/freud-sigmund/brill-abraham-arden/1919/09/15. Freud to Jones, October 24, 1919, in *Complete Correspondence*, letter 290. Bernays, *Biography of an Idea*, 253–254. Freud to Brill, October 5, 1919, Sigmund Freud Papers: General Correspondence, 1871–1996; A.A. Brill, from Freud; Transcripts and translations; 1912–1919, in Library of Congress; translation viewed at https://www.freud-edition.net/ briefe/freud-sigmund/brill-abraham-arden/1919/10/05.

14. Bernays, *Biography of an Idea*, 253. Bernays to Freud, August 8, 1920, Bernays Papers, Library of Congress, Box 1 (I have silently corrected the transcriber's misspellings of proper names in this quotation). *New York Times*, March 10, 1980.

15. Freud to Bernays, July 20, 1920, in Sigmund Freud Papers at the Library of Congress: Family Papers 1851–1978, Correspondence between Sigmund Freud and Edward Bernays, photocopies and transcripts; 1919 to 1921 as translated in Bernays, *Biography of an Idea*, 259. Jones to Freud, July 9, 1920, and May 6, 1921, in *Complete Correspondence*.

16. A.J. Portenar, "'Vacations' in the Printing Industry in New York City." *Monthly Labor Review* 10 (January 1920): 270–279. Bernays to Liveright, February 5 and August 5, 1920, in Bernays Papers at Library of Congress, Box 120.

17. Bennett Cerf, "Horace Liveright. An Obituary—Unedited," *Publishers Weekly*, October 7, 1933, 1230. Bernays, *Biography of an Idea*, 277.

18. Edward Bernays, "Promotion Expert Urges New Sales Methods for Books," *Publishers Weekly,* March 20, 1920, 933–936.

19. Bernays, *Biography of an Idea*, 282 and 284.

20. W.W. Norton & Company records 1923–1967 at Columbia University, Series III: Boni and Liveright, Inc./Horace Liveright, Inc. records, Accounts—Cr–Gi, Box III.2.

21. W.W. Norton & Company records 1923–1967 at Columbia University, Series III: Boni and Liveright, Inc./Horace

Liveright, Inc. records, Accounts—Cr–Gi, Box III.2.

22. W.W. Norton & Company records 1923–1967 at Columbia University, Series III: Boni and Liveright, Inc./Horace Liveright, Inc. records, Accounts—Cr–Gi, Box III.2. There are minor discrepancies among the figures given by Bernays in his autobiography, those surviving in royalty reports in his unpublished papers, and Boni and Liveright's records. I have relied on the publisher's accounting ledgers at Columbia.

23. Freud to Bernays, April 24, 1921, quoted in Tye, *Father of Spin*, 190. Jones, *Complete Correspondence*, letter 310. Bernays Papers at Library of Congress, Box 120.

24. Jones, *Complete Correspondence*, letter 310. Freud, *A General Introduction to Psychoanalysis* (New York: Horace Liveright Inc, 1935), [13]. W.W. Norton & Company records 1923–1967 at Columbia University, Series III: Boni and Liveright, Inc./Horace Liveright, Inc. records, Accounts—Cr–Gi, Box III.2.

25. *Publishers Weekly*, March 6, 1948. W.W. Norton & Company records 1923–1967 at Columbia University, Series III: Boni and Liveright, Inc./Horace Liveright, Inc. records, Accounts—Cr–Gi, Box III.2.

26. *Publishers Weekly*, March 6 and July 24, 1948. Hyde Park Books, "Paperback Publisher: Permabooks—1951," http://paperbarn.www1.50megs.com/Paperbacks/paperbackpub2.html, viewed on July 6, 2022. Ronelle K.H. Thompson, "Permabooks" in Peter Dzwonkoski, ed., *Dictionary of Literary Biography, vol. 46: American Literary Publishing Houses, 1900–1980* (Detroit: Gale, 1986), 284–285. The verso of the title page of the August 1954 Doubleday Permabooks paperback edition lists the reprints, 1938–1854. W.W. Norton & Company records 1923–1967 at Columbia University, Series III: Boni and Liveright, Inc./Horace Liveright, Inc. records, Accounts—Cr–Gi, Box III.2. Beam, *A Great Idea at the Time*, 106 and 135.

27. Satterfield, *World's Best Books*, 161–162. Schick, *Paperbound Book in America*, found that in the 1940s and 1950s Anchor print runs were usually 20,000–37,000 (181), Beacon's were 10,000 (238), Pocket Books were initially 10,000 (125), and Vintage were originally 20,000 (187).

28. Ernest Jones, *The Life and Work of Sigmund Freud: Years of Maturity, 1901–1919* (New York: Basic Books, 1955), 196–197. Sigmund Freud and Oskar Pfister, *Psychoanalysis and Faith: The Letters of Sigmund Freud and Oskar Pfister* (New York: Basic Books, 1964), 65.

29. Bernays, *Biography of an Idea*, 256–258. G.C. Meynell, "Freud TranslateD," 307. Freud to Brill, October 5, 1919, in Sigmund Freud Papers: General Correspondence, 1871–1996; A.A. Brill, from Freud; Transcripts and translations; 1912–1919 at Library of Congress; translation viewed at https://www.freud-edition.net/briefe/freud-sigmund/brill-abraham-arden/1919/10/05. Jones to Freud, February 9, 1924, *Complete Correspondence*, letter 419.

30. *New York Tribune*, September 19, 1920, 10.

31. Ann Freud, "Personal Memories of Ernest Jones," *International Journal of Psychoanalysis* 60 (1979): 285–287. Bernays, *Biography of an Idea*, 256–261.

32. M. Grotjahn, "The Rundbriefe between Sigmund Freud and the Committee During the Years 1920–1924," *Annual of Psychoanalysis* 2 (1974): 31. Jelliffe to White, December 27, 1921, in Records of St. Elizabeths Hospital, National Archives, Washington D.C.: Record Group 418.3.3 Records of Superintendent William Alanson White, Personal correspondence 1906–37, box 22.

33. Roudinesco, *Freud*, 219, quoting his 1926 interview with George Sylvester Viereck, and 236, quoting Anglo-American psychologist William McDougall.

34. *Bloomsbury/Freud: The Letters of James and Alix Strachey, 1924–1925*, ed. Perry Meisel and Walter Kendrick (New York: Basic Books, 1985), 3. James Strachey, "Obituary. Joan Riviere (1883–1962)," *The International Journal of Psycho-Analysis* 44 (1963): 228–229. Tyler Johansson, "Caroline Jane Mary Hubback," *Modernist Archives Publishing Project* at https://www.modernistarchives.com/person/caroline-jane-mary-hubback, viewed May 24, 2022. [Ernest Jones], "Editorial Preface," *Beyond the Pleasure Principle* (London, 1922).

35. Freud to Jones, July 14, 1921, *Complete Correspondence*, letters 318 and 352–354.

36. Woolf to John Rickman, December 12, 1936, in Leonard Woolf, *Letters*, ed. Frederic Spotts (New York: Harcourt Brace Jovanovich, 1989), 328.

37. Woolf to Unwin, August 7, 1924, in Woolf, *Letters*, 287; Unwin to Woolf, *Letters*, footnote.

38. Bernays, *Biography of an Idea*, 268. Laura Marcus, "European Dimensions of the Hogarth Press" in *The Reception of Virginia Woolf in Europe*, ed. Mary Ann Caws, et al. (London: Bloomsbury, 2008), 238.

39. John H. Willis, *Leonard and Virginia Woolf as Publishers: The Hogarth Press, 1917–41* (Charlottesville: University Press of Virginia, 1992), 298–301. Virginia Woolf, *The Letters of Virginia Woolf, Volume III: 1923–1928* (New York: Harcourt Brace Jovanovich, 1977), 119.

40. Leonard Woolf, interview with Kurt Eissler, July 10, 1956, in Sigmund Freud Papers: Interviews and Recollections 1914–1998, Box 123, Library of Congress; viewed online at https://www.loc.gov/item/mss3999001586, August 2, 2022.

41. Jones to Freud, April 11 and May 30, 1924, in *Complete Correspondence*, letters 423 and 428. Roazen, *Freud and His Followers*, 405. Boni and Liveright accounts ledgers, W.W. Norton & Company records 1923–1967 (MS#0938), Columbia University Rare Book and Manuscript Library, box III.3.

42. *New York Times Book Review*, September 7, 1924. *Time*, October 27, 1924, 20 and 22. Rank to Freud July 11, 1924, *The Letters of Sigmund Freud and Otto Rank: Inside Psychoanalysis*, ed. E. James Lieberman and Robert Kramer (Baltimore: Johns Hopkins University Press, 2012), 206. Correspondence between Liveright Publishing and the Hogarth Press 1949–1951 online at the Modernist Archives Publishing Project, viewed July 21, 2022, at https://www.modernistarchives.com/work/group-psychology-and-the-analysis-of-the-ego. Boni and Liveright accounts ledgers, W.W. Norton & Company records 1923–1967 (MS#0938), Columbia University Rare Book and Manuscript Library, box III.1 and III.3.

43. Bernays, *Biography of an Idea*, 285.

44. Anderson, *Memoirs*, 357.

Chapter 11

1. H.V. Kaltenborn, "A Talk with Dr. Freud, Psycho-Analyst," *Brooklyn Daily Eagle*, December 18, 1921, 18. Though famous while alive, Tridon has received little scholarly attention since. The best treatment is in Hale's *The Rise and Crisis of Psychoanalysis*, 69–72.

2. Hale, *Rise and Crisis of Psychoanalysis*, 69. *New York Times*, November 23, 1922. *Publishers Weekly*, December 2, 1922. Allan Antliff, *Anarchist Modernism*, 102–105. Hippolyte Havel, *Proletarian Days* (La Vergne: AK Press eBook, 2018), note 498. "Bankruptcy Notices," *New York Times*, June 1, 1915, 20. OCLC WorldCat.

3. Tridon to Dreiser throughout 1919, in the Theodore Dreiser Papers at the University of Pennsylvania, Box 107, folder 6213. *New York Times* events notices 1919–1922. Tridon to Brill, November 20, 1919, in the Brill Papers at the Library of Congress, Box 120.

4. Tridon to Dreiser, September 21, 1919, in Theodore Dreiser Papers at the University of Pennsylvania, Box 107, folder 6213. Andre Tridon, *Psychoanalysis, Its History, Theory and Practice* (New York: B.W. Huebsch, 1919), vii–viii.

5. *The International Journal of Psycho-analysis* 1 (1920): 477. Andre Tridon, *Psychoanalysis*, copyright page of 1923 edition. Hale, *Rise and Crisis of Psychoanalysis*, 70, citing his interview with B. W. Huebsch on May 6, 1960.

6. Lecture series advertisement reproduced without date in *Joint Legislative Committee Investigating Seditious Activities, filed April 24, 1920, in the Senate of the State of New York* (Albany: J. B. Lyon, 1920), 2322. Tridon to Dreiser, January 3, 1919, in the Theodore Dreiser Papers at the University of Pennsylvania, Box 107, folder 6213.

7. OCLC WorldCat.

8. *New York Times* obituary, February 6, 1952. *Publishers Weekly*, February 24 and December 28, 1912, April 5 and 19, 1919.

9. OCLC WorldCat. Ads in *Publishers Weekly*, 1919–1923. *Publishers Weekly*, February 9, 1924.

10. Amanda Reid, "Claiming the Copyright," *Yale Law & Policy Review* 34, no. 2 (2016): 437–438. G.B. Neavill, "Canonicity,

Reprint Series, and Copyright" in J. Spiers, ed., *The Culture of the Publisher's Series, 1: Authors, Publishers and the Shaping of Taste* (London: Palgrave Macmillan, 2011), 88–105.

11. *International Journal of Psycho-Analysis* 3 (March 1922): 114–115.

12. Freud, *Dream Psychology*, x–xi.

13. Library of Congress, Copyright Office, *Catalog of Copyright Entries, 1922: Books For the Year 1922* (Washington, D.C.: Government Printing Office, 1922), 11.

14. Unwin to Brill, March 13, 1921, in the Brill Papers at the Library of Congress, Box 4, folder 15.

15. Brill to Unwin, April 4, 1921, in the Brill Papers at the Library of Congress, Box 4, folder 15. Jones, *Complete Correspondence*, letters 310 and 340.

16. E. Jones, *Complete Correspondence*, letters 328, 331, 340, 342, 343.

17. *The International Journal of Psycho-Analysis* 3 (March 1922): 114–115. Unwin to Brill, November 14, 1922, in the Brill Papers at the Library of Congress, Box 4, folder 15.

18. *New York Times*, November 23, 1922. *Publishers Weekly*, December 2, 1922. *A Brief History of Coward-McCann, 1928–1953* (New York: Coward-McCann, 1953[?]), 1–6. *New York Times*, February 6, 1952.

Chapter 12

1. Manuel Komroff, "The Liveright Story" in the Manuel Komroff Papers 1897-1979 (MS#0723), Rare Book & Manuscript Library, Columbia University, box 15.

2. Gordon Neavill, *The Modern Library Series: A Dissertation* (Chicago: University of Chicago, 1984), 67.

3. Louis Kronenberger, "Gambler in Publishing: Horace Liveright," *Atlantic* 215 (January 1965): 95.

4. Charles Egleston, *The House of Boni & Liveright, 1917–1933: A Documentary Volume* (Detroit: Gale, 2004), 24, 28. George Andes, *A Descriptive Bibliography of the Modern Library: 1917–1970* (Boston: Boston Book Annex, 1989), 8 (spring 1918 catalog illustration). Bennett Cerf, *At Random*, 40.

5. Bennett Cerf, *Oral History Interview Transcripts, 1967-1968*, Columbia University Oral History Research Office, session 2, 100 and 102. Henry Toledano, *The Modern Library Price Guide, 1917–1995*. (Dexter, MI: Thomson-Shore, 1995), 102.

6. Bernays, *Biography of an Idea*, 51–52 and 266. Freud, *Complete Correspondence*, letters 335–336.

7. *Publishers Weekly*, July 7, 1923. *Bookseller and Stationer*, August 15, 1923. Rank/Freud correspondence, July–August 1924, in *Letters of Sigmund Freud and Otto Rank*, 206–208.

8. Bernays, *Biography of an Idea*, 273. Rank/Freud correspondence, July–August 1924, in *Letters of Sigmund Freud and Otto Rank*, 206–208.

9. *United States World War I Draft Registration Cards, 1917–1918: Massachusetts*. Image 733 on NARA microfilm M1509 (Washington, D.C.: National Archives and Records Administration, n.d.). James Van Teslaar, *When I Was a Boy in Roumania* (Boston: Lothrop, Lee and Shepard, 1917), 175–176.

10. Van Teslaar, *When I Was a Boy*, 176. American Medical Association, *United States Deceased Physician File (AMA), 1864-1968* at National Library of Medicine, viewed May 28, 2022, at https://www.familysearch.org/search/collection/2061540. Hale, *James Jackson Putnam*, 152. Van Teslaar, *Outline of Psychoanalysis*, ix. *Clark University Directory of Alumni, Faculty and Students* (Worcester, MA, 1915), 26.

11. Van Teslaar, "Religion and Sex," *Psychoanalytic Review* 2, no. 1 (1915): 82–92. Paul Roazen, "George Wilbur: Otto Rank and Hanns Sachs," *Psychoanalysis and History* 8, no. 1 (2006): 57. Van Teslaar, *Outline of Psychoanalysis*, viii–ix.

12. Toledano, *Modern Library Price Guide*, 54–55. G.B. Neavill, "The Modern Library Series: Format and Design, 1917–1977," *Printing History* 1, no. 1 (1979): 26–37.

13. Satterfield, *World's Best Books*, 127–128. "Modern Library Sales" in box 765, Random House Records 1925-1999 (Ms. #1048), Rare Book and Manuscript Library, Columbia University Library; also printed in Neavill, *The Modern Library: A Dissertation*, 561. Earl Witenberg to Jess Stein, December 13, 1955. *Random House*

Records 1925-1999, Columbia University, Box 776. The usually thorough Random House records at Columbia do not appear to contain any other data on this title.

14. Satterfield, *World's Best Books*, 35-36. Egleston, *House of Boni & Liveright, 1917-1933*, 70 and 80. Bennett Cerf, Oral History Interview Transcripts, 1967-1968. Columbia University Oral History Research Office. Session 3, 140 and 150.

15. Satterfield, *World's Best Books*, 41-43 and 51-57.

16. Cerf to Brill quoted in Neavill, *The Modern Library: A Dissertation*, 207. Cerf to Dodd Mead quoted in Satterfield, *World's Best Books*, 129. Brill to Jelliffe, October 22, 1937, in S.E. Jelliffe Papers at the Library of Congress Box 3, folder 2.

17. Brill to Freud, December 15, 1938, in Sigmund Freud Papers at Library of Congress: General Correspondence, Brill to Freud, Transcripts https://www.loc.gov/item/mss3999000471/.

18. Freud, *Basic Writings* (New York: Modern Library, 1938), 185. Random House records, 1925-1999 Rare Book and Manuscript Library, Columbia University Library, Box 81.

19. *Publishers Weekly*, December 18, 1937.

20. *Publishers Weekly*, February 19, May 14, July 16, 1938. Fred H. Tracht, "College Store and Town Store," *Publishers Weekly*, October 29, 1938. Neavill, *Modern Library: A Dissertation*, 207.

21. Brill to Freud, November 25 and December 15, 1938, and May 2, 1939, in Sigmund Freud Papers at Library of Congress: General Correspondence, Brill to Freud, Transcripts, https://www.loc.gov/item/mss3999000471/, and Freud to Brill, December 4, 1938, Sigmund Freud Papers at Library of Congress: General Correspondence, Freud to Brill, Transcripts, https://www.loc.gov/item/mss3999000468/ in the Freud Papers at the Library of Congress.

22. Cerf quoted in Satterfield, *World's Best Books*, 243, citing John T. Frederick, "Of Men and Books: The Classics are Contemporary," *Northwestern University on the Air* 2 (January 16, 1943): 4. Richard L. Simon, "Trade Winds: Try and Stop Them," *Saturday Review of Literature* 33 (December 23, 1950): 40. Neavill, *Modern Library: A Dissertation*, 207-208.

Epilogue

1. Sigmund Spaeth, *Read 'Em and Weep: The Songs You Forgot to Remember* (New York: Doubleday Page, 1927), 245-246.

2. *Interpretation of Dreams*: Brill Papers at the Library of Congress, boxes 4 and 15; *Psychopathology*: Brill Papers at the Library of Congress, boxes 5 and 15; *Wit*: Brill Papers at the Library of Congress, box 15 and Dodd, Mead Mss. (Moffat Yard) at the Lilly Library, box 15; *Leonardo*: Dodd, Mead Mss. (Moffat Yard) at the Lilly Library, box 15; *Dream or Delusion*: Dodd, Mead Mss. (Moffat Yard) at the Lilly Library, box 15; *Totem & Taboo*: Brill Papers at the Library of Congress, box 15 and Dodd, Mead Mss. (Moffat Yard) at the Lilly Library, box 15; *General Introduction*: W.W. Norton & Company records 1923-1967 at Columbia University, Series III: Boni and Liveright, Inc./Horace Liveright, Inc. records, Accounts—Cr-Gi, Box III.2. *Group Psychology* and *Beyond the Pleasure Principle*: Jones and Freud, *Complete Correspondence*, letters 423 and 428. *Outline of Psychoanalysis*: Neavill dissertation.

3. Alice Payne Hackett and James Henry Burke, *80 Years of Best Sellers: 1895-1975* (New York: R.R. Bowker Company, 1977), 22, 96-98. Matthew Joseph Bruccoli, *F. Scott Fitzgerald: A Descriptive Bibliography*. rev. ed. (Pittsburgh: University of Pittsburgh Press, 1987), 65-67.

4. Woolf to Ernest Jones, October 7, 1932, in Woolf, *Letters*, 312.

5. Emmanuel Haldeman-Julius, *The First Hundred Million* (New York: Simon & Schuster, 1928), 19-20 and 265. Jake Gibbs, *Little Blue Book Bibliography*, 3, 15-16, and 20 and unpaginated bibliography section; viewed online at https://www.littlebluebooksbibliography.com/, September 22, 2022. William J. Fielding, *All the Lives I Have Lived* (Philadelphia: Dorrance, 1972), 149-151.

6. Martin Waugh, ed. *Fruition of an Idea: Fifty Years of Psychoanalysis in New York* (New York: International Universities Press, 1962), 45-46. Hale, *Rise and Crisis*, 124-127. Laura Fermi, *Illustrious Immigrants: The Intellectual Migration from Europe, 1930-1941* (Chicago: University of Chicago Press, 1968), 151-161.

7. W.H. Auden, "In Memory of

Sigmund Freud," *Collected Poems*, ed. Edward Mendelson (New York: Vintage, 1991), 273–276. Roudinesco, *Freud*, 399–406.

8. Scull, *Desperate Remedies*, 225–226.

9. May E. Romm, "Abraham Arden Brill, 1874–1948. First American Translator of Freud" in *Psychoanalytic Pioneers*, ed.Franz Alexander, Samuel Eisenstein and Martin Grotjahn (New York: Basic Books, 1966), 222.

10. A.A. Brill, "Chaos," 158. Theodore Dreiser Papers, Ms. Coll. 30, box 14, University of Pennsylvania.

11. Scull, *Desperate Remedies*, 225–226. The pope analogy had been used as early as 1919 by William Alanson White. Huxley anecdote is documented in Cynthia Carson Bisbee et al., *Psychedelic Prophets: The Letters of Aldous Huxley and Humphry Osmond* (Montreal: McGill-Queen's University Press, 2018), x.

12. Frank L. Schick, *The Paperbound Book in America* (New York: R. R. Bowker, 1958), 132. Scull, *Desperate Remedies*, 230–231.

13. Charles Allan Madison, *Book Publishing in America* (New York: McGraw-Hill, 1966), 376–377.

14. Beam, *A Great Idea at the Time*, 2–4 and 106.

15. Schick, *Paperbound Book in America*, found that in the 1940s and 1950s Anchor print runs were usually 20,000–37,000 (181), Beacon's were 10,000 (238), Pocket Books were initially 10,000 (125), and Vintage were originally 20,000 (187). See also Satterfield, *World's Best Books*, 161–163, and Kenneth C. Davis, *Two-Bit Culture: the Paperbacking of America* (Boston: Houghton Mifflin, 1984), 208.

16. Madison, *Book Publishing in America*, 376–377. "Arthur Rosenthal, 93, Dies; Published Academic Books." *New York Times*, July 9, 2013, B10.

17. John Tebbel, *A History of Book Publishing in the United States*, vol. 3, 180. Dzwonkoski, *American Literary Publishing Houses 1900–1980*, 16.

18. Leonard Woolf, *Downhill All the Way* (London: Hogarth Press, 1969), 167–168.

19. Willis, *Leonard and Virginia Woolf as Publishers*, 310–319 and 327–328. Leonard Woolf, *Downhill All the Way* (London: Hogarth Press, 1969), 167–168.

20. Sir Peter Medawar, quoted in Louis Menand, "Why Freud Survives," *New Yorker*, August 28, 2017. Freud, *The Question of Lay Analysis* (New York: Norton, 1969). 43. Mary Jo Buhle, *Feminism and Its Discontents: A Century of Struggle with Psychoanalysis* (Cambridge: Harvard University Press, 1998), 230–239. An excellent summary of the historiography of Freud is given in Roudinesco, *Freud*, 420–427.

21. Seymour Fisher and Roger P. Greenberg, *Freud Scientifically Reappraised: Testing the Theories and Therapy* (New York: Wiley & Sons, 1996).

22. Anne Harrington, *Mind Fixers: Psychiatry's Troubled Search for the Biology of Mental Illness* (New York: W.W. Norton, 2019), 247–270. Freud, "An Outline of Psychoanalysis," *Standard Edition*, vol. 23 (London: Hogarth Press, 1964), 182. Scull, *Desperate Remedies*, 277–282 and 338. D.J. Brody and Q. Gu, "Antidepressant Use Among Adults: United States, 2015–2018," *NCHS Data Brief* 377 (Hyattsville, MD: National Center for Health Statistics, 2020). Sarah Lewis, "The Top 50 Drugs Prescribed in the United States." Published September 29, 2022, at https://www.healthgrades.com/right-care/patient-advocate/the-top-50-drugs-prescribed-in-the-united-states. Viewed December 11, 2022.

23. Scull, *Desperate Remedies*, 262–265 and 375–378.

24. Mark Edmundson, *The Death of Sigmund Freud* (New York: Bloomsbury, 2007), 225.

1. Brill Papers at Library of Congress, Box 4 folder 15. *Records of George Allen & Unwin Ltd, 1884–1983*, folder AU FSC 20/127/2, University of Reading.

2. Dodd, Mead Mss., Lilly Library, Indiana University, boxes 8 and 15.

3. Dodd, Mead Mss., Lilly Library, Indiana University, boxes 8 and 15.

4. Dodd, Mead Mss., Lilly Library, Indiana University, boxes 8 and 15.

5. Dodd, Mead Mss., Lilly Library, Indiana University, Box 8.

6. Dodd, Mead Mss., Lilly Library, Indiana University, Box 8 and Box 15.

7. W.W. Norton & Company records 1923–1967 at Columbia University, Series III: Boni and Liveright, Inc./Horace Liveright, Inc. records, Accounts—Cr–Gi, Box III.2.

8. Jones to Freud, April 11 and May 30, 1924, in *Complete Correspondence*, letters 423 and 428.

9. Jones to Freud, April 11 and May 30, 1924, in *Complete Correspondence*, letters 423 and 428.

10. Freud to Brill, March 24, 1924, in the Freud Papers at the Library of Congress, https://www.loc.gov/resource/mss39990.0 1905/?sp=18&r=-0.39,0.007,1.928,0.738,0 translation viewed August 11, 2022, at wwwfreud-edition.net t/briefe/freud-sig-mund/brill-abraham-arden/1924/03/24.

Bibliography

Archives and Unpublished Records

Allen and Unwin. "Letters from Macmillan & Company, 1904–1914." AU FSC 20/127/2. *Records of George Allen & Unwin Ltd, 1884–1983.* University of Reading, Reading, Berkshire, United Kingdom.

American Medical Association, Chicago. "United States Deceased Physician File (AMA): 1864–1968." Viewed throughout 2021–2022 online at http://FamilySearch.org.

Bernays, Edward L. *Edward L. Bernays Papers.* Mss. 12534, Library of Congress, Washington, D.C. Series 1, Family Correspondence, and Series 3, Client, Institution, and Organization File, 1916–1964, Box I:120 (Boni and Liveright, 1919–1926) and Box I:201 (International Psycho-Analytical Press, 1920–1922).

Bernays, Edward L. "My Uncle Sigi" (undated typescript). *Sigmund Freud Papers,* Library of Congress, Washington, D.C. Series: Family Papers, 1851–1978; Subject File, 1851–1978. Viewed online at https://www.loc.gov/resource/mss39990.01354/?sp=6&r=-0.129, 0.339,1.442,0.614,0.

Boni and Liveright. *Albert and Charles Boni, Inc. Records, ca. 1916–1974.* University of California–Los Angeles.

Boni and Liveright. *Boni and Liveright Correspondence.* University of Pennsylvania, Philadelphia.

Brill, Abraham A. *Abraham Arden Brill Papers,* Library of Congress, Washington, D.C. Correspondence: Box 4: Dodd, Mead & Co., 1916– (Moffat & Yard) and George Allen & Unwin, 1912; Box 5: Nervous and Mental Disease Publishing Co., 1909–1947, and Unwin, T. Fisher, 1913–1937; Box 15– Royalty statements, 1913–1937.

Brill, Abraham A. "Chaos" (transcript of dialogue between Brill and Theodore Dreiser taken down by Brill's stenographer September 23, 1932). *Theodore Dreiser Papers,* Ms. Coll. 30, box 14, University of Pennsylvania.

Brill, Abraham A. Letters to Freud in the *Sigmund Freud Papers: General Correspondence, 1871–1996; Brill, A.A.; To Freud; Transcripts, 1908–1939.* Library of Congress, Washington, D.C. Online at https://www.loc.gov/resource/mss39990.01908/?st=list.

Cerf, Bennett. *Oral History Interview Transcripts, 1967–1968.* Columbia University Oral History Research Office. Viewed throughout 2021–2022 online at http://www.columbia.edu/cu/lweb/digital/collections/nny/cerfb/toc.html.

Dodd, Mead Mss., 1855–1992. Box 8: Authors, Publishers, and Other Correspondents, Freud, Sigmund; Box 15: Moffat, Yard and Company: Agreements, correspondence, bills, catalogs, royalty reports, etc. Lilly Library, Indiana University, Bloomington, IN.

Dreiser, Theodore. *Theodore Dreiser Papers, ca. 1890–1965.* Box 14: Correspondence between Dreiser and Brill. University of Pennsylvania Libraries, Philadelphia, PA.

Eissler, Kurt. "Interviews and Recollections recorded by Kurt Eissler." *Sigmund Freud Papers at the Library of Congress: Interviews and Recollections, 1914–1998.* Interviews

191

consulted: Anna Freud, Martin Grotjahn, Belinda Jelliffe, Clarence Oberndorf, Joan Riviere, Rudolph von Urbantschitsch, George S. Viereck, and Leonard Woolf.

Fielding, William J. *William John Fielding Papers, 1911–1986.* Box 3: Correspondence with William J. Robinson and André Tridon. Tamiment Library, New York University, New York, NY. TAM.069.

Freud, Sigmund. *Sigmund Freud Papers,* Library of Congress, Washington, D.C. Viewed online throughout 2021–2022 at http://hdl.loc.gov/loc.mss/collmss.ms000051.

Freud, Sigmund. *Sigmund Freud, Letters to Abraham Brill.* English translations viewed online throughout 2021–2022 at https://www.freud-edition.net/briefe/freud-sigmund/brill-abraham-arden .

Hall, G. Stanley. *G. Stanley Hall Papers.* Clark University, Worcester, MA.

Hogarth Press. *The Modernist Archives Publishing Project.* Online archive of Hogarth Press records at https://www.modernistarchives.com.

Huebsch, Benjamin W. "Reminiscences of Ben W. Huebsch, 1955." Interview, Columbia Center for Oral History, Rare Book and Manuscript Library, Columbia University Libraries. Transcript viewed online at https://clio.columbia.edu/catalog/15197742.

Jellliffe, S.E. *Smith Ely Jelliffe Papers, 1882–1977,* MSS57018. Series 1: Correspondence, 1889–1944, Box 3 (Brill). Library of Congress, Manuscript Division, Washington, D.C.

Komroff, Manuel. *Manuel Komroff Papers, 1897–1979.* Columbia University, New York, NY.

Liveright, Horace. *Horace Liveright Papers, 1902–1932.* University of Pennsylvania, Philadelphia, PA.

Macmillan Co. (London). *Macmillan Records 1889–1960: Correspondence with Macmillan Company (N.Y.).* New York Public Library, New York, NY.

Macmillan Company (New York). *Records 1889–1960.* Series I: General Correspondence, 1892–1914, and II: Foreign Correspondence Files, 1898–1914. New York Public Library, New York, NY.

Random House. *Records, 1925–1999.* Box 81: Series II: Box 181-Manufacturing Department Correspondence-Dead File, 1932–1949-Freud, Sigmund; Box 776-Jess Stein files, 1948–1956-*Outline of Psychoanalysis.* Columbia University Library, New York, NY.

Sumner, John S. *John Saxton Sumner Papers, 1904–1961.* "Monthly reports, New York Society for the Suppression of Vice." Wisconsin Historical Society, Madison, WI.

Tucker, Benjamin R. *Benjamin R. Tucker Papers, 1860s–1970s.* MssCol 3040. "The Life of Benjamin R. Tucker Disclosed by Himself in the Principality of Monaco at the Age of 74." Series: Scrapbooks & Miscellaneous Papers, Box 8. New York Public Library, Manuscripts and Archives Division, New York, NY.

W.W. Norton & Company Records, 1923–1967. MS#0938. Series III: Boni and Liveright, Inc./Horace Liveright, Inc. Records, Series III.1 Accounts, 1920–1960s: Boxes III.1-III.5. Columbia University, New York, NY.

Publications by or about Freud Prior to His September 1909 American Visit

The 63 items in this section are arranged chronologically to facilitate browsing. The earliest mention of psychoanalysis is an 1894 abstract by William James of Freud and Breuer's "Über den Psychischen Mechanismus Hysterischer Phänomene" in the *Psychological Review.* The first American review of a book by Freud appeared in *American Journal of Psychology* in July 1899. The first discussion of Freud's ideas outside the medical press was "Mystery of Dreams Revealed" in the *San Francisco Call* on March 18, 1900. The first separate publication of Freud's work in the U.S. was the pamphlet *What Are Dreams?* printed in April 1900 in New York (see Appendix). The first popular account of Freud's ideas in a mainstream magazine was Frederick Peterson's "The New Divination of Dreams" in *Harper's Monthly* for August 1907.

1882. "The Structure of Living Nerves and Nerve Cells." *Journal of Nervous & Mental Disease* 9 (October 1882): 784–785. Refers to Freud's early research on the nervous system of freshwater crayfish.

1883. "The Acoustic Nucleus and the Interolivary Tract." *Journal of Nervous & Mental Disease* 12 (July 1883): 386. Abstracts a neurology article by Freud originally published in *Neurologisches Centralblatt*, June 15, 1885.

1883. Freud, Sigmund (unsigned). "Spina's Studies on the Bacillus of Tuberculosis." *Medical News* (April 7, 1883): 401–402. A two-column (13-paragraph) review of *Studien über Tuberculose* by Arnold Spina (Vienna: W. Braumüller, 1883). Attributed to Freud by Alexander Grinstein.

1884. Freud, Sigmund (unsigned). "Vienna—From Our Special Correspondent. Cocaine." *Medical News* (November 1, 1884): 502. Four paragraphs. Attributed to Freud by Alexander Grinstein.

1884. Freud, Sigmund (unsigned). "Coca." *St. Louis Medical & Surgical Journal* 47 (1884): 502–505. Reprints *Medical News* article of November 1, 1884.

1884. Freud, Sigmund (unsigned). "Vienna—From Our Special Correspondent. The Bacillus of Syphilis." *Medical News* (December 13, 1884): 673–674. Attributed to Freud by Alexander Grinstein.

1884. Freud, Sigmund. "A New Histological Method for the Study of Nerve Tracts in the Brain and Spinal Cord." *Brain, A Journal of Neurology* 7 (April 1884): 86–88.

1885. "Coca." *Alienist and Neurologist* 6, no. 2 (April 1, 1885): 265. Abstracts a paper by Freud on cocaine, citing "*Centralbl. f. d. Ges. Therap., 1884, VII. Heft—Ueber Coca.*"

1885. "The Different Cocaine Preparations and Their Efficacy." *Medical Age* (September 25, 1885): 419–421. Translates an 11-paragraph article from *Wiener Medicinishe Presse* of August 9, 1885.

1886. "The Connections of the Inferior Peduncle of the Cerebellum with the Posterior Columns of the Spinal Cord." *Journal of Nervous and Mental Disease* 13 (April–May 1886): 246. Abstracts an article by Freud and L. Darkschewitsch from "*Neurol. Centralbl., no. 6, 1886.*"

1888. Upson, Henry S. "On Gold as a Staining Agent for Nerve Tissues." *Journal of Nervous & Mental Disease* 15 (November 1888): 685. One-paragraph description of Freud's method.

1893. "Nocturnal Enuresis in Children." *Medical Times and Register* 26 (December 23, 1893): 1175. Abstract of an article by Freud (citing "*Neurol. Centrallbl., Nov. 21, 1893*") on incontinence in children.

1894. James, William. "Über den Psychischen Mechanismus Hysterischer Phänomene." *Psychological Review* 1 (March 1894): 199. One-paragraph abstract of Freud and Breuer's article. Signed only with initials.

1894. Leszynsky, W.M. "On a Symptom That Frequently Accompanies Nocturnal Enuresis in Children." *Journal of Nervous & Mental Disease* 21 (1894): 112. One paragraph abstract of an article by Freud cited as "(*Neurolog. Centrbl., 1893, No. 21*)." Signed only with initials.

1894. Newmark, Leo. "The Relation of Abnormal Birth to Certain Cerebral Affections in Children." *Pacific Medical Journal* 37, no. 7 (1894): 401–412. Contains several brief references to Freud's neurological research.

1895. Edes, Robert T. "The New England Invalid." *Boston Medical & Surgical Journal* 133 (July 18, 1895): 56. Contains one brief reference to Freud and Breuer's work on hysteria.

1895. Onuf, Bronislaw. "The Warding-Off Neuro-Psychoses (Die Abwehr Neuro-Psychosen.)" *Journal of Nervous & Mental Disease* 22 (February 1895): 129. Nearly full-page abstract of "an attempt at a psychological theory of acquired hysteria, many phobias and certain hallucinatory psychoses—Freud "(*Neurolog. Centrallbl., 1894. Nos. 10 and 11*)."

1895. Putnam, James Jackson. "Remarks on the Psychical Treatment of Neurasthenia." *Boston Medical & Surgical Journal* 122 (May 23, 1895): 505–511. Discusses the methods of Janet, Breuer, and Freud in passing.

1895. Sachs, Bernard. *A Treatise on the Nervous Diseases of Children for Physicians and Students*. New York: William Wood and Co., 1893. Contains many brief references to Freud's neurological research.

1896. "Etiology of Hysteria." *Alienist and Neurologist* 17, no. 3 (October 1, 1896): 519–520. Summarizes Freud's article of the same title, citing "Wien. Klin. Runsch., Nos. 22 to 26."

Rejects Freud's claim that hysteria and other neuroses have sexual origins and condemns "the absurdity of such wildly conjectural, unproved and unprovable conclusions."

1896. "Paresthetic Neuralgia." *Boston Medical & Surgical Journal* 134, no. 4 (January 23, 1896): 85–86. Contains two paragraphs discussing Freud's neurological research.

1898. "Sexual Origin of Neurasthenia and Psycho-Neurosis." *Alienist and Neurologist* 19, no. 4 (1898): 673–674. One-paragraph abstract of Freud's research, citing "The Medical Times."

1898. "Sexual Origin of Neurasthenia and Psychoneurosis." *Medical and Surgical Reporter* 78, no. 6 (May 16, 1898): 190. Six-paragraph abstract of Freud's research.

1898. Ellis, Havelock. "Hysteria in Relation to the Sexual Emotions." *Alienist and Neurologist* 19, no. 4 (1898): 599–615. Devotes seven pages to a summary of the research by Freud and Breuer which is to "form part of Vol. II of [Ellis's] *Studies in the Psychology of Sex.*"

1898. Mills, Charles Karsner. *The Nervous System and Its Diseases*. Philadelphia, Lippincott, 1898. Contains 10 references to Freud's pre-psychoanalytic writings.

1898. Stieglitz, Leopold. "Multiple Sclerosis in Childhood, with a Report of Three Cases." *American Journal of the Medical Sciences* 115, no. 2 (1898): 146–161. Several brief references to Freud's early neurological research on pp. 151–153.

1898. Zenner, Philip. "Neurasthenia." *Cincinnati Lancet and Clinic* 40, no. 26 (June 25, 1898): 643–650. Brief reference to Freud's theory of the sexual origins of neurasthenia on p. 644.

1899. "Sexuality in the Etiology of the Neuroses." *Medical News* 74, no. 2 (1899): 47–48. Abstract of Freud's research, citing "*Central-bl. f. inner. Med.*, November 5, 1898."

1899. "Sigmund Freud's Foolish Conclusion." *Alienist and Neurologist* 20 (1899): 113–114. Condemns Freud's claim of the sexual origins of hysteria and neuroses as exemplifying "the absurd lengths to which medical men will go in their conclusions, either when seeking medical notoriety or when they take leave of their reason."

1899. Forel, August. "Hypnotism and Cerebral Activity." *Clark University 1889–1899 Decennial Celebration*. Worcester, MA, 1899, 412–413. Brief summary of Freud and Breuer's theory of the sexual etiology of hysteria.

1899. Putnam, James Jackson. "The Shattuck Lecture: Not the Disease Only, But Also the Man. Article II. Delivered June 13, 1899." *Medical Communications of the Massachusetts Medical Society* 18 (1899–1901): 47–79. Brief summary of Freud's and Breuer's techniques on pp. 70–71.

1899. Runkle, Erwin W. "Studien Uber Hysterie Von Dr. Jos. Brewer [sic] und Dr. Sigm. Freud." *American Journal of Psychology* 10, no. 4 (July 1899): 592–93. Long positive review, the first review of one of Freud's books in the U.S.

1900. "Mystery of Dreams Revealed." *San Francisco Call*, March 18, 1900, 8. Unsigned review of the German edition of *The Interpretation of Dreams*. See chapter 1.

1900. *What Are Dreams?* New York: Tucker Publishing Co., 1900. Sixteen-page pamphlet reprinting a long review with substantial excerpts from *The Interpretation of Dreams*, "originally printed in '*Die Grenzboten*,' Leipzig, March 15, 1900." See Chapter 1.

1900. Metzentin, Carl. "Wissenschaftliche Traumdetung." *Der Deutsche Correspondent*, January 21, 1900. Reprints a review of *The Interpretation of Dreams* from *Die Gegenwart* (Berlin) 56 (16 December1899): 386–89. See Chapter 1.

1903. Myers, Frederic. *Human Personality and Its Survival of Bodily Death*. New York: Longmans, 1903, vol. I, 50–52. Summarizes the case of Lucy R. from Freud's and Breuer's *Studies on Hysteria*.

1903. Politzer, Adam. *A Text-Book of the Diseases of the Ear for Students and Practitioners*. Philadelphia, Lea Bros, 1902. Three brief references to Freud's neurological research on pp. 700–701.

1904. Edes, Robert T. "Mind Cures from the Standpoint of the General Practitioner." *Medical Communications of the Massachusetts Medical Society* 19 (1904): 659–678. Freud's and Breuer's early psychoanalytic work is discussed on pp. 673–674.

1904. Hall, G. Stanley. *Adolescence: Its Psychology and Its Relations to Physiology, Anthropology, Sociology, Sex, Crime, Religion and Education*. New York: D. Appleton and

Company, 1904. Two volumes. Quotes and discusses Freud's theory of the sexual origins of neuroses several times.

1904. Putnam, James Jackson. "A Consideration of Mental Therapeutics as Employed by Special Students of the Subject." *Medical Communications of the Massachusetts Medical Society* 19 (1904): 681–693. Freud's and Breuer's early psychoanalytic work is briefly mentioned on p. 687.

1905. "Obsessions and Sexual Life." *Lancet-Clinic* 93 (1905): 57. Brief mention of Freud in a short review of another author's work.

1905. Clarke, J. Mitchell. Review of *Studien über Hysterie*. *Brain* 19 (March 10, 1905): 401–414. Long analysis of Freud's and Breuer's book on the 10th anniversary of its original publication in German.

1906. Elllis, Havelock. *Studies in the Psychology of Sex*, vol. 5. Philadelphia: Davis, 1906. Discusses Freud's *Three Essays on the Theory of Sex* on p. 133.

1906. Forel, August. *Hypnotism, or Suggestion and Psychotherapy*. New York: Rebman, 1906. One paragraph on p. 208 discusses Freud's work on hysteria.

1906. Putnam, James Jackson. "Recent Experiences in the Study and Treatment of Hysteria at the Massachusetts General Hospital, with Remarks on Freud's Method of Treatment by 'Psychoanalysis.'" *Journal of Abnormal Psychology* 1 (1906–07): 26–41. Reports on the author's use of Freud's techniques; refers to all Freud's major works published up to that time.

1907. Jelliffe, Smith Ely. "The Signs of Pre-Dementia Praecox: Their Significance and Pedagogic Prophylaxis." *American Journal of the Medical Sciences* 134, no. 2 (1907): 157–182. Two passing references to Freud, apparently Jelliffe's first.

1907. Peterson, Frederick. "The New Divination of Dreams." *Harper's Monthly Magazine* 115 (August 1907): 448–452. Summarizes Freud's main points in *The Interpretation of Dreams* without citing the book or naming him. The first discussion of Freud's ideas in a popular American magazine.

1908. "Freud's Method of Psychotherapy." *Pacific Medical Journal* 51, no. 5 (1908): 283. One-paragraph abstract of L. Pierce Clarke on Freud, citing *Medical Record*, March 21, 1908.

1908. Allen, Leo B. "Psychotherapy." *University of Pennsylvania Medical Bulletin* 21 (May 1, 1908): 76–80. Summarizes techniques then in use, devoting two pages to Freud.

1908. Brill, A.A. "Psychological Factors in Dementia Praecox." *Journal of Abnormal Psychology* 3, no. 4 (October 1, 1908): 219–239. A few passing references to Freud, but mainly a description of Jung's methods applied to one case.

1908. Clark, L. Pierce. "Freud's Method of Psychotherapy." *Medical Record* 73, no. 12 (March 21, 1908): 481–482. Abstract of a paper given at the New York Neurological Society meeting, January 7, 1908, summarizing Freud's theories and methods.

1908. Clark, L. Pierce. "Freud's Method of Psychotherapy." *Journal of Nervous & Mental Disease* 35 (June 1, 1908): 391–392. Brief report on the paper given January 7, 1908, at New York Neurological Society meeting.

1908. Dercum, Francis Xavier. "An Analysis of Psychotherapeutic Methods." *Therapeutic Gazette* 52 (May 13, 1908): 305–316. A paper read before the Philadelphia Medical Society, March 25, 1908; discusses Freud on pp. 310–315.

1908. Jones, Ernest. "Rationalization in Everyday Life." *Journal of Abnormal Psychology* 3 (August 1908): 161–169. Refers to Freud throughout.

1908. Lull, Cabot. "Remarks on Psychotherapy." *Alabama Medical Journal* 20 (June 1908): 394–400. Brief mention of Freud on p. 400.

1908. Onuf, Bronislaw. "Psychotherapy." *Journal of the American Medical Association* 50, no. 23 (June 6, 1908): 1892–1897. Discusses Freud's theories and methods throughout.

1909. Allen, C.L. "Some Consideration with Regard to Present Popular Interest in Psycho- and Religio-Therapy." *Southern California Practitioner* 24 (July 1, 1909): 343–346. Brief reference to Freud on p. 345.

1909. Barlow, W. Jarvis. "Psychotherapy." *California State Journal of Medicine* 7 (August 1, 1909): 274–279. A paper "read at the Thirty-ninth Annual Meeting of State Society, San Jose, April, 1909" that makes four short references to Freud.

1909. Brill, A.A. "A Case of Schizophrenia." *American Journal of Insanity* 66, no. 1 (July 1909): 53–70. Many references to Freud throughout.

1909. Brill, A.A. "Freud's Method of Psychoanalysis" in Parker, William B. *Psychotherapy, A Course of Reading in Sound Psychology, Sound Medicine and Sound Religion.* New York: Centre Publishing Co., 1909, vol. 2, 36–47. An overview of Freud's theories and methods.

1909. Brill, A.A. "A Contribution to the Psychopathology of Everyday Life" in Parker, William B. *Psychotherapy, A Course of Reading in Sound Psychology, Sound Medicine and Sound Religion.* New York: Centre Publishing Co., 1909, vol. 3, 5–20. Long, thorough article on Freud's basic concepts and methods, using several examples from Brill's own practice.

1909. Jones, Ernest. "Psychoanalysis in Psychotherapy." *Journal of Abnormal Psychology* 4 (June 1, 1909): 140–150. Many references to Freud throughout.

Primary Sources Published After Freud's September 1909 American Visit

Acher, Rudolph. "Recent Freudian Literature." *American Journal of Psychology* 22 (1911): 408–43.

Albrecht, Albert. "Prof. Sigmund Freud. The Eminent Vienna Psycho-Therapeutist Now in America." *Boston Evening Transcript,* September 11, 1909, p. 31.

Allen & Unwin. *Archives of George Allen & Co., 1893–1915* in *British Publisher's Archives on Microfilm* (Thetford: Chadwyck-Healey, 1974).

Alumni Horae (Concord, New Hampshire, St. Paul's School).

Anderson, Sherwood. *Memoirs.* New York: Harcourt Brace, 1942.

Ayer & Son's American Newspaper Annual and Directory. Philadelphia: N.W. Ayer, 1910–1915.

Bernays, Edward. *Biography of an Idea: Memoirs of Public Relations Counsel.* New York: Simon & Schuster, 1965.

_____. "Promotion Expert Urges New Sales Method for Books." *Publishers Weekly,* March 20, 1920: 933–936.

_____. "Uncle Sigi." *Journal of the History of Medicine and Allied Sciences* 35, no. 2 (1980): 216–223.

Bok, Edward. *The Americanization of Edward Bok.* New York: Scribner's, 1920.

"Boston Radicals—As Mild-Mannered Men and Women as Ever Scuttled the Ship of State." *Boston Globe,* Sunday, April 5, 1891, p. 28.

Brett, George P. "Publisher, Book Seller and Reader: Changing Currents in the World of Books." *The Independent* 76, no. 3390 (November 20, 1913): 344.

A Brief History of Coward-McCann, 1928–1953. New York: Coward-McCann, 1953[?].

Brill, Abraham A. "Adjustment of the Jew to the American Environment." *Mental Hygiene* 2 (1918): 219–231.

_____. "Dreams and Their Relations to the Neurosis." *New York Medical Journal* 91 (April 23, 1910): 842–846.

_____. "Freud's Conception of Psychoneurosis." *Medical Record* 76 (December 25, 1909): 1065–1069.

_____. *Freud's Contributions to Psychiatry.* New York: W.W. Norton, 1944.

_____. "In Memoriam. Sigmund Freud, 1856–1939." *American Journal of Psychiatry* 96, no. 3 (November 1939): 760–764.

_____. "In Memoriam. Smith Ely Jelliffe. October 27, 1866–September 25, 1945." *Journal of Nervous and Mental Disease* 106, no. 3 (September 1947): 220–227.

_____. "The Introduction and Development of Freud's Works in the United States." *American Journal of Sociology* 45 (November 1939): 318–325.

_____. "Introduction" in Jung, C.G. *Psychology of Dementia Praecox.* Princeton: Princeton University Press, 1974 [originally published 1936].

_____. "Introduction" in *The Basic Writings of Sigmund Freud.* New York: Modern Library, 1938.

_____. "Jelliffe, the Psychiatrist and Psychoanalyst." *Journal of Nervous and Mental Disease* 89 (1939): 536.

_____. "Masturbation: Its Causes and Sequelae." *American Journal of Urology* 12 (1916): 214–222.

_____. "Professor Freud and Psychiatry." *Psychoanalytic Review* 18 (1931): 241–246.

_____. "A Psychoanalyst Scans His Past." *Journal of Nervous & Mental Disease* 95, no. 5 (1942): 537–549.

_____. "Psychoanalytic Fragments from a Day's Work." *Journal of Abnormal Psychology* 8, no. 5 (1913): 310–321.

_____. "Psychological Factors in Dementia Praecox." *Journal of Abnormal Psychology* 3 (1908): 219–239.

_____. "Psychotherapies I Encountered." *Psychiatric Quarterly* 21 (1947): 575–591.

_____. "Reflections, Reminiscences of Sigmund Freud" in Ruitenbeek, Hendrik Marinus. *Freud As We Knew Him*. Detroit: Wayne State University Press, 1973.

_____. "Science Discovers Reality of Dreams." *New York Times*, May 8, 1910.

_____. "Thoughts on Life and Death." *Psychiatric Quarterly* 21 (1947): 199–211.

Brill, Abraham A., and Smith Ely Jelliffe. "Statistical Summary of Cases in Department of Neurology, Vanderbilt Clinic for Ten Years—1900 to 1909." *Journal of Nervous and Mental Disease* 38, no. 7 (July 1911): 391–412.

Brooks, Van Wyck. *The Confident Years, 1885–1915*. New York: Dutton, 1952.

Bruce, H. Addington. "Masters of the Mind." *American Magazine* (November 1, 1910): 71–81.

_____. "Some Books on Mental Healing." *Forum* 43 (March 1, 1910): 316.

Burrow, Trigant. *A Search for Man's Sanity: The Selected Letters of Trigant Burrow, with Biographical Notes*. New York: Oxford University Press, 1958.

Cattell, J. McKeen. "Some Psychological Experiments: Address of the Retiring President of the American Association for the Advancement of Science, Given at Kansas City on December 28, 1925." *Science* (January 1, 1926): 1–8.

Cerf, Bennett. *At Random: The Reminiscences of Bennett Cerf*. New York: Random House, 1977.

_____. "Horace Liveright. An Obituary—Unedited." *Publishers Weekly*, October 7, 1933, p. 1230.

Chase, Harry W. "Freud's Theories of the Unconscious." *Popular Science Monthly* 78 (April 1, 1911): 355–363.

Clark University. *Lectures and Addresses Delivered Before the Departments of Psychology and Pedagogy in Celebration of the Twentieth Anniversary of the Opening of Clark University September 1909*. Worcester, MA: [no publisher identified], 1910. See Chapter 3.

Clark University Directory of Alumni, Faculty and Students. Worcester, MA: Clark University, 1915.

Columbia University. "Directory of Students" in *Catalogue 1920–1921*. New York: Columbia University, [1920].

Columbia University Libraries. *University Bibliography 1909*. New York, 1910.

Comstock, Anthony. "The Work of the New York Society for the Prevention of Vice and Its Bearing on the Morals of the Young." *Proceedings of the Child Conference for Research and Welfare*. New York: G.E. Stechert, 1910: 91–109.

Coriat, Isador. "Some Reminiscences of Psychoanalysis in Boston." *Psychoanalytic Review* 32 (January 1945): 1–8.

DeForest, Henry P. "William J. Robinson: Eulogy." *Medical Review of Reviews* 42, no. 2 (February 1936): 52–56.

Dell, Floyd. *Homecoming: An Autobiography*. New York: Farrar & Rinehart, 1933.

"Die Gegenwart." *Wikipedia* (German edition). Viewed March 4, 2022, at https://de.wikipedia.org/wiki/Die_Gegenwart_(1872%E2%80%931931).

Dreiser, Theodore. "The Mercy of God." *American Mercury* II (August 1924): 457.

_____. *Twelve Men*. New York: Modern Library, 1928.

Eastman, Max. *Enjoyment of Living*. New York: Harper, 1948.

Ellis, Havelock. "Freud's Influence on the Changed Attitude Toward Sex." *American Journal of Sociology* 45, no. 3 (November 1939): 309–317.

_____. "The Symbolism of Dreams." *Popular Science Monthly*, July 1910, 42–55.
Everett, Patricia R. *Corresponding Lives: Mabel Dodge Luhan, A.A. Brill, and the Psychoanalytic Adventure in America*. New York: Routledge, 2019.
Frank, Waldo (under the pseudonym "Search-Light"). "Joyful Wisdom." *New Yorker*, October 17, 1925: 11–12.
"Freud and Freudism." *TIME Magazine* 4, no. 17 (October 27, 1924): 20. Viewed August 16, 2022, at https://tinyurl.com/5ctdpxdf.
Freud, Anna. "Personal Memories of Ernest Jones." *International Journal of Psychoanalysis* 60 (1979): 285–287.
Freud, Sigmund. *An Autobiographical Study*. London: Hogarth Press and Institute for Psycho-Analysis, 1935.
_____. *The Basic Writings of Sigmund Freud*. New York: Modern Library, May 1938.
_____. *Beyond the Pleasure Principle*. New York: Boni and Liveright, September 1924.
_____. *The Complete Correspondence of Sigmund Freud and Ernest Jones, 1908–1939*. Cambridge: Harvard University Press, 1993.
_____. *The Complete Correspondence of Sigmund Freud and Karl Abraham: 1907–1925*. London: Karnac, 2002.
_____. *The Complete Letters of Sigmund Freud to Wilhelm Fliess, 1887–1904*. Cambridge: Harvard University Press, 1985.
_____. *The Correspondence of Sigmund Freud and Saindor Ferenczi*. Cambridge: Harvard University Press, 1994–2000.
_____. *Delusion and Dream: An Interpretation in the Light of Psychoanalysis of Gradiva, a Novel*. New York: Moffat, Yard, 1917.
_____. *Dream Psychology: Psychoanalysis for Beginners*. New York: The James A. McCann Co., 1920.
_____. *Freud/Jung Letters*. Ed. William McGuire. Princeton: Princeton University Press, 1974.
_____. *A General Introduction to Psychoanalysis*. New York: Boni and Liveright, 1920.
_____. *A General Selection from the Works of Sigmund Freud*. Ed. John Rickman. London: Hogarth Press, 1937.
_____. *Group Psychology and the Analysis of the Ego*. New York: Boni and Liveright, 1924.
_____. *History of the Psychoanalytic Movement*. New York: Nervous and Mental Disease Publishing Co., 1917.
_____. *The Interpretation of Dreams*. New York: Macmillan Co., 1913.
_____. *The Interpretation of Dreams*. Second edition. New York: Macmillan, 1932.
_____. *Leonardo da Vinci, A Psychosexual Study of an Infantile Reminiscence*. New York: Moffat, Yard & Co., 1916.
_____. *The Letters of Sigmund Freud and Otto Rank: Inside Psychoanalysis*. Ed. E. James Lieberman and Robert Kramer. Baltimore: Johns Hopkins University Press, 2012.
_____. *Letters of Sigmund Freud*. New York: Basic Books, 1960.
_____. *The Major Works of Sigmund Freud*. Chicago: Encyclopædia Britannica, 1952.
_____. *Modern Sexual Morality and Modern Nervousness*. New York: Critic and Guide Co., 1915.
_____. *On Dreams*. New York: Rebman Company, 1914.
_____. "The Origin and Development of Psychoanalysis" in *Lectures and Addresses Delivered Before the Departments of Psychology and Pedagogy in Celebration of the Twentieth Anniversary of the Opening of Clark University. September, 1909*. Worcester, MA, 1910.
_____. *Psychoanalysis and Faith: The letters of Sigmund Freud and Oskar Pfister*. New York: Basic Books, 1963.
_____. *Psychopathology of Everyday Life*. New York: Macmillan, 1914.
_____. *Reflections on War and Death*. New York: Moffat, Yard, 1918.
_____. *Selected Papers on Hysteria and Other Psychoneuroses*. New York: The Nervous & Mental Disease Publishing Co., 1909.
_____. *The Standard Edition of the Complete Psychological Works of Sigmund Freud*. 24 volumes. London: Hogarth Press and Institute for Psycho-Analysis, 1953–1974.

_____. *Three Contributions to the Sexual Theory*. New York: Nervous and Mental Disease Publishing Co., 1910.

_____. *Totem and Taboo, Resemblances between the Psychic Lives of Savages and Neurotics*. New York: Moffat, Yard & Co., 1918.

_____. *Wit and Its Relation to the Unconscious*. New York: Moffat, Yard & Co., 1916.

"Freud's Discovery of the Lowest Chamber of the Soul." *Current Opinion* 50 (May 1, 1911): 512–514.

Goldman, Emma. *Anarchism and Other Essays*. New York: Mother Earth, 1910.

_____. *Living My Life*. Salt Lake City: G.M. Smith, 1982.

"Greenberg: Publisher Celebrates Twenty-Fifth Anniversary." *Publishers Weekly* (October 1, 1949): 1569–1571.

Hale, Nathan G., ed. *James Jackson Putnam and Psychoanalysis: Letters Between Putnam and Sigmund Freud, Ernest Jones, William James, Sandor Ferenczi, and Morton Prince, 1877–1917*. Cambridge: Harvard University Press, 1971.

Hall, G. Stanley. *Life and Confessions of a Psychologist*. New York: Appleton, 1924.

_____ "Recent Freudian Literature in English." *American Journal of Psychology* 28, no. 2 (April 1917): 306–307.

[Hall, G. Stanley]. "Twentieth Anniversary of Clark University." *Nation* 89 (September 23, 1909): 284–285.

Hapgood, Hutchins. *A Victorian in the Modern World*. New York: Harcourt Brace, 1939.

Havel, Hippolyte. *Proletarian Days*. La Vergne: AK Press eBook, 2018.

Ishill, Joseph. "Benjamin R. Tucker: In Appreciation" in *Free Vistas II* (Berkeley Heights, NJ: Oriole Press, 1937[?]), 261–308.

Jelliffe, Smith E. "The Editor Himself and His Adopted Child." *Journal of Nervous and Mental Disease* 89 (April 1939): 545–589.

_____. "Glimpses of a Freudian Odyssey." *Psychoanalytic Quarterly* 2, no. 2 (1933): 318–329.

_____. "Sigmund Freud and Psychiatry: A Partial Appraisal." *American Journal of Sociology* 45, no. 3 (November 1939): 326- 340.

_____. "Some Notes on his Earlier Neurobiological and Clinical Neurological Studies." *Journal of Nervous and Mental Disease* 85 (1937): 696–711.

Jelliffe: American Psychoanalyst and Physician. His Correspondence with Sigmund Freud and C.G. Jung. Ed. John C. Burnham and William McGuire. Chicago: University of Chicago Press, 1983.

Jones, Bobby. "The Story of Greenwich Village. Part VI." *Greenwich Village Quill* 13, no. 1 (July 1923) and no. 6 (December 1923).

Jones, Ernest. *Free Associations: Memories of a Psycho-Analyst*. New York: Basic Books, 1959.

_____. *Life and Work of Sigmund Freud*. 3 volumes. London: Hogarth Press, 1953–1957.

_____. *Life and Work of Sigmund Freud*. One-volume edition abridged by Lionel Trilling and Steven Marcus. New York: Basic Books, 1961.

_____. "Psycho-Analytic Notes on a Case of Hypomania." *American Journal of Insanity* 66, no. 3 (October 1909): 203–218.

_____. "Reminiscent Notes on the Early History of Psycho-Analysis in English-Speaking Countries." *International Journal of Psycho-Analysis* 26 (1945): 8.

_____. *Sandor Ferenczi—Ernest Jones Letters 1911–1933*. New York: Routledge, 2013.

Kaltenborn, H.V. "A Talk with Dr. Freud, Psycho-Analyst." *Brooklyn Daily Eagle*, December 18, 1921, 18.

Kearney, Patrick. "Taboos of the Vice Agents." *Freeman* 1 (August 18, 1920): 542–543.

Kronenberger, Louis. "Gambler in Publishing: Horace Liveright." *Atlantic* 215 (January 1965): 94–104.

Library of Congress. Copyright Office. *Catalog of Copyright Entries*. Washington, D.C.: Government Printing Office, 1900–1938.

Lloyd, William J. "Memories of Benjamin R. Tucker" in *Free Vistas II*. Berkeley Heights, NJ: Oriole Press, 1937[?], 279–283.

Luhan, Mabel Dodge. *The Dreams of Mabel Dodge: Diary of an Analysis with Smith Ely Jelliffe*. Ed. Patricia Everett. New York: Routledge, 2021.

_____. *European Experiences.* New York: Harcourt, Brace, 1935.

_____. *A History of Having a Great Many Times Not Continued to Be Friends: the Correspondence Between Mabel Dodge and Gertrude Stein, 1911–1934.* Albuquerque: University of New Mexico Press, 1996.

_____. *Movers and Shakers.* Albuquerque: University of New Mexico Press, 1985.

_____. *The Suppressed Memoirs of Mabel Dodge Luhan: Sex, Syphilis, and Psychoanalysis in the Making of Modern American Culture.* Albuquerque: University of New Mexico Press, 2012.

Macfarlane, Peter Clark. "Diagnosis by Dreams." *Good Housekeeping* 60 (February and March 1915): 215–133 and 278–286.

"Medical Report from a New Psychological World." *Current Literature* 50 (February 1, 1911): 167–169.

"Memorial Number to William Josephus Robinson, [December 8, 1867–January 6, 1936]." *Medical Review of Reviews* 42, no 2 (February 1936).

Menninger, Karl. "Contributions of A.A. Brill to Psychiatry." *Bulletin of the Menninger Clinic* 13, no. 5 (1949): 185–187.

Meyer, Adolf. "A Few Trends in Modern Psychiatry." *Psychological Bulletin* I (June 15, 1904): 217–240.

Mumby, F.A., and F.H.S. Stallybrass. *From Swan Sonnenschein to George Allen & Unwin, Ltd.* London: George Allen & Unwin, 1955.

New York. *Joint Legislative Committee Investigating Seditious Activities, filed April 24, 1920, in the Senate of the State of New York.* Albany: J.B. Lyon, 1920.

Oberndorf, C.P. *An Autobiographical Sketch.* Ithaca: Cornell University Press, 1958.

_____. *A History of Psychoanalysis in America.* New York: Grune and Stratton, 1953.

_____. "History of the Psychoanalytic Movement in America." *Psychoanalytic Review* 14 (1927): 281–297.

_____. "Obituary: Abraham Arden Brill." *Psychoanalytic Review* 35 (January 1, 1948): 389–393.

_____. "Smith Ely Jelliffe [obituary]." *International Journal of Psycho-Analysis* 26 (1945): 186–188.

Overton, Grant. *Portrait of a Publisher.* New York: Appleton, 1925.

Peterson, Frederick. "Some New Fields and Methods in Psychology." *New York Medical Journal* 90 (November 13, 1909): 945–948.

Pierce, A.H. "Proceedings of the Eighteenth Annual Meeting of the American Psychological Association, Boston, December 29, 30 and 31, 1909." *Psychological Bulletin* 7 (1910): 37–64.

Portenar, A.J. "'Vacations' in the Printing Industry in New York City." *Monthly Labor Review* 10 (January 1920): 270–279.

"Psychanalysis [sic]," *Scientific American Supplement* 71 (April 15, 1911): 256.

"Psychologists at Clark: Important Scientific Papers Read at the University Anniversary." *Springfield Republican,* September 8, 1909, 9.

Putnam, James Jackson. "Personal Impressions of Sigmund Freud and His Work, with Special Reference to His Recent Lectures at Clark University." *Journal of Abnormal Psychology* 4–5 (December 1909 and March 1910): 293–310 and 372–379.

Read, Stanford. "The International Psycho-Analytical Press." *International Journal of Psychoanalysis* 2 (1921): 149.

_____. "Review of the Recent Psycho-Analytical Literature in English." *International Journal of Psychoanalysis* 1 (1920): 68–85.

Reeve, Arthur B. "The Dream Doctor." *Cosmopolitan,* August 1913, 325–334.

_____. "The Psychic Scar." *Cosmopolitan,* April 1918, 85–88, 128–34.

_____. "The Soul-Analysis." *Cosmopolitan,* May 1916, 869–81.

Reitman, Ben. "William J. Robinson: Estimate." *Medical Review of Reviews* 42, no. 2 (February 1936): 61.

[Robinson, Fred.] "A Review of the 'Medical Review of Reviews'" in *Medical Review of Reviews* 22 (January 1916): 1–4.

Robinson, William J. *A Doctor's Views on Life.* London: Allen & Unwin, 1927.

_____. *A Few Minutes in the Confessional: A Page from My Inner Life.* New York: Altrurians, n.d. [1910?].

_____. *Fewer and Better Babies, or, the Limitation of Offspring.* New York: Race Betterment League, 1916.

_____. *If I Were God.* New York: Freethought Press, 1930.

_____. *Psychoanalysis or the Freudian Philosophy: A Popular Exposition of Its Truths and Errors.* New York: Critic & Guide, 1924.

_____. "Suppressing Sex Information." *Appeal to Reason,* May 14, 1921.

_____. *Voice in the Wilderness, 1917–1920.* Westport, CT: Greenwood, 1970.

Ruitenbeek, Hendrik Marinus. *Freud As We Knew Him.* Detroit: Wayne State University Press, 1973.

Schumm, George. "Benj. R. Tucker—A Brief Sketch of His Life and Work." *Freethinkers Magazine* XI (July 1893): 436–440.

Schwab, Sidney. "An Estimate of Freud's Theory of the Neuroses and Its Value to the Neurologist." *Interstate Medical Journal* 18 (September 1911): 938.

_____. "Some New Freudian Literature." *Interstate Medical Journal* 17 (September 1910): 697–700.

"Science Discovers Reality of Dreams." *New York Times Sunday Magazine,* May 8, 1910, p. 14.

Scripture, E.W. "Neurology in Zurich." *Medical Record* 78, no. 26 (December 24, 1910): 1129–1135.

Simon, Richard L. "Trade Winds: Try and Stop Them." *Saturday Review of Literature* 33 (December 23, 1950): 4–6, 40.

Sommer's Newspaper Manual, containing a Carefully Compiled List of Newspapers and Periodicals ... Published in the U.S., with their Circulation ... 1903. Newark: F.N. Sommer, 1903.

Stearns, Harold, ed. *Civilization in the United States, an Inquiry by Thirty Americans.* New York: Harcourt, Brace, 1922.

Steffens, L. *Autobiography of Lincoln Steffens.* New York: Harcourt Brace, 1931.

Strachey, James. "List of English Translations of Freud's Works." *International Journal of Psycho-Analysis* 26 (1945): 67–76.

_____. "Obituary. Joan Riviere (1883–1962)." *The International Journal of Psycho-Analysis* 44 (1963): 228–229.

Strachey, James, and Alix. *Bloomsbury/Freud: The Letters of James and Alix Strachey, 1924–1925.* Ed. Perry Meisel and Walter Kendrick. New York: Basic Books, 1985.

Sumner, James S. "The New York Society for the Suppression of Vice." *Publishers Weekly,* May 17, 1930, 2516–2518.

Tracht, Fred H. "College Store and Town Store." *Publishers Weekly,* October 29, 1938, 1591–1592.

Traubel, Horace. *With Walt Whitman in Camden.* Boston: Small, Maynard, 1906.

Tridon, André. *Psychoanalysis, Its History, Theory and Practice.* New York: B.W. Huebsch, 1919.

Trow Copartnership and Corporation Directory of Boroughs of Manhattan and the Bronx. New York: Trow Directory, Printing and Bookbinding Co., 1906–1916.

Tucker, Benjamin. "Are Anarchists Thugs?" *New York Tribune,* December 4, 1898.

United States World War I Draft Registration Cards, 1917–1918: Massachusetts. Microfilm M1509. Washington, D.C.: National Archives and Records Administration, n.d.

Unwin, Stanley. *The Truth about a Publisher: An Autobiographical Record.* London: Unwin, 1960.

U.S. Bureau of the Census. *Occupations at the Twelfth Census.* Washington, D.C.: Government Printing Office, 1904.

Van Teslaar, James. "Freud and Our Frailties." *Forum,* November 1921, 406–411.

_____. "Religion and Sex: An Account of the Erotogenetic Theory of Religion as Formulated by Theodore Schroeder." *Psychoanalytic Review* 2, no. 1 (1915): 82–92.

_____. *When I Was a Boy in Roumania.* Boston: Lothrop, Lee and Shepard, 1917.

Van Teslaar, James, ed. *An Outline of Psychoanalysis.* New York: Boni and Liveright, Modern Library, 1924.

Victor Robinson Memorial Volume. New York: Froben Press, 1948.
Vienna Psychoanalytic Society. *Minutes of the Vienna Psychoanalytic Society, 1906–1911*. New York: International Universities Press, 1962–1974.
Viereck, George S. *Confessions of a Barbarian*. New York: Jackson, 1910.
_____. "Surveying Life at Seventy" [Interview with Freud]. *American Monthly* 20, no. 7 (October 1927): 8.
White, William A. *The Autobiography of a Purpose*. New York: Doubleday, 1938.
_____. *Forty Years of Psychiatry*. New York: Nervous and Mental Disease Publishing Co., 1933.
Williams, Frankwood E. *A Selected List of Books on Mental Hygiene and Allied Subjects*. New York: National Committee for Mental Hygiene, 1924.
Wittels, Fritz. "Brill: The Pioneer." *Psychoanalytic Review* 35 (1948): 394–398.
_____. *Sigmund Freud: His Personality, His Teaching, & His School*. London: Allen & Unwin, 1924.
Wood, Clement. *Modern Sexual Morality*. Girard, KS: Haldeman-Julius, 1924. Little Blue Book no. 717.
Woolf, Leonard. *Beginning Again*. London: Hogarth Press, 1964.
_____. *Downhill All the Way*. London: Hogarth Press, 1967.
_____. *Letters* Ed. Frederic Spotts. San Diego: Harcourt Brace Jovanovich, 1989.
Woolf, Virginia. *The Letters of Virginia Woolf, Volume III: 1923–1928*. New York: Harcourt Brace Jovanovich, 1977.
Yard, Robert Sterling. *The Publisher*. Boston: Houghton Mifflin, 1913.
A Young Girl's Diary. New York: Thomas Seltzer, 1921.

Secondary Sources

Andes, George. *Descriptive Bibliography of the Modern Library: 1917–1970*. Boston: Boston Book Annex, 1989.
Apmann, Sarah Bean. "Anarchy in the East Village! The Ferrer Modern School." *Off the Grid* (Greenwich Village Society for Historic Preservation), September 24, 2015.
Ashley, Mike. "Blue Book—The Slick in Pulp Clothing." *Pulp Vault* 14 (2011): 210–253.
Atkin, Samuel. "The New York Psychoanalytic Society and Institute: Its Founding and Development" in Quen, Jacques M,. and Eric T. Carlson, *American Psychoanalysis: Origins and Development*. New York: Brunner/Mazel, 1978, 73–86.
Auden, W.H. "In Memory of Sigmund Freud." *Collected Poems*, ed. Edward Mendelson. New York: Vintage, 1991, 273–276.
Avrich, Paul. *Anarchist Voices: An Oral History of Anarchism in America*. Princeton: Princeton University Press, 1995.
Beam, Alex. *A Great Idea at the Time: the Rise, Fall, and Curious Afterlife of the Great Books*. New York: Public Affairs, 2008.
Bisbee, Cynthia Carson, et al. *Psychedelic Prophets: The Letters of Aldous Huxley and Humphry Osmond*. Montreal: McGill-Queen's University Press, 2018.
Brody, D.J., and Gu. Q. "Antidepressant Use Among Adults: United States, 2015–2018." *NCHS Data Brief* 377. Hyattsville, MD: National Center for Health Statistics, 2020.
Brown, Junius F. "Freud's Influence on American Psychology." *Psychoanalytic Quarterly* 9 (1940): 283–292.
Bruccoli, Matthew Joseph. *F. Scott Fitzgerald: A Descriptive Bibliography*. Rev. ed. Pittsburgh: University of Pittsburgh Press, 1987.
Bruyère, Claire. "From Boston, MA, to Kingsport, TN: Joseph Hamblen Sears (1865–1946): A Forgotten Figure in American Publishing." *Papers of the Bibliographical Society of Canada* 52, no. 1 (2014): 293–321.
Bry, Ilse, and Alfred Rifkin. "Freud and the History of Ideas: Primary Sources, 1886–1900" in Masserman, Jules, *Science and Psychoanalysis 5: Psychoanalytic Education*. New York: Grune & Stratton, 1962, 6–36.
Burnham, John. *After Freud Left: A Century of Psychoanalysis in America*. Chicago: University of Chicago Press, 2012.

_____. "The Impact of Psychoanalysis Upon American Culture" in Quen, Jacques M., and Eric T. Carlson, *American Psychoanalysis: Origins and Development*. New York: Brunner/Mazel, 1978.

_____. *Psychoanalysis and American Medicine, 1894–1918*. New York: International Universities Press, 1967.

Burnham, John C. "From Avant-Garde to Specialism: Psychoanalysis in America." *Journal of the History of the Behavioral Sciences* 15 no. 2 (1979): 128–134.

Christie's [Auction House, New York]. *The Haskell F. Norman Library of Science and Medicine Part III: The Modern Age*. Christie's, October 29, 1998.

Covert, Catherine L. *Freud on the Front Page: Transmission of Freudian Ideas in the American Newspapers of the 1920s*. PhD dissertation, Syracuse University, 1975.

Cromer, Ward, and Paula Anderson, "Freud's Visit to America: Newspaper Coverage." *Journal of the History of the Behavioral Sciences* 6 (1970): 549–557.

Curry, William Lee. *Comstockery: A Study in the Rise and Decline of a Watchdog Censorship*. PhD dissertation, Columbian University, 1957.

Cutlip, Scott. *The Unseen Power. Public Relations, A History*. Hillsdale, NJ: Lawrence Erlbaum Associates, 1994.

Dardis, Tom. *Firebrand, The Life of Horace Liveright*. New York: Random House, 1995.

Davies, J.K., and G. Fichtner. *Freud's Library: A Comprehensive Catalogue*. London: Freud Museum, 2006.

Davis, Kenneth C. *Two-Bit Culture: The Paperbacking of America*. Boston: Houghton Mifflin, 1984.

Dennis, P.M. "Psychology's First Publicist." *Psychological Reports* 68, no. 3 (1991): 755–765.

Drell, Martin J. "Hermine Hug-Hellmuth, A Pioneer in Child Analysis." *Bulletin of the Menninger Clinic* 46, no. 2 (1982): 139–150.

Dzwonkoski, Peter, ed. *Dictionary of Literary Biography, vol. 46: American Literary Publishing Houses, 1900–1980*. Detroit: Gale, 1986.

Edmundson, Mark. *The Death of Sigmund Freud*. New York: Bloomsbury, 2007.

Egleston, Charles. *The House of Boni and Liveright, 1917–1933: A Documentary Volume*. Detroit: Gale, 2004.

Evans, R.B., and W.A. Koelsch. "Psychoanalysis Arrives in America: The 1909 Psychology Conference at Clark University." *American Psychologist* 40, no. 8 (1985): 942–948.

Everett, Patricia R. *Corresponding Lives: Mabel Dodge Luhan, A.A. Brill, and the Psychoanalytic Adventure in America*. New York: Routledge, 2016.

Falzeder, Ernst. "Brill and His Correspondence with Sigmund Freud," accessed May 15, 2022, www.freud-edition.net.

_____. "'A Fat Wad of Dirty Pieces of Paper': Freud on America, Freud in America, Freud and America" in Burnham, John, *After Freud Left: A Century of Psychoanalysis in America*. Chicago: University of Chicago Press, 2012, 85–109.

_____. "Is There Still an Unknown Freud? A Note on the Publications of Freud's Texts and On Unpublished Documents." *Psychoanalysis and History* 9, no. 2 (2007): 201–232.

Fass, Paula. *A.A. Brill—Pioneer and Prophet*. MS thesis, Columbia University, 1969.

Ffytche, Matt. *Sigmund Freud*. London: Reaktion Books, 2022.

Fielding, William J. *All the Lives I Have Lived*. Philadelphia: Dorrance, 1972.

Fishbein, Leslie. "Freud and the Radicals: The Sexual Revolution Comes to Greenwich Village." *Canadian Review of American Studies* 12, no. 2 (1981): 173–189.

Freedman, Forence B. *William Douglas O'Connor: Walt Whitman's Chosen Knight*. Athens: Ohio University Press, 1985.

Gainor, J. Ellen. *Susan Glaspell in Context*. Ann Arbor: University of Michigan, 2004.

Gay, Peter. *Freud: A Life for Our Time*. New York: W.W. Norton, 1988; revised, 2006.

Gertzman, Jay. *Bookleggers and Smuthounds: The Trade in Erotica, 1920–1940*. Philadelphia: University of Pennsylvania Press, 2001.

Gibbs, Jake. *Little Blue Book Bibliography*. Published online at https://www.littlebluebooksbibliography.com/, viewed September 22, 2022.

Gilmer, Walker. *Horace Liveright*. New York: David Lewis, 1970.

Gitre, Edward J.K. "Importing Freud: First-Wave Psychoanalysis, Interwar Social Sciences, and the Interdisciplinary Foundations of an American Social Theory." *Journal of the History of the Behavioral Sciences* 46 (2010): 239–262.

Green, Christopher D. "Where Did Freud's Iceberg Metaphor of Mind Come from?" *History of Psychology, Psychology and Psychiatry in the Global World* 22, no. 4, Part II (November 2019): 369–372.

Grinstein, Alexander. "Freud's First Publications in America." *Journal of the American Psychoanalytic Association* 19, no. 2 (1971): 241–264.

_____. *Sigmund Freud's Writings: A Comprehensive Bibliography.* New York: International Universities Press, 1977.

Grotjahn, M. "The Rundbriefe between Sigmund Freud and the Committee During the Years 1920–1924." *Annual of Psychoanalysis* 2 (1974): 24–39.

Hackett, Alice Payne, and James Henry Burke. *80 Years of Bestsellers: 1895–1975.* New York: R.R. Bowker, 1977.

Hale, Nathan G. *Freud and the Americans: The Beginnings of Psychoanalysis in the United States, 1876–1917.* New York: Oxford University Press, 1971.

_____. "From Berggasse XIX to Central Park West: The Americanization of Psychoanalysis, 1919–1940." *Journal of the History of the Behavioral Sciences* 14, no. 4 (October 1978): 299–315.

_____. *The Rise and Crisis of Psychoanalysis in the United States, 1917–1980.* New York: Oxford University Press, 1995.

Hare, Steve. *Penguin Portrait: Allen Lane and the Penguin Editors, 1935–1970.* London: Penguin, 1995.

Harrington, Anne. *Mind Fixers: Psychiatry's Troubled Search for the Biology of Mental Illness.* New York: W.W. Norton, 2019

Hatcher, Jessamyn. "Psychoanalysis and Everyday Life: The Popularization and Popular Use of Psychoanalysis in the United States, 1909–1935." PhD dissertation, Duke University, 2004.

Hecksher, August. *St. Paul's: The Life of a New England School.* New York: Scribner's, 1980.

Heller, Adele, and Lois Rudnick, eds. *1915, The Cultural Moment: The New Politics, the New Woman, the New Psychology, the New Art, and the New Theatre in America.* New Brunswick: Rutgers University Press, 1991.

Henry, Susan. *Anonymous in Their Own Names: Doris E. Fleischman, Ruth Hale, and Jane Grant.* Nashville: Vanderbilt University Press, 2012.

Henry, Susan. "'There Is Nothing in This Profession … That a Woman Cannot Do': Doris E. Fleischman and the Beginnings of Public Relations," *American Journalism* 16, no. 2 (April 1, 1999): 85–111.

Hobman, J.B., ed. *David Eder: Memoirs of a Modern Pioneer.* London: Gollancz, 1945.

Hoffman, Frederick J. *Freudianism and the Literary Mind.* Baton Rouge: Louisiana State University Press, 1945.

Horowitz, Helen Lefkowitz. "Victoria Woodhull, Anthony Comstock, and Conflict over Sex in the United States in the 1870s." *Journal of American History* 87, no. 2 (September 2000): 403–434.

Hulme, Peter. "The Liberal Club and Its Jamaican Secretary" (March 2017), accessed April 10, 2022 at www.academia.edu.

Irmscher, Christoph. "'I Regret America': Max Eastman Meets Sigmund Freud" in Zacharasiewicz, Waldemar, and David Staines, *Narratives of Encounters in the North Atlantic Triangle* (NED-New edition, Vol. 865). Vienna: Austrian Academy of Sciences Press, 2015, 226.

_____. *Max Eastman: A Life.* New Haven: Yale University Press, 2018.

Jacoby, Russell. "When Freud Came to America." *Chronicle of Higher Education,* September 21, 2009.

Johansson, Tyler. "Caroline Jane Mary Hubback." Modernist Archives Publishing Project, accessed June 1, 2022, at https://www.modernistarchives.com/node/312

Johnson, Niel M. *George Sylvester Viereck: Pro-German Publicist in America, 1910–1945.* PhD dissertation, University of Iowa, 1971.

Johnson, Richard Colles, and G. Thomas Tanselle. "The Haldeman-Julius 'Little Blue

Books' as a Bibliographical Problem." *Papers of the Bibliographical Society of America* 64 (1970): 29–78.

Keller, Phyllis. "George Sylvester Viereck: The Psychology of a German-American Militant." *Journal of Interdisciplinary History* 2, no. 1 (1971): 59–108.

Knight, Robert P. "The Present Status of Organized Psychoanalysis in the United States." *Journal of the American Psychoanalytic Association* 1, no. 2 (1953): 197–221.

Koelsch, William A. *Incredible Day-Dream: Freud and Jung at Clark, 1909.* Worcester, MA: Clark University, Friends of the Goddard Library, 1984.

Kramer, Dale. *Ross and the New Yorker.* New York: Doubleday, 1952.

Kramer, Milton. "Sigmund Freud's The Interpretation of Dreams: The initial response (1899–1908." *Dreaming* 4, no. 1 (March 1994): 47–52.

Kuhn, P. "The Sexual Life of Our Time: Medical Censorship in Early-20th-Century England." *History of Psychology* 23 (2020): 40–61.

Kuhn, Philip. "Subterranean Histories: The Dissemination of Freud's Works into the British Discourse on Psychological Medicine, 1904–1911." *Psychoanalysis and History* 16, no. 2 (July 2014): 153–214.

Kwarer, Jay S. "Origin, Theory, and Practice: 1943-Present." William Alanson White Institute. Web page viewed July 24, 2022, at https://www.wawhite.org/about-us/our-history.

Lamme, Margot Opdycke. "Outside the Prickly Nest: Revisiting Doris Fleischman." *American Journalism* 24, no. 3 (2007): 85–107.

Leinenberger, Charles. "Introduction" to *Dr. Robinson's Voice in the Wilderness, 1917–1920.* Westport, CT: Greenwood, 1970.

Levin, Alexandra Lee. "Thomas Seltzer: Publisher, Fighter for Freedom of the Press, and the Man Who 'Made' D. H. Lawrence." *American Jewish Archives* 41, no. 2 (1989): 217.

Levitas, Irving. *The Unterrified Jeffersonian: Benjamin R. Tucker.* PhD dissertation, New York University, 1974.

Lewin, B.D. "Reminiscences and Retrospect" in Waugh, M., *Fruition of an Idea: Fifty Years of Psychoanalysis in New York.* New York: International Universities Press, 1962.

Lewis, Nolan D.C. "Smith Ely Jelliffe 1866–1945: Psychosomatic Medicine in America" in Alexander, Franz, Samuel Eisenstein, and Martin Grotjahn, *Psychoanalytic Pioneers.* New York: Basic Books, 1966, 234–234.

Lewis, Sarah. "The Top 50 Drugs Prescribed in the United States." Published September 29, 2022, at https://www.healthgrades.com/right-care/patient-advocate/the-top-50-drugs-prescribed-in-the-united-states. Viewed December 11, 2022.

Library of Congress. "About Der Deutsche Correspondent." *Chronicling of America* Web page, accessed March 4, 2022, at https://chroniclingamerica.loc.gov/lccn/sn830450 81/.

_____. "About *The San Francisco Call*." *Chronicling of America* Web page, accessed March 4, 2022, at https://chroniclingamerica.loc.gov/lccn/sn85066387/.

Maddox, Brenda. *Freud's Wizard: Ernest Jones and the Transformation of Psychoanalysis.* Cambridge: Da Capo Press, 2006.

Madison, Charles A. "Benjamin R. Tucker: Individualist and Anarchist." *New England Quarterly* 16, no. 3 (September 1943): 444–467.

_____. *Book Publishing in America.* New York: McGraw-Hill, 1966.

_____. *Critics and Crusaders.* New York: Henry Holt, 1947.

Marcus, Laura. "European Dimensions of the Hogarth Press" in Caws, Mary Ann, and Nicola Luckhurst, *The Reception of Virginia Woolf in Europe.* New York: Continuum, 2002, 328–357.

Martin, James J. *Men Against the State: The Expositors of Individualist Anarchism in America, 1827–1908.* New York: Libertarian Book Club, 1957.

Matthews, F.H. "The Americanization of Sigmund Freud: Adaptations of Psychoanalysis before 1917." *Journal of American Studies* 1 (April 1967): 39–62.

May, Henry. *The End of American Innocence.* New York: Knopf, 1959.

McElroy, Wendy. "Benjamin Tucker, 'Liberty,' and Individualist Anarchism. *Independent Review* 2, no. 3 (Winter 1998): 421–434.

McElroy, Wendy. "Bibliographical Essay: Benjamin Tucker, Individualism, & Liberty."

Online Library of Liberty, accessed February 28, 2022, at https://oll.libertyfund.org/
page/benjamin-tucker-and-liberty-a-bibliographical-essay-by-wendy-mcelroy.

McElroy, Wendy. "Comprehensive Index to Liberty ... 1881–1908." The Memory Hole, 2013
accessed February 28, 2022, at https://web.archive.org/web/20131009015702/http://tmh.
floonet.net/articles/ind_intr.html

Menninger, Karl. "Contributions of A.A. Brill to Psychiatry." *Bulletin of the Menninger
Clinic* 13, no. 5 (1949).

Meynell, G.C. "Freud Translated: An Historical and Bibliographical Note." *Journal of the
Royal Society of Medicine* 74 (April 1981): 306–309.

Morgan, Charles. *The House of Macmillan*. London: Macmillan, 1943.

Mott, Frank Luther. *A History of American Magazines*. 5 volumes. Cambridge: Harvard
University Press, 1938–1968.

Murchison, C., ed. *The Psychological Register III*. Worcester, MA: Clark University Press,
1932, 591–605.

Neavill, Gordon B. "Canonicity, Reprint Series, and Copyright." in Spiers, J., *The Culture of
the Publisher's Series, vol. 1: Authors, Publishers and the Shaping of Taste*. London: Palgrave Macmillan, 2011, 88–105.

_____. *The Modern Library Series*. PhD dissertation, University of Chicago, 1984.

_____. "The Modern Library Series: Format and Design, 1917–1977." *Printing History* 1, no.
1 (1979): 26–37.

Norman, Jeremy, Fielding H. Garrison, and Leslie T. Morton. *An Interactive Annotated
World Bibliography of Printed and Digital Works in the History of Medicine and the Life
Sciences from Circa 2000 BCE to 2022*. Accessed June 20, 2022, at https://www.history-
ofmedicine.com/.

Norman, Jeremy M., and Diana H. Hook. *The Haskell Norman Library of Science & Medicine*, volume II. San Francisco: Jeremy Norman & Co., 1991.

Paskauskas, Richard A. *Ernest Jones: A Critical Study of his Scientific Development*. PhD
dissertation, University of Toronto, 1986.

Perkons, Renate. *Benjamin R. Tucker—A Fighter Against his Age: An Interpretation of the
Dominant Spokesman for Individualist Anarchism in America, 1881–1908*. PhD dissertation, California State University, Fullerton, 1989.

Perrone, Frenanda. *Inventory to the Modern School Collection*. Brunswick: Rutgers University Libraries, 1996.

Quen, Jacques M., and Eric T. Carlson. *American Psychoanalysis: Origins and Development*. New York: Brunner/Mazel, 1978.

Ray, Royal Henderson. *Concentration of Ownership and Control in the American Daily
Newspapers Industry*. PhD dissertation, Columbia University, 1950.

Reid, Amanda. "Claiming the Copyright." *Yale Law & Policy Review* 34, no. 2 (2016): 425–470.

Richards, Arnold D. "A.A. Brill and the Politics of Exclusion." *Journal of the American Psychoanalytic Association* 47, no. 1 (1999): 9–28.

Richwine, Keith N. *The Liberal Club: Bohemia and the Resurgence in Greenwich Village,
1912–1918*. PhD dissertation, University of Pennsylvania, 1968.

Rickman, John. *Index Psychoanalyticus 1893–1926... Being an Authors' Index of Papers on
Psycho-analysis*. London: Hogarth Press and Institute of Psycho-Analysis, 1928.

Rieber, Robert W. *Freud on Interpretation*. New York: Springer, 2012.

Roazen, Paul. *Freud and His Followers*. New York: Alfred A. Knopf, 1974.

_____. "George Wilbur: Otto Rank and Hanns Sachs." *Psychoanalysis and History* 8, no. 1
(2006): 43–63.

Romm, May E. "Abraham Arden Brill, 1874–1948. First American Translator of Freud" in
Franz, Alexander, Samuel Eisenstein, and Martin Grotjahn, *Psychoanalytic Pioneers*.
New York: Basic Books, 1966, 210–223.

Rosenzweig, Saul. *Freud, Jung and Hall the King-Maker: The Expedition to America (1909)*.
St. Louis: Rana House, 1992.

Rothgeb, Carrie Lee. *Abstracts of the Standard Edition of the Complete Psychological Works
of Sigmund Freud*. Rockville, MD: U.S. Department of Health Education and Welfare,
1972.

Roudinesco, Élisabeth. *Freud: In His Time and Ours*. Cambridge: Harvard University Press, 2017.

Rudnick, Lois P. *Mabel Dodge Luhan: New Woman, New Worlds*. Albuquerque: University of New Mexico Press, 1984.

Ruitenbeek, Hendrick M. *Freud In America*. New York: Macmillan, 1966.

St. John, John. *William Heinemann: a Century of Publishing, 1890–1990*. London: Heinemann, 1990.

Satterfield, Jay Corey. *"The World's Best Books": Taste, Culture, and the Modern Library*. Amherst: University of Massachusetts Press, 2002.

Scull, Andrew. *Desperate Remedies: Psychiatry's Turbulent Quest to Cure Mental Illness*. Cambridge: Harvard University Press, 2022.

Showalter, Elaine. "A Freudian Fraud?" *Times Literary Supplement*, July 6, 1990.

Shulkin, Jeremy. "When Sigmund Came to Clark." *Worcester Magazine*, November 12, 2009.

Silverman, Al. *The Time of Their Lives: The Golden Age of Great American Book Publishers, Their Editors, and Authors*. New York: St. Martins, 2008.

Simpson, Jon. "Finding Brand Success in the Digital World." *Forbes Community Voice*, August 25, 2017.

Skues, Richard. "Clark Revisited: Reappraising Freud in America" in Burnham, John, *After Freud Left: A Century of Psychoanalysis in America*. Chicago: University of Chicago Press, 2012, 49–84.

Spaeth, Sigmund. *Read 'Em and Weep: The Songs You Forgot to Remember*. New York: Doubleday Page, 1927.

Steel, Ronald. *Walter Lippmann and the American Century*. London: Bodley Head, 1980.

Steiner, Riccardo. "'A World Wide International Trade Mark of Genuineness?' Some Observations on the History of the English Translation of the Work of Sigmund Freud, Focusing Mainly on His Technical Terms." *International Review of Psycho-Analysis* 14, no. 1 (1987): 33–102.

Stendler, Celia Burns. "New Ideas for Old: How Freudianism Was Received in the United States" *Journal of Educational Psychology* 38, no. 4 (1947): 193–206.

Sullivan, Mark. *Our Times; the United States, 1900–1925*. New York: Scribner's, 1936.

Sulloway, Frank. *Freud: Biologist of the Mind*. New York: Basic Books, 1979.

Tanselle, G. Thomas. "The Bibliographical Concepts of 'Issue' and 'State.'" *Papers of the Bibliographical Society of America* 69, no. 1 (1975): 17–66.

_____. "The Thomas Seltzer Imprint." *Papers of the Bibliographical Society of America* 58, no. 4 (1964): 380–448.

Tebbel, John. *A History of Book Publishing in the United States: Vol. 2—The Expansion of an Industry, 1865–1919*. New York: Bowker, 1972.

_____. *A History of Book Publishing in the United States: Vol. 3—The Golden Age Between the Two Wars, 1920–1940*. New York: Bowker, 1978.

Thompson, Ronelle K.H. "Permabooks" in Dzwonkoski, Peter, *Dictionary of Literary Biography, vol. 46: American Literary Publishing Houses, 1900–1980*. Detroit: Gale, 1986, 284–285.

Toledano, Henry. *The Modern Library Price Guide, 1917–1995*. Dexter, MI: Thomson-Shore, 1995.

Torrey, E. Fuller. *Freudian Fraud*. New York: Harper Perennial, 1993.

Tye, Tom. *Firebrand: The Life of Horace Liveright*. New York: Random House, 1995.

Tyson, Alan, and James Strachey. "A Chronological Hand List of Freud's Works." *International Journal of Psycho-Analysis* 37 (1956): 19–33.

Unwin, Philip. *The Publishing Unwins*. London: Heinemann, 1972.

Wagner, Rob. *Hollywood Bohemia*. Santa Maria, CA: Janeway Books, 2019.

Watner, Carl. "Benjamin Tucker's Liberty." *Reason Magazine* (April 1979), accessed February 28, 2022, at https://reason.com/1979/04/01/benjamin-tuckers-liberty/.

Watson, Steven. *Strange Bedfellows: The First American Avant-Garde*. New York: Abbeville Press, 1991.

Waugh, M. *Fruition of an Idea: Fifty Years of Psychoanalysis in New York*. New York: New York University Press. 1962.

Wertheim, Arthur F. *The New York Little Renaissance.* New York: New York University Press, 1976.

Whitelaw, Nancy. *William Randolph Hearst and the American Century.* Greensboro, NC: Morgan Reynolds, 2000.

William Alanson White: The Washington Years, 1903–1937: The Contributions to Psychiatry, Psychoanalysis, and Mental Health by Dr. White While Superintendent of Saint Elizabeth's Hospital. Washington, D.C.: U.S. Department of Health, Education, and Welfare, Public Health Service, Alcohol, Drug Abuse, and Mental Health Administration, 1976.

Willis, John H. *Leonard and Virginia Woolf as Publishers: The Hogarth Press, 1917–41.* Charlottesville: University Press of Virginia, 1992.

Wineapple, Brenda. *Sister Brother: Gertrude and Leo Stein.* New York: Putnam, 1996.

Wittenberger, Gerhard. "The Circular Letters (Rundbriefe) as a Means of Communication of the 'Secret Committee' of Sigmund Freud." *International Forum of Psychoanalysis* 5, no. 2 (1996): 111–121.

Index

Numbers in *bold italics* indicate pages with illustrations